REGULATING AVERSION

REGULATING AVERSION

Tolerance in the Age of Identity and Empire

■ ■ ■ ■

Wendy Brown

PRINCETON UNIVERSITY PRESS
PRINCETON AND OXFORD

Third printing, and first paperback printing, 2008
Paperback ISBN: 978-0-691-13621-9

The Library of Congress has cataloged the cloth edition of this book as follows
Brown, Wendy.
Regulating aversion : tolerance in the age of identity and empire / Wendy Brown.
p. cm.
Includes index.
ISBN-13: 978-0-691-12654-8 (hardcover : alk. paper)
ISBN-10: 0-691-12654-2 (hardcover : alk. paper)
1. Toleration. I. Title.
HM1271.B76   2006
179′.9—dc22   2005036547

British Library Cataloging-in-Publication Data is available

This book has been composed in Sabon

Printed on acid-free paper. ∞
press.princeton.edu
Printed in the United States of America
7 9 10 8 6

For Lila and Gail

CONTENTS

ACKNOWLEDGMENTS

Over six years of working intermittently on this book, I have acquired many debts. Rainer Forst sparked the project with his invitation to revisit Marcuse's essay "Repressive Tolerance" for his own edited volume on tolerance. Val Hartouni made the first visit to the Simon Wiesenthal Museum of Tolerance with me and brought her subtle intelligence to bear on my early efforts to conceptualize the strange province of tolerance. Neve Gordon took time to answer my questions about Hebrew terms and (the general absence of) tolerance discourse in Israel. Lila Abu-Lughod gave me things to read, spotted errors in my arguments, and put gentle pressure on my Euro-Atlantic habits of seeing and thinking. Joan W. Scott, Elizabeth Weed, Barry Hindess, Michel Feher, Caroline Emcke, and William Connolly each engaged carefully with one or more chapters. Judith Butler, Melissa Williams, and an anonymous reviewer read the entire manuscript in draft; their criticisms were invaluable as I revised.

In his discerning and disarming way, Stuart Hall suggested that I loosen rather than tighten the analytic noose around liberalism that I was readying in the final two chapters. His reminder that colonial discourse cannot be wholly resolved into liberalism saved me from foolishness. Around the same time, Mahmood Mamdani reminded me that the discursive practices emanating from the settler-native encounter are distinct from a liberal democracy's practices for managing its internal others. These convergent readings strengthened the book's argument that tolerance discourse is continuously remade and redirected by encounters with new historical turns and new objects.

At the penultimate phase of revising, Gail Hershatter provided me with an office, plied me with her wondrous cooking, and, during one early morning run in the woods, persuaded me not to start the book over. Judith Butler's own work, her reading of mine, and our persistent disagreements have enriched my thinking more than anything else over the past fifteen years. That I am also graced by her love is fortune beyond measure.

Many audiences have responded usefully to presentations of this work in progress; I am particularly grateful for the rich engagements with it in Canada and England, two lands that have become second intellectual homes for me. I have also had wonderful research assistance. Catherine Newman scouted background information on the Museum of Tolerance. Robyn Marasco completed citations, located speeches based on phrases I recalled from radio newscasts, tracked down odd facts and sources, and much more. Colleen Pearl did a final cleanup on the manuscript that left me in awe; she also prepared the index. Ivan Ascher good-naturedly lent me his French fluency to study Foucault's untranslated lectures.

Ian Malcolm of Princeton University Press, one of the finest editors in the trade, handled this book expertly. My debts to Alice Falk, my copyeditor, are too large to repay in this lifetime.

Initial institutional support for this project came from the Division of Humanities and the Academic Senate Committee on Research at the University of California, Santa Cruz. Later, I was the recipient of a Humanities Research Fellowship from the University of California, Berkeley; an American Council of Learned Societies Fellowship; and a residential fellowship at the Institute for Advanced Study in Princeton. Anyone who has spent a year at the Institute knows what an incomparable environment it is for thinking and writing. For this, I am especially indebted to Michael Walzer and Joan W. Scott.

Portions of this book have appeared, in different form, in the following publications: Parts of chapter 1 and 2 draw on "Reflexionen über Toleranz im Zeitalter der Identität," in *Toleranz: Philosophische Grundlagen und gesellschäftliche Praxis einer umstrittenen Tugend*, ed. Rainer Forst (Frankfurt/Main: Campus Verlag, 2000), also published as "Reflections on Tolerance in the Age of Identity," in *Democ-*

racy and Vision: Sheldon Wolin and the Vicissitudes of the Political, ed. Aryeh Botwinick and William E. Connolly (Princeton University Press, 2001). An early version of chapter 3 was published in *Differences: A Journal of Feminist Cultural Studies* 15.2 (Summer 2004), and republished in *Going Public: Feminism and the Shifting Boundaries of the Private Sphere,* ed. Joan W. Scott and Debra Keates (University of Illinois Press, 2004). And chapter 7 was adapted from "Tolerance As/In Civilizational Discourse," *Finnish Yearbook of Political Science* (2004).

REGULATING AVERSION

■　■　■　■

TOLERANCE AS A DISCOURSE
OF DEPOLITICIZATION

Can't we all just get along?
— Rodney King

An enemy is someone whose story you have not heard.
— epigraph of "Living Room Dialogues
on the Middle East"

Tolerance is not a product of politics, religion or culture.
Liberals and conservatives, evangelicals and atheists,
whites, Latinos, Asians, and blacks . . . are equally capable of tolerance and intolerance. . . . [T]olerance has much
less to do with our opinions than with what we feel and
how we live.
— Sarah Bullard, *Teaching Tolerance*

How did tolerance become a beacon of multicultural justice and civic peace at the turn of the twenty-first century? A mere
generation ago, tolerance was widely recognized in the United States
as a code word for mannered racialism. Early in the civil rights era,
many white northerners staked their superiority to their southern
brethren on a contrast between northern tolerance and southern bigotry. But racial tolerance was soon exposed as a subtle form of Jim
Crow, one that did not resort to routine violence, formal segregation,
or other overt tactics of superordination but reproduced white supremacy all the same. This exposé in turn metamorphosed into an ar-
tifact of social knowledge: well into the 1970s, racial tolerance remained a term of left and liberal derision, while religious tolerance
seemed so basic to liberal orders that it was as rarely discussed as it
was tested. Freedom and equality, rather than tolerance, became the

watchwords of justice projects on behalf of the excluded, subordinated, or marginalized.

Since the mid-1980s, however, there has been something of a global renaissance in tolerance talk. Tolerance surged back into use in the late twentieth century as multiculturalism became a central problematic of liberal democratic citizenship; as Third World immigration threatened the ethnicized identities of Europe, North America, and Australia; as indigenous peoples pursued claims of reparation, belonging, and entitlement; as ethnically coded civil conflict became a critical site of international disorder; and as Islamic religious identity intensified and expanded into a transnational political force. Tolerance talk also became prominent as domestic norms of integration and assimilation gave way to concerns with identity and difference on the left and as the rights claims of various minorities were spurned as "special" rather than universal on the right.

Today, tolerance is uncritically promoted across a wide range of venues and for a wide range of purposes. At United Nations conferences and in international human rights campaigns, tolerance is enumerated, along with freedom of conscience and speech, as a fundamental component of universal human dignity. In Europe, tolerance is prescribed as the appropriate bearing toward recent Third World immigrants, Roma, and (still) Jews and as the solution to civil strife in the Balkans. In the United States, tolerance is held out as the key to peaceful coexistence in racially divided neighborhoods, the potential fabric of community in diversely populated public schools, the corrective for abusive homophobia in the military and elsewhere, and the antidote for rising rates of hate crime. Tolerance was the ribbon hung around the choice of an orthodox Jew for the Democratic vice presidential nominee in the 2000 presidential elections and the rubric under which George W. Bush, upon taking office in his first term, declared that appointees in his administration would not have their sexual orientations scrutinized . . . or revealed. Schools teach tolerance, the state preaches tolerance, religious and secular civic associations promulgate tolerance. The current American "war on terrorism" is being fought, in part, in its name. Moreover, even as certain contemporary conservatives identify tolerance as a codeword for endorsing homosexuality, tolerance knows no political party: it is what liberals and leftists reproach a religious, xenophobic, and homophobic right for lacking, but also what evangelical Christians claim that secular liberals refuse them and what conservative foreign policy ideologues claim America cherishes and "radical Islamicists" abhor.[1] Combined with this bewildering array of sites and calls for tolerance is an impressive range of potential objects of tolerance, including cultures, races, ethnicities, sexualities, ideologies, lifestyle and fashion choices, political positions, religions, and even regimes.

Moreover, tolerance has never enjoyed a unified meaning across the nations and cultures that have valued, practiced, or debated it. It has a variety of historical strands, has been provoked or revoked in relation to diverse conflicts, and has been inflected by distinct political traditions and constitutions. Today, even within the increasingly politically and economically integrated Euro-Atlantic world, tolerance signifies differently and attaches to different objects in different national contexts; for example, tolerance is related to but not equivalent to *laïcité* in France, as the recent French debate over the *hijab* made clear. And practices of tolerance in Holland, England, Canada, Australia, and Germany not only draw on distinct intellectual and political lineages but are focused on different contemporary objects—sexuality, immigrants, or indigenous peoples—that themselves call for different modalities of tolerance. That is, modalities of tolerance talk that have issued from postcolonial encounters with indigenous peoples in settler colonies do not follow the same logics as those that have issued from European encounters with immigrants from its former colonies or those that are centered on patriarchal religious anxieties about insubordinate gender and sexual practices. Similarly, an Islamic state seeking to develop codes of tolerance inflects the term differently than does a Euro-Atlantic political imaginary within which the nation-states of the West are presumed always already tolerant.

Given this proliferation of and variation in agents, objects, and political cadences of tolerance, it may be tempting to conclude that it is too polymorphous and unstable to analyze as a political or moral discourse. I pursue another hypothesis here: that the semiotically polyvalent, politically promiscuous, and sometimes incoherent use of tolerance in contemporary American life, closely considered and critically theorized, can be made to reveal important features of our political time and condition. The central question of this study is not "What is tolerance?" or even "What has become of the idea of tolerance?" but, What kind of political discourse, with what social and political effects, is contemporary tolerance talk in the United States? What readings of the discourses of liberalism, colonialism, and imperialism circulating through Western democracies can analytical scrutiny of this talk provide? The following chapters aim to track the social and political work of tolerance discourse by comprehending how this discourse constructs and positions liberal and nonliberal subjects, cultures, and regimes; how it figures conflict, stratification, and difference; how it operates normatively; and how its normativity is rendered oblique almost to the point of invisibility.

These aims require an appreciation of tolerance as not only protean in meaning but also historically and politically discursive in character. They require surrendering an understanding of tolerance as a transcendent or universal concept, principle, doctrine, or virtue so that it can be considered instead as a political discourse and practice of *governmentality* that is historically and geographically variable in purpose, content, agents, and objects. As a consortium of para-legal and para-statist practices in modern constitutional liberalism—practices that are associated with the liberal state and liberal legalism but are not precisely codified by it—tolerance is exemplary of Foucault's account of governmentality as that which organizes "the conduct of conduct" at a variety of sites and through rationalities not limited to those formally countenanced as political. Absent the precise dictates, articulations, and prohibitions associated with the force of law, tolerance nevertheless produces and positions subjects, orchestrates meanings and practices of identity, marks bodies, and conditions political subjectivities. This production, positioning, orchestration, and conditioning is achieved not through a rule or a concentration of power, but rather through the dissemination of tolerance discourse across state institutions; civic venues such as schools, churches, and neighborhood associations; ad hoc social groups and political events; and international institutions or forums.[2]

When I commenced this study in the late 1990s, I was almost exclusively concerned with *domestic* tolerance talk. My interest in the subject was piqued by the peculiar character of the discourse of tolerance in contemporary civic and especially pedagogical culture in the United States. As multicultural projects of enfranchisement, cooperation, and conflict reduction embraced the language of tolerance, clearly both the purview and purpose of tolerance had undergone changes from its Reformation-era concern with minoritarian religious belief and modest freedom of conscience. In its current usage, tolerance seemed less a strategy of protection than a telos of multicultural citizenship, and focused less on belief than on identity broadly construed. The genuflection to tolerance in the literatures, mottos, and mission statements of schools, religious associations, and certain civic institutions suggested that what once took shape as an instrument of civic peace and an alternative to the violent exclusion or silencing of religious dissidents had metamorphosed into a generalized language of antiprejudice and now betokened a vision of the good society yet to come. And if this vision was promulgated by actors across the political spectrum, its praises as likely to be sung by a neoconservative American president or attorney general as by a United Nations chief or a leftist community organizer, tolerance was clearly having a strange new life at the turn of the century.

In the context of this profusion of subjects and objects of tolerance, this uncritical embrace of tolerance across a diverse ideological field, and this apparent conversion of tolerance from a particular form of protection against violent persecution to a late-twentieth-century vision of the good society, my questions were these: What kind of governmental and regulatory functions might tolerance discourse perform in contemporary liberal democratic nation-states? What kind of civil order does tolerance configure or envision? What kind of social subject does it produce? What kind of citizen does it hail, with what orientation to politics, to the state, and to fellow citizens? What kind of state legitimation might it supply and in response to what legitimation deficits? What kind of justice might it promise and what kinds might it compromise or displace? What retreat from stronger ideals of justice is conveyed by giving tolerance pride of place in a moral-political vision of the good? What kind of fatalism about the persistence of hostile and irreconcilable differences in the body politic might its promulgation carry?

The original project, then, was to be a consideration of the constructive and regulatory effects of tolerance as a discourse of justice, citizenship, and community in late modern, multicultural liberal democracies, with a focus on the United States. However, in the aftermath of September 11, political rhetorics of Islam, nationalism, fundamentalism, culture, and civilization have reframed even domestic discourses of tolerance—the enemy of tolerance is now the weaponized radical Islamicist state or terror cell rather than the neighborhood bigot—and have certainly changed the cultural pitch of tolerance in the international sphere. While some of these changes have simply brought to the surface long-present subterranean norms in liberal tolerance discourse, others have articulated tolerance for genuinely new purposes. These include the legitimation of a new form of imperial state action in the twenty-first century, a legitimation tethered to a constructed opposition between a cosmopolitan West and its putatively fundamentalist Other. Tolerance thus emerges as part of a civilizational discourse that identifies both tolerance and the tolerable with the West, marking nonliberal societies and practices as candidates for an intolerable barbarism that is itself signaled by the putative intolerance ruling these societies. In the mid–nineteenth through mid–twentieth centuries, the West imagined itself as standing for civilization against primitivism, and in the cold war years for freedom against tyranny; now these two recent histories are merged in the warring figures of the free, the tolerant, and the civilized on one side, and the fundamentalist, the intolerant, and the barbaric on the other.

As it altered certain emphases in liberal discourse itself, so, too, did the post–September 11 era alter the originally intended course of this study. The new era demanded that questions about tolerance as a domestic governmentality producing and regulating ethnic, religious, racial, and sexual subjects be supplemented with questions about the operation of tolerance in and as a civilizational discourse distinguishing Occident from Orient, liberal from nonliberal regimes, "free" from "unfree" peoples. Such questions include the following: If tolerance is a political principle used to mark an opposition between liberal and fundamentalist orders, how might liberal tolerance discourse function not only to anoint Western superiority but also to legitimate Western cultural and political imperialism? That is, how might this discourse actually promote Western supremacy and aggression even as it veils them in the modest dress of tolerance? How might tolerance, the very virtue that Samuel Huntington advocates for preempting a worldwide clash of civilizations, operate as a key element in a civilizational discourse that codifies the superiority and legitimates the superordination of the West? What is the work of tolerance discourse in a contemporary *imperial* liberal governmentality? What kind of subject is thought to be capable of tolerance? What sort of rationality and sociality is tolerance imagined to require and what sorts are thought to inhibit it—in other words, what anthropological presuppositions does liberal tolerance entail and circulate?

In the end, the effort to understand tolerance as a domestic discourse of ethnic, racial, and sexual regulation, on the one hand, and as an international discourse of Western supremacy and imperialism on the other, did not have to remain permanently forked. Contemporary domestic and global discourses of tolerance, while appearing at first blush to have relatively distinct objects and aims, are increasingly melded in encomiums to tolerance, such as those featured in the Simon Wiesenthal Museum of Tolerance discussed in chapter 4, and are also analytically interlinked. The conceit of secularism undergirding the promulgation of tolerance within multicultural liberal democracies not only legitimates their intolerance of and aggression toward nonliberal states or transnational formations but also glosses the ways in which certain cultures and religions are marked in advance as ineligible for tolerance while others are so hegemonic as to not even register *as* cultures or religions; they are instead labeled "mainstream" or simply "American." In this way, tolerance discourse in the United States, while posing as both a universal value and an impartial practice, designates certain beliefs and practices as civilized and others as barbaric, both at home and abroad; it operates from a conceit of neutrality that is actually thick with bourgeois Protestant norms. The moral autonomy of the individual at the heart of liberal tolerance discourse is also critical in drawing the line between the tolerable and the intolerable, both domestically and globally, and thereby serves to sneak liberalism into a civilizational discourse that claims to be respectful of all cultures and religions, many of which it would actually undermine by "liberalizing," and, conversely, to sneak civilizational discourse into liberalism. This is not to say that tolerance in civilizational discourse is reducible to liberalism; in fact, it is strongly shaped by the legacy of the colonial settler-native encounter as well as the postcolonial encounter between white and indigenous, colonized, or expropriated peoples. This strain in the lexicon and ethos of tolerance, while not reducible to a liberal grammar and analytics, is nonetheless mediated by them and also constitutes an element in the constitutive outside of liberalism over the past three centuries.[3] Tolerance is thus a crucial analytic hinge between the constitution of abject domestic subjects and barbarous global ones, between liberalism and the justification of its imperial and colonial adventures.

Put slightly differently, tolerance as a mode of late modern governmentality that iterates the normalcy of the powerful and the deviance of the marginal responds to, links, and tames both unruly domestic identities or affinities and nonliberal transnational forces that tacitly or explicitly challenge the universal standing of liberal precepts. Tolerance regulates the presence of the Other both inside and outside the liberal democratic nation-state, and often it forms a circuit between them that legitimates the most illiberal actions of the state by means of a term consummately associated with liberalism.

TOLERANCE AS A DISCOURSE OF POWER AND A PRACTICE OF GOVERNMENTALITY

As will already be apparent, the questions with which this study is concerned place it to one side of contemporary philosophical, historical, political-theoretical, and legal considerations of tolerance as a benignly positive, if difficult, individual and collective practice. In philosophy and ethics, tolerance is typically conceived as an individual virtue, issuing from and respecting the value of moral autonomy, and acting as a sharp rein on the impulse to legislate against morally or religiously repugnant beliefs and behaviors.[4] Political theorists debate the appropriate purview and limits of tolerance and probe the problem of nonreciprocity between more and less tolerant individuals, cultures, or regimes.[5] In Western history, while scholars have unearthed premodern pockets of tolerance practice, tolerance as a political principle is mostly treated as the offspring of classical liberalism and, more precisely, as a product of the bloody early modern religious wars that initiated the prising apart of political and religious authority and the carving out of a space of individual autonomy from both.[6] In comparative cultural and political analysis, the standard contrast is between the millet system of tolerance famously associated with the Ottoman Empire (also practiced in limited ways in ancient Greece and Rome, medieval England, medieval China, and modern India), which divided society into communities grouped by religion, and the form of Protestant tolerance, with its emphasis on individual conscience, that flowered in the West. In American law, tolerance is either First Amendment territory or is placed on the relatively newer legal terrain of group rights and sovereignty claims.[7] In international law, tolerance is among the panoply of goods promised by a universal doctrine of human rights.

While benefiting substantially from these literatures, this study also works to one side of them. Rather than treating tolerance as an independent or self-consistent principle, doctrine, or practice of cohabitation, it aims to comprehend political deployments of tolerance as historically and culturally specific discourses of power with strong rhetorical functions.[8] Above all, it seeks to track the complex involvement of tolerance with power. As a moral-political practice of governmentality, tolerance has significant cultural, social, and political effects that exceed its surface operations of reducing conflict or of protecting the weak or the minoritized, and that exceed its formal goals and self-representation. These include contributions to political and civic subject formation and to the articulation of the political, the social, citizenship, justice, the nation, and civilization. Tolerance can function as a substitute for or as a supplement to formal liberal equality or liberty; it can also overtly block the pursuit of substantive equality and freedom. At times, tolerance shores up troubled orders of power, repairs state legitimacy, glosses troubled universalisms, and provides cover for imperialism. There are mobilizations of tolerance that do not simply alleviate but rather circulate racism, homophobia, and ethnic hatreds; likewise, there are mobilizations that legitimize racist state violence. Not all deployments of tolerance do all of these things all the time. But the concern of this study is to consider how, when, and why these effects occur as part of the operation of tolerance, rather than to ignore them or treat them as "externalities" vis-à-vis tolerance's main project.

Does such a relentlessly critical set of concerns mean that this is a book "against tolerance"? Comprehending tolerance in terms of power and as a productive force—one that fashions, regulates, and positions subjects, citizens, and states as well as one that legitimates certain kinds of actions—does not lead to a roundly negative judgment. To reveal the operations of power, governance, and subject production entailed in particular deployments of tolerance certainly divests them of a wholly blessed status, puncturing the aura of pure goodness that contemporary invocations of tolerance carry; but this fall from grace does not strip tolerance of all value in reducing violence or in developing certain habits of civic cohabitation. The recognition that discourses of tolerance inevitably articulate identity and difference, belonging and marginality, and civilization and barbarism, and that they invariably do so on behalf of hegemonic social or political powers, does not automatically negate the worth of tolerance in attenuating certain kinds of violence or abuse. Without question tolerance has been adduced at times for such purposes, from early modern efforts to stop the burning alive of religious heretics and bloody civil wars to the contemporary willingness of people who disapprove of racial mixing to forswear attempts to impose their views on others or enact them as law. Conversely, all encomiums to tolerance need not be aimed at limiting violence or subordination for some to have this aim, and degrees and forms of subordination and abjection in tolerance discourse vary substantially. For example, though tolerance of homosexuals today is often advocated as an alternative to full legal equality, this stance is significantly different from promulgating tolerance of homosexuals as an alternative to harassing, incarcerating, or institutionalizing them; the former opposes tolerance to equality and bids to maintain the abject civic status of the homosexual while the latter opposes tolerance to cruelty, violence, or civic expulsion.

To remove the scales from our eyes about the innocence of tolerance in relation to power is not thereby to reject tolerance as useless or worse. Rather, it changes the status of tolerance from a transcendental virtue to a historically protean element of liberal governance, a re-situating that casts tolerance as a vehicle for producing and organizing subjects, a framework for state action and state speech, and an aspect of liberalism's legitimation. Yet the initial counterintuitiveness of this claim, our commonplace inclination to view tolerance as a moral rather than political practice, reminds us what an unusual figure tolerance is in liberal democracy today. Like civility, with which it is often linked, tolerance is a political value and sometimes even a dictum, but it is not precisely formulated or enshrined in law.[9] While the First Amendment may be understood as a constitutional codification of tolerance in the United States, it is significant that the word appears nowhere in the amendment itself; in addition, most contemporary domestic iterations of tolerance pertain to race, ethnicity, sexuality, culture, or "lifestyle," none of which is among the freedoms expressly guaranteed by this amendment. Moreover, liberal democracies feature no "right to tolerance," although their liberties of religion, assembly, and speech may together be considered to promote a tolerant regime or a tolerant society. Nor is there a "crime of intolerance," even as intolerance is often linked to "hate crime" and is also invoked to cast aspersion on regimes or societies figured as dangerous in their orthodoxy or fundamentalism. Thus, within secular liberal democratic states it is safe to say that tolerance functions politically and socially, but not legally, to propagate understandings and practices regarding how people within a nation, or regimes within an international system, can and ought to cohabit. So while tolerance may be a state or civic principle, while it may figure prominently in the preambles of constitutions or policy documents and may conceptually undergird laws and judicial decisions concerning freedom of religion, speech, and association, tolerance as such is not legally or doctrinally codified.[10] Nor can it be, both because the meaning and work of tolerance is bound to its very plasticity—to when, where, and how far it will stretch—and because its legitimating goodness is tied to virtue, not to injunction or legality. Virtue is exercised and emanates from within; it cannot be organized as a right or rule, let alone commanded.

Conventionally, tolerance is adduced for beliefs or practices that may be morally, socially, or ideologically offensive but are not in direct conflict with the law. Thus, law constitutes one limit of the reach of tolerance, designating its purview as personal or private matters within the range of what is legal. Laws, of course, may be changed in the name of greater tolerance, as in the repeal of antimiscegenation or antisodomy laws, or in the name of less tolerance, as in laws banning same-sex marriage or restricting abortion. But in each case, the negotiation is between what is deemed a private or individual choice appropriately beyond the reach of law (hence tolerable) and what is deemed a matter of the public interest (hence not a matter of tolerance).[11] Again, tolerance is generally a civic or social practice that may be sanctioned by law but is not precisely encoded or regulated by it; we are tolerant not by law but in addition to the law. Nor are there today laws of tolerance as there are laws, say, of equality, liberty, or the franchise; and when we glance back at edicts of tolerance in past centuries, they appear incompatible with contemporary standards of egalitarianism, since they did not merely protect but simultaneously stigmatized and overtly regulated the group they targeted. This suggests that the legal codification of tolerance necessarily recedes as the purview of formal equality is expanded. But it does not follow that tolerance as governmentality therefore declines or disappears; rather, it is resituated to the para-legal and para-statist status described above.

What are the implications of the fact that the cultural-political field of tolerance as a civic practice is largely *inside* the domain demarcated as legal? First, that position makes it difficult to see the extent to which tolerance at times functions as a supplement to liberal legalism and liberal egalitarianism, a function discussed at length in chapters 3 and 4. Second, the identification of the virtue of tolerance with voluntary rather than coerced or mandated behavior makes it difficult to see tolerance as a practice of power and regulation—in short, as a practice of governmentality. Third, insofar as the legal and the political are generally conflated in liberal democratic thought, the practice of tolerance occurs off the radar screen of the formally political, in a space remaindered by liberal legalism. All of these factors contribute to the depoliticizing functions of tolerance and the depoliticization of tolerance, matters to which we now turn.

TOLERANCE AND/AS DEPOLITICIZATION

Some scholars of tolerance have attempted to distinguish *tolerance*, the attitude or virtue, from *toleration*, the practice.[12] For this study, a different distinction is useful, one that is both provisional and porous but that may stem the tendency, mentioned earlier, to mistake an insistence on the involvement of tolerance with power for a rejection or condemnation of tolerance. The distinction is between a personal ethic of tolerance, an ethic that issues from an individual commitment and has objects that are largely individualized, and a political discourse, regime, or governmentality of tolerance that involves a particular mode of depoliticizing and organizing the social. A tolerant individual bearing, understood as a willingness to abide the offensive or disturbing predilections and tastes of others, is surely an inarguable good in many settings: a friend's irritating laugh, a student's distressing attire, a colleague's religious zeal, the repellant smell of a stranger, a neighbor's horrid taste in garden plants—these provocations do not invite my action, or even my comment, and the world is surely a more gracious and graceful place if I can be tolerant in the face of them. Every human being, perhaps even every sentient animal, routinely exercises tolerance at this level. But tolerance as a political discourse concerned with designated modalities of diversity, identity, justice, and civic cohabitation is another matter. It involves not simply the withholding of speech or action in response to contingent individual dislikes or violations of taste but the enactment of social, political, religious, and cultural norms; certain practices of licensing and regulation; the marking of subjects of tolerance as inferior, deviant, or marginal vis-à-vis those practicing tolerance; and a justification for sometimes dire or even deadly action when the limits of tolerance are considered breached. Tolerance of this sort does not simply address identity but abets in its production; it also abets in the conflation of culture with ethnicity or race and the conflation of belief or consciousness with phenotype. And it naturalizes as it depoliticizes these processes to render identity itself an object of tolerance. These are consequential achievements.

In cautiously distinguishing an individual bearing from a political discourse of tolerance, I am not arguing that the two are unrelated, nor am I suggesting that the former is always good, benign, or free of power while the latter is bad, oppressive, or power-laden. Not only does tolerance as a public value have its place, and not only does the political discourse give shape to the individual ethos and vice versa, but even an individual bearing of tolerance in nonpolitical arenas carries authority and potential subjection through unavowed norms. Almost all objects of tolerance are marked as deviant, marginal, or undesirable by virtue of being tolerated, and the action of tolerance inevitably affords some access to superiority, even as settings or dynamics of mutual tolerance may complicate renderings of superordination and superiority as matters of relatively fixed status.

Again, if tolerance is never innocent of power or normativity, this serves only to locate it solidly in the realm of the human and hence make it inappropriate for conceptualizations of morality and virtue that fancy themselves independent of power and subjection. Of itself, however, this revaluation does not yet indicate what the specifically political problematics of tolerance are. These are set not by the presence of power in the exercise of tolerance but, rather, by the historical, social, and cultural particulars of this presence in specific deployments of tolerance as well as in discourses with which tolerance intersects, including those of equality, freedom, culture, enfranchisement, and Western civilization. Tolerance as such is not the problem. Rather, the call for tolerance, the invocation of tolerance, and the attempt to instantiate tolerance are all signs of identity production and identity management in the context of orders of stratification or marginalization in which the production, the management, and the context themselves are disavowed. In short, they are signs of a buried order of politics.

Part of the project of this book, then, is to analyze tolerance, espe-cially in its recently resurgent form, as a strand of depoliticization in liberal democracies. Depoliticization involves construing inequality, subordination, marginalization, and social conflict, which all require political analysis and political solutions, as personal and individual, on the one hand, or as natural, religious, or cultural on the other. Tol-erance works along both vectors of depoliticization—it personalizes and it naturalizes or culturalizes—and sometimes it intertwines them. Tolerance as it is commonly used today tends to cast instances of in-equality or social injury as matters of individual or group prejudice. And it tends to cast group conflict as rooted in ontologically natural hostility toward essentialized religious, ethnic, or cultural difference. That is, tolerance discourse reduces conflict to an inherent friction among identities and makes religious, ethnic, and cultural difference itself an inherent site of conflict, one that calls for and is attenuated by the practice of tolerance. As I will suggest momentarily, tolerance is hardly the cause of the naturalization of political conflict and the on-tologization of politically produced identity in liberal democracies, but it is facilitated by and abets these processes.

Although depoliticization sometimes personalizes, sometimes cul-turalizes, and sometimes naturalizes conflict, these tactical variations are tethered to a common mechanics, which is what makes it possible to speak of depoliticization as a coherent phenomenon.[13] Depoliti-cization involves removing a political phenomenon from comprehen-sion of its *historical* emergence and from a recognition of the *powers* that produce and contour it. No matter its particular form and me-chanics, depoliticization always eschews power and history in the rep-resentation of its subject. When these two constitutive sources of social relations and political conflict are elided, an ontological naturalness or essentialism almost inevitably takes up residence in our understand-ings and explanations. In the case at hand, an object of tolerance an-alytically divested of constitution by history and power is identified as naturally and essentially different from the tolerating subject; in this difference, it appears as a natural provocation to that which tolerates it. Moreover, not merely the parties to tolerance but the very scene of tolerance is naturalized, ontologized in its constitution as produced by the problem of difference itself. When, for example, middle and high schoolers are urged to tolerate one another's race, ethnicity, culture, religion, or sexual orientation, there is no suggestion that the differences at issue, or the identities through which these differences are negotiated, have been socially and historically constituted and are themselves the effect of power and hegemonic norms, or even of certain discourses about race, ethnicity, sexuality, and culture.[14] Rather, difference itself is what students learn they must tolerate.

In addition to depoliticization as a mode of dispossessing the constitutive histories and powers organizing contemporary problems and contemporary political subjects—that is, depoliticization of *sources* of political problems—there is a second and related meaning of depoliticization with which this book is concerned: namely, that which substitutes emotional and personal vocabularies for political ones in formulating *solutions* to political problems. When the ideal or practice of tolerance is substituted for justice or equality, when sensitivity to or even respect for the other is substituted for justice for the other, when historically induced suffering is reduced to "difference" or to a medium of "offense," when suffering as such is reduced to a problem of personal feeling, then the field of political battle and political transformation is replaced with an agenda of behavioral, attitudinal, and emotional practices. While such practices often have their value, substituting a tolerant attitude or ethos for political redress of inequality or violent exclusions not only reifies politically produced differences but reduces political action and justice projects to sensitivity training, or what Richard Rorty has called an "improvement in manners."[15] A justice project is replaced with a therapeutic or behavioral one.

One sure sign of a depoliticizing trope or discourse is the easy and politically crosscutting embrace of a political project bearing its name. As we have seen, tolerance, like diversity, democracy, and family, is endorsed across political lines in liberal societies, a phenomenon that has intensified in recent years as tolerance has come to belong collectively rather than selectively to Westerners and as intolerance has become a code word not merely for bigotry or investments in whiteness but for a fundamentalism identified with the non-West, with barbarism, and with anti-Western violence. Even Westerners who oppose certain kinds of tolerance—conservative Christians who argue against tolerating sexual libertinism, "humanism," or atheism; self-anointed patriots who would limit political dissent; or progressives who argue against tolerating cultural or religious practices they judge abusive to women or children—even these positions are not arrayed against tolerance as such but only against extending tolerance to the obscene or the barbaric. If tolerance today is considered synonymous with the West, with liberal democracy, with Enlightenment, and with modernity, then tolerance is what distinguishes "us" from "them." Chandran Kukathas has taken this so far as to instantiate tolerance as the *first* virtue of liberal political life; prior to equality, freedom, or any other principle of justice is the liberty of conscience and association that toleration protects.[16]

By no means is tolerance the only or even the most significant discourse of depoliticization in contemporary liberal democracies. In fact, the widespread embrace of tolerance today, especially in the United States, is facilitated by its convergence with other sources of discursive depoliticalization. These sources include long-standing tendencies in liberalism itself and in the peculiarly American ethos of individualism. They include the diffusion of market rationality across the political and social spheres precipitated by the ascendency of neoliberalism. And they include the more recent phenomenon that Mahmood Mamdani has named the "culturalization of politics."[17] Each of these will be considered below.

Liberalism. The legal and political formalism of liberalism, in which most of what transpires in the spaces designated as cultural, social, economic, and private is considered natural or personal (in any event, independent of power and political life), is a profound achievement of depoliticization. Liberalism's excessive freighting of the individual subject with self-making, agency, and a relentless responsibility for itself also contributes to the personalization of politically contoured conflicts and inequalities. These tendencies eliminate from view various norms and social relations—especially those pertaining to capital, race, gender, and sexuality—that construct and position subjects in liberal democracies. In addition, the reduction of freedom to rights, and of equality to equal standing before the law, eliminates from view many sources of subordination, marginalization, and inequality that organize liberal democratic societies and fashion their subjects. Liberal ideology at its most generic, then, always already eschews power and history in its articulation and comprehension of the social and the subject.

Individualism. The American cultural emphasis on the importance of individual belief and behavior, and of individual heroism and failure, is also relentlessly depoliticizing. An identification of belief, attitude, moral fiber, and individual will with the capacity to make world history is the calling card of the biographical backstories and anecdotes that so often substitute for political analyses and considerations of power in American popular culture.[18] From Horatio Algers to demonized welfare mothers, from Private Jessica Lynch to Private Lynndie England, from mythohistories to mythobiographies, we are awash in the conceits that right attitudes produce justice, that willpower and tenacity produce success, and that everything else is, at most, background, context, luck, or accidents of history.[19] It is a child's view of history and politics: idealist, personal, and replete with heroes and villains, good values and bad.

Market rationality. A third layer of depoliticization is added to the contemporary American context by the saturation of every feature of social and political life with entrepreneurial and consumer discourse, a saturation inaugurated by capitalism in its earlier modality but taken to new levels by neoliberal political rationality. When every aspect of human relations, human endeavor, and human need is framed in terms of the rational entrepreneur or consumer, then the powers constitutive of these relations, endeavors, and needs vanish from view. As the political rationality of neoliberalism becomes increasingly dominant, its depoliticizing effects combine with those of classical political liberalism and American cultural narratives of the individual to make nearly everything seem a matter of individual agency or will, on the one hand, or fortune or contingency on the other.[20]

Tolerance as a depoliticizing discourse gains acceptance and legitimacy by being nestled among these other discourses of depoliticization, and it draws on their techniques of analytically disappearing the political and historical constitution of conflicts and subjects. Moreover, as is the case with liberalism, the American culture of individualism, and neoliberal market rationality, tolerance masks its own operation as a discourse of power and a technology of governmentality. Popularly defined as respect for human difference or for "opinions and practices [that] differ from one's own,"[21] there is no acknowledgment of the norms, the subject construction, the subject positioning, or the civilizational identity at stake in tolerance discourse; likewise, there is no avowal of the means by which certain peoples, nations, practices, or utterances get marked as beyond the pale of tolerance, or of the politics of line drawing between the tolerable and the intolerable, the tolerant and the intolerant.

Culturalization of politics. We have already noted ambiguity in the meaning and purview of tolerance: Is it respect? acceptance? repressed violence? Is it a posture? a policy? a moral principle? an ethos? a politics? Does it promote moral autonomy? equality? the protection of difference? freedom? But more than being merely ambiguous, tolerance today is often invoked in a manner that equates or conflates non commensurable subjects and practices, including religion, culture, ethnicity, race, and sexual norms. In tolerance talk, ethnicity, race, religion, and culture are especially interchangeable. For example: In her discussion of how and why "culture" oppresses women and ought therefore to be constrained and regulated by liberal juridicism rather than always tolerated, Susan Okin slides indiscriminately between (patriarchal) culture and (patriarchal) religion, effectively conflating them.[22] And in a film on terror at the Simon Wiesenthal Museum of Tolerance, the narrative moves directly from a discussion of the threat posed by "Islamic extremists" to a question about the appropriateness of "racial and ethnic profiling" to manage this threat, thereby conflating religion, ethnicity, and race. Similarly, the interchangeability of "Arab American" and "Muslim" in American political discourse is as routine as is elision of the fact that many Palestinians are Christians and some Israelis are Arabs. And fundamentalism as one name for the post–cold war enemy of the "free world" is assigned a shifting site of emanation that floats across culture, religion, state, region, and regime.

These conflations and slides are not simply the effect of historical and political ignorance or of a sloppy multiculturalist discourse in which all marked identities are rendered analytically equivalent. They are, rather, symptoms of the culturalization of politics, the assumption "that every culture has a tangible essence that defines it and then explains politics as a consequence of that essence."[23] This reduction of political motivations and causes to essentialized culture (where *culture* refers to an amorphous polyglot of ethnically marked religious and nonreligious beliefs and practices) is mobilized to explain everything from Palestinian suicide bombers to Osama bin Laden's world designs, mass death in Rwanda and Sudan, and the failure of democracy to take hold in the immediate aftermath of Saddam Hussein's Iraq. It is what George W. Bush draws on when he insists that a gruesome event in the Middle East "reminds us of the *nature* of our enemy."[24] The culturalization of politics analytically vanquishes political economy, states, history, and international and transnational relations. It eliminates colonialism, capital, caste or class stratification, and external political domination from accounts of political conflict or instability. In their stead, "culture" is summoned to explain the motives and aspirations leading to certain conflicts (living by the sword, religious fundamentalism, cultures of violence) as well as the techniques and weapons deployed (suicide bombing, decapitation). Samuel Huntington offers the premier inscription for the culturalization of politics: since the end of the cold war, he argues, "the iron curtain of ideology" has been replaced by a "velvet curtain of culture."[25] Critically reworded, the West's cold war reduction of political conflict to ideology has been replaced by its post–cold war reduction of political conflict to culture.

Importantly, however, this reduction bears a profound asymmetry. The culturalization of politics is not evenly distributed across the globe. Rather, culture is understood to drive Them politically and to lead them to attack our culture, which We are not driven by but which we do cherish and defend. As Mamdani puts it, "The moderns make culture and are its masters; the premoderns are said to be but conduits."[26] This division into those who are said to be ruled by culture and those who are said to rule themselves but enjoy culture renders culture not simply a dividing line between various peoples or regimes or civilizations, and not simply the explanation for political conflict, but itself the problem for which liberalism is the solution. How does this work?

The notion that culture—whatever one means by it—is political is old news. But the notion that liberalism, as a politics, is cultural, is catachrestic. The reasons for this nonreciprocity are several. There is, first, liberalism's conceit about the universality of its basic principles: secularism, the rule of law, equal rights, moral autonomy, individual liberty. If these principles are universal, then they are not matters of culture, which is identified today with the particular, local, and provincial.[27] There is, second, liberalism's unit of analysis, the individual, and its primary project, maximizing individual freedom, which together stand antithetically to culture's provision of the coherence and continuity of groups—an antithesis that positions liberal principles and culture as mutual antagonists. This leads to the third basis on which liberalism represents itself as cultureless: namely, that liberalism presumes to master culture by privatizing and individualizing it, just as it privatizes and individualizes religion. It is a basic premise of liberal secularism and liberal universalism that neither culture nor religion are permitted to govern publicly; both are tolerated on the condition that they are privately and individually enjoyed.

Contemporary liberal political and legal doctrine thus positions culture as its Other and also as necessarily antagonistic to its principles unless it is subordinated—that is, unless culture is literally "liberalized" through privatization and individualization. Moreover, liberalization is taken to attenuate the claims of culture by making what are otherwise authoritative and automatically transmitted meanings, practices, behaviors, and beliefs into matters of individual attachment. Liberalism presumes to convert culture's collectively binding powers, its shared and public qualities, into individual and privately lived choices. Liberalism, in other words, presumes culture and politics to be fused unless culture is conquered—politically neutered—by the universal, hence noncultural, principles of liberalism. Without liberalism, culture is conceived by liberals as oppressive and dangerous not only because of its disregard for individual rights and liberties and for the rule of law, but also because the inextricability of cultural principles from power, combined with the nonuniversal nature of these principles, renders it devoid of judicial and political accountability. Hence culture must be contained by liberalism, forced into a position in which it makes no political claim and is established as optional for individuals. Rather than a universe of organizing ideas, values, and modes of being together, culture must be shrunk to the status of a house that individuals may enter and exit. Liberalism represents itself as the sole mode of governance that can do this.

In short, in our time, the conceit of the relative autonomy of the political, the economic, and the cultural within liberal democracies—a conceit shared by liberals ranging from Habermas to Huntington—has replaced the nineteenth-century conceit of the autonomy of the state from civil society. Liberal democratic governance is imagined by liberals to operate relatively independently of both capital and cultural values. This putative autonomy of liberal political principles and institutions is incarnated in the liberal insistence on the universality and hence supervenience of human rights, an insistence that runs from Jimmy Carter to Michael Ignatieff to George W. Bush. Not only does this formulation free human rights from the stigma of cultural imperialism, it also allows them to be coherently invoked as a means of protecting culture.[28]

But liberalism *is* cultural. This is not simply to say that liberalism promotes a certain culture—say, of individualism or of entrepreneurship—though certainly these are truisms. Nor is it simply to say that liberalism is always imbricated with what we call national cultures, although it is and too little contemporary liberal theory has considered what this imbrication implies, even as our histories of political thought have routinely compared the liberalisms emerging from different parts of Europe and the Americas. Nor is it simply to say that there is no pure liberalism but only varieties of it—republican, libertarian, communitarian, social democratic. Nor is it only to say that all liberal orders harbor, affirm, and instantiate in law nonliberal values and practices, although this is also so. Rather, the theoretical claim here is that both the constructive and repressive powers we call those of culture—the powers that produce and reproduce subjects' relations and practices, beliefs and rationalities, and that do so without their express choice or consent—are neither conquered by liberalism nor absent from liberalism. Liberalism is not only itself a cultural form, it also is striated with nonliberal culture wherever it is institutionalized and practiced. Even in the texts of its most abstract analytic theorists, it is impure, hybridized, and fused to values, assumptions, and practices unaccounted by it and unaccountable within it. Liberalism involves a contingent, malleable, and protean set of beliefs and practices about being human and being together; about relating to self, others, and world; about doing and not doing; about valuing and not valuing select things. And liberalism is also always institutionalized, constitutionalized, and governmentalized in articulation with other cultural norms—those of kinship, race, gender, sexuality, work, politics, leisure, and more. This is one reason why liberalism, a protean cultural form, is not analytically synonymous with democracy, a protean political practice of sharing power and governance. The double ruse on which liberalism relies to distinguish itself from culture—on the one hand, casting liberal principles as universal; on the other, juridically privatizing culture—ideologically figures liberalism as untouched by culture and thus as incapable of cultural imperialism. In its self-representation as the sole political doctrine that can harbor culture and religion without being conquered by them, liberalism casts itself as uniquely tolerant of culture from its position above culture. But liberalism is no more above or outside culture than is any other political form, and culture is not always elsewhere from liberalism. Both the autonomy and the universality of liberal principles are myths, crucial to liberalism's reduction of questions about its imperial ambitions or practices to questions about whether forcing others to be free is consonant with liberal principles.

In sum, the contemporary "culturalization of politics" reduces nonliberal political life (including radical identity claims within liberal regimes) to something called culture at the same time that it divests liberal democratic institutions of any association with culture. Within this logic, tolerance is invoked *as* a liberal democratic principle but *for* what is named the cultural domain, a domain that comprises all essentialized identities, from sexuality to ethnicity, that produce the problem of difference within contemporary liberalism. Thus, tolerance is invoked as a tool for managing what are construed as (non-

liberal because "different" and nonpolitical because "essential") culturalized identity claims or identity clashes. As such, tolerance reiterates the depoliticization of those claims and clashes, at the same time
depicting itself as a norm-free tool of liberal governance, a mere means
for securing freedom of conscience or (perhaps more apt today) freedom of identity.

This book seeks to lay bare this political landscape. It contests the
culturalization of politics that tolerance discourse draws from and
promulgates, and contests as well the putatively a-cultural nature of
liberalism. The normative premise animating this contestation is that
a more democratic global future involves affirming rather than denying and disavowing liberalism's cultural facets and its imprint by particular cultures. Such an affirmation would undermine liberalism's
claims to universalism and liberalism's status as culturally neutral in
brokering the tolerable. This erosion, in turn, would challenge the
standing of liberal regimes as uniquely, let alone absolutely, tolerant,
revealing them instead to be as self-affirming and Other-rejecting as
many other regimes. It would also reveal liberalism's proximity to and
bouts of forthright engagement with fundamentalism.

The recognition of liberalism as cultural is more than a project of
debunking its airs of superiority or humiliating its hubristic reach.
Rather, insofar as it makes explicit the inherent hybridity or impurity
of every instantiation of liberalism, it underscores the impossibility of
any liberalism ever being "only liberalism" and the extent to which
both form and content are potted, historical, local, lived. It reveals liberalism as always already being the issue of miscegenation with its fundamentalist Other, as containing this Other within, and thus as having a certain potential for recognizing and connecting with this Other
without. In this possibility may be contained liberalism's prospects for
renewal, even for redemption, or at the very least for more modest and
peaceful practices.

■ ■ ■ ■

TOLERANCE AS A DISCOURSE
OF POWER

Despite its pacific demeanor, tolerance is an internally unharmonious term, blending together goodness, capaciousness, and conciliation with discomfort, judgment, and aversion. Like patience, tolerance is necessitated by something one would prefer did not exist. It involves managing the presence of the undesirable, the tasteless, the faulty—even the revolting, repugnant, or vile. In this activity of management, tolerance does not offer resolution or transcendence, but only a strategy for coping. There is no *Aufhebung* in the operation of tolerance, no purity and no redemption. As compensation, tolerance anoints the bearer with virtue, with standing for a principled act of permitting one's principles to be affronted; it provides a gracious way of allowing one's tastes to be violated. It offers a robe of modest superiority in exchange for yielding.

The *Oxford English Dictionary* identifies the Latin root of tolerance as *tolerare*, meaning to bear, endure, or put up with and implying a certain moral disapproval. The *OED* offers three angles on tolerance as an ethical or political term: (1) "the action or practice of *enduring* pain or hardship"; (2) "the action of *allowing*; license, permission granted by an authority"; and (3) "the *disposition to be patient with or indulgent to* the opinions or practices of others; freedom from bigotry . . . in judging the conduct of others; forbearance; catholicity of spirit."[1] From these three definitions—"enduring," "licensing," and "indulging"—it is clear that tolerance entails suffering something one would rather not, but being positioned socially such that one can determine whether and how to suffer it, what one will allow from it. Not simply power, then, but authority is a presupposition of tolerance as a moral and political value.[2] It is this positioning, power, and authority that make possible the third dimension of tolerance listed above— a posture of indulgence toward what one permits or licenses, a posture that softens or cloaks the power, authority, and normativity in the act of tolerance. Tolerance is thus an act of power that inherently entails this softening disguise, this "catholicity of spirit." Magnanimity is always a luxury of power; in the case of tolerance, it also disguises power.[3]

The *OED* definitions together make clear that tolerance involves neither neutrality toward nor respect for that which is being tolerated. Rather, tolerance checks an attitude or condition of disapproval, disdain, or revulsion with a particular kind of overcoming—one that is enabled either by the fortitude to throw off the danger or by the capaciousness to incorporate it or license its existence. Thus, tolerance carries within it an antagonism toward alterity as well as the capacity for normalization. Developed into a civic ethos and social practice in modernity, and more recently attached to all manner of cultural identities, tolerance appears as an element in the formation Foucault named *biopower*: a distinctly modern form of power that involves the subjugation of bodies and control of populations through the regulation of life rather than the threat of death.[4]

This dimension of tolerance appears all the more vividly if we leave generic dictionary definitions and consider how the term is used in various technical fields. In plant physiology, "drought tolerance" or "shade tolerance" refers to the amount of deprivation of a fundamental substance (water or sun) that a plant can bear and still survive. In medicine, tolerance of drugs, implants, and organ transplants pertains to a combination of how the body handles what is foreign or strange and how it endures what is patently toxic. In human physiology more generally, the concept of alcohol tolerance or histamine or glucose tolerance identifies the body's capacity to absorb, metabolize, or process a threatening element, sometimes alien but sometimes, like histamines and glucose, internally generated.[5] In policing and prosecution, the notion of "zero tolerance" has been adopted in the United States and Canada for highly moralized crimes—from illicit drugs to domestic abuse—identified as intolerable threats to a neighborhood or a community considered worthy of preservation. Statistical tolerances establish the margin of error that can be sustained by statistical claims without nullifying or falsifying them. And in engineering, mechanics, and minting, tolerance refers to the acceptable distances, mismeasures, or degrees of deviation that can be allowed, the gaps and flaws that can be borne without creating structural weakness or invalidating some output. In every lexicon, tolerance signifies the limits on what foreign, erroneous, objectionable or dangerous element can be allowed to cohabit with the host without destroying the host— whether the entity at issue is truth, structural soundness, health, community, or an organism. The very invocation of tolerance in each domain indicates that something contaminating or dangerous is at hand, or something foreign is at issue, and the limits of tolerance are determined by how much of this toxicity can be accommodated without destroying the object, value, claim, or body. Tolerance appears, then, as a mode of incorporating and regulating the presence of the threatening Other within. In this regard, tolerance occupies the position of Derridean supplement; that which conceptually undermines the binary of identity/difference or inside/outside yet is crucial to the conceit of the integrity, autarky, self-sufficiency, and continuity of the dominant term.[6]

If tolerance poses as a middle road between rejection on the one side and assimilation on the other, this road, as already suggested, is paved by necessity rather than virtue; tolerance, as Nietzsche would say, becomes a virtue only retroactively and retrospectively. As a practice concerned with managing a dangerous, foreign, toxic, or threatening difference from an entity that also demands to be incorporated, tolerance may be understood as a unique way of sustaining the *threatened* entity. This understanding is at odds with the conventional view of civic or political tolerance as protecting the weak or minoritized, though it does not deny the possibility of such protection as one effect of tolerance.[7] Generically, however, tolerance is less an extension toward a potentially intrusive or toxic difference than the management of the threat represented by that difference. It is a singular form of such management insofar as it involves the simultaneous incorporation and maintenance of the otherness of the tolerated element; again, this is what distinguishes tolerance from digestion, assimilation, or solubility, on the one side, and rejection, negation, or pollution on the other. What is tolerated remains distinct even as it is incorporated. Since the object of tolerance does not dissolve into or become one with the host, its threatening and heterogenous aspect remains alive inside the tolerating body. As soon as this ceases to be the case, tolerance ceases to be the relevant action.[8] Tolerance as a term of justice, then, crucially sustains a status of outsiderness for those it manages by incorporating; it even sustains them as a potential danger to the civic or political body. This suggests that the adoption of tolerance by multiculturalist discourse reveals that discourse as figuring something other than a happy community of differences. It indicates as well the importance of understanding both the norms and the antagonists at stake in this conception of contemporary civic bodies, in order to see what is valued and what is considered threatening to that value, to see what relations of enmity and of permanent alterity are imagined, and to see how these relations are to be handled.

Insofar as tolerance does not resolve but manages antagonism or hostility toward difference, the psychic costs of this particular management technique may mount in the form of palpable social effects when tolerance becomes a ubiquitous ideology or an element of governance. Designated objects of tolerance are invariably marked as undesirable and marginal, as liminal civil subjects or even liminal humans; and those called upon to exercise tolerance are asked to repress or override their hostility or repugnance in the name of civility, peace, or progress. Psychically, the former is the material of abjection and one variety of resentment (that associated with exclusion); the latter is the material of repressed aggression and another variety of resentment (that associated with forsworn strength or domination). Because tolerance is, among other things, a breeding ground for such resentments, it does not simply respond to but produces a troubling and unstable psychic landscape for liberal multiculturalism. This aspect of the action of tolerance is likely to be glossed by formulations of it as an individual ethical virtue, a collective social ethos, or a civic instrument of peacekeeping.

Tolerance not only produces, organizes, and marks subjects, it also delineates a purview and the availability of alternatives to tolerance. We do not tolerate what is outside of our reach, what is irrelevant to us, or what we cannot do anything about. And tolerance is a selected alternative to actions or reactions of a different sort: rejection, quarantine, prohibition, repression, exile, or extermination. If these are not viable, expedient, or morally acceptable responses, if we have little or no choice about living with peoples or practices to which we object, then we cannot properly speak of tolerating what threatens or repels us; rather we are subjected, oppressed, or undone by their presence. Tolerance is an accommodation that may indeed compromise the well-being of its host, but at its heart tolerance fundamentally expresses choice or ability; it is canceled by mandate on one side and passivity on the other.

Tolerance thus involves two kinds of boundary drawing and a practice of licensing. Its invocation involves drawing spatial boundaries of dominion and relevance, as well as moral boundaries about what can and cannot be accommodated within this domain. The licensing action specifies the conditions within which the tolerated practice remains tolerable. So, for example, some Americans who personally believe abortion to be morally wrong tolerate its conditioned legality because they believe that this moral question is an individual one, though they may regard "late-term abortions" as intolerable. Others, believing abortion to be murder and equating ethical action with the prevention of murder, cannot tolerate the practice under any circumstances and may go beyond opposing the legality of abortion to actively seeking to prevent abortions from taking place. In just these two positions, one can see boundaries of dominion and relevance shift from individual to society, and it is possible to see as well a practice of licensing that sets out what kinds of abortions—for whom and at what point in a pregnancy—may or may not be considered tolerable.[9]

GENEALOGY

Thus far, we have been reflecting on the general implications of tolerance drawn from its dictionary meanings and common usages. But to make good on the recognition that tolerance is always a specific discursive practice, these meanings need to be supplemented by those emerging from the distinctive genealogy of the governmentality of tolerance in the West. Neither the dictionary meanings nor this genealogy can tell us how tolerance is deployed today, with what political effects and implications, but both contribute to understanding diverse possibilities for its involvement with power, and both suggest as well the range of legitimation strategies it draws on for its present work.

Tolerance as a principle of governance in the West is inaugurated with the Renaissance humanist counsel of toleration of heretics in the fifteenth and sixteenth centuries. Humanists advocating tolerance in this notably intolerant period sought acceptance of those suspected of religious heresy by granting them full membership in the church while acknowledging their deviation from certain church principles. The idea was that religious dissenters who disagreed about nonessentials but accepted the fundamentals of faith should be allowed their disagreements while remaining within the church. In late-seventeenth-century England, this type of toleration was termed "comprehension," because it sought to include or "comprehend" nonconformists within Anglicanism. Comprehension is distinguished from toleration insofar as the former applies to denominations inside the church and the latter to denominations outside. But the early humanists would not have embraced such a distinction, for they did not recognize the permanent fragmentation of Christianity.[10]

It is, of course, the Reformation rather than the Renaissance that produced the doctrine widely considered to be the origins of tolerance in liberalism. Concern with tolerance during and after the Reformation varied according to the hegemonic religions, monarchical powers, and particular religious dissenters at issue from decade to decade and nation to nation. Protestants in France presented a different problem from either Puritans or Catholics in Stuart England, and English Presbyterians confronting an upsurge of sects in the 1640s produced a mode of intolerance different from the religious persecution ensuing from the revocation of the French Edict of Nantes in 1685.

The number of thinkers writing on toleration during these years is extraordinary: Baruch Spinoza, John Milton, Gotthold Ephraim Lessing, Pierre Bayle, Roger Williams, and John Goodwin are only the better known.[11] Post-Reformation toleration doctrine, however, is most famously codified by John Locke in his "Letter Concerning Toleration."[12] Published anonymously during the Exclusion Crisis in 1689 but emerging from years of thinking about and writing on toleration, it is also significant for having been written while Locke was in exile in the Netherlands, a land that had undergone a century of its own political crises over religion in the aftermath of Spanish rule and was then the main destination of French Protestants fleeing persecution. Locke's aim in the "Letter" is not simply to plead for toleration but to articulate a sharp distinction between civil and political society, on the one hand, and religious life on the other. "He jumbles heaven and earth together—the things most remote and opposite—who mixes these two societies," Locke polemicizes, and then proceeds to specify the remoteness and opposition of these two spheres (403). Religion is for the achievement of an afterlife (in heaven) and concerns the salvation of souls. Political society is for the organization of this life (on earth) and concerns worldly goods—"life, liberty, health, and indolency of body, and the possession of outward things—money, lands, houses, furniture . . . public justice, equity, etc." (393).

This sharp attenuation of the bearing of religion on everyday civil and political life enables Locke in the same gesture to privatize religious belief, to render it an individual rather than common matter. The "care . . . of every man's soul belongs unto himself," Locke declares (405), signaling the emergence of an intensely individualistic and privatistic believer, one who will become the signature figure, or at least the stick figure, of modernity.[13] Clearly, one effect of privatizing religious belief is to reduce its truth claim, inevitably imbuing it with the quality of subjective belief that undergirds ordinances of religious toleration today.[14] Thus, Locke's formulation signals a paradox emerging with modern toleration doctrine: that which is most vital to individuals qua individuals—personal belief or conscience—is not only that which is divorced from public life but that which is divorced from the standing of shared Truth. Tolerance of diverse beliefs in a community becomes possible to the extent that those beliefs are phrased as having no public importance; as being constitutive of a private individual whose private beliefs and commitments have minimal bearing on the structure and pursuits of political, social, or economic life; and as having no reference to a settled common epistemological authority. Two things are simultaneously achieved by this privatization, individualization, and subjectivization of religious belief and of moral or ethical values more generally. Civil and political power are rendered technical, material, juridical, or practical—divested of moral, religious, or spiritual meaning or grounding. In addition, religion and all matters of conscience are rendered private and individual, divested of political or communal bearing, thus making the notion of political morality something of an oxymoron. Moreover, community in political life must be radically reduced—it cannot have a thick fabric to it without invoking the very belief structures that must be limited and private if they are not to be mandated by authority. And religious and ethical life must stay sharply bounded, minimizing their claims on public ways of life or public issues. For Locke, "churches stand in the same relation to each other as private persons among themselves, thus have no jurisdiction over one another" (400)—a claim that establishes not merely individual belief but organized religion as private rather than public matters, and as rightly and severely contained in their powers.

Locke's proposed radical compromise of the claims of religious and ethical truth, of conscience and belief, hardly coincided with either the dominant or minority sects of the age. Locke offered a strategy for peace that satisfied almost no one at the time, given their passionate investments in religious orthodoxy and absolutism and deep convictions about the exhaustive reach of religion. Thus, tolerance was initially embraced not as a moral or principled conviction but as a practical solution to an impossible impasse, a fact too rarely recalled about another crucial moment in the genealogy of modern toleration—the American founding. It is commonplace to frame the founding of the United States as coterminous with an embrace of toleration: as they fled from an intolerant religious and political culture in the Old World, the Puritans are credited with establishing a new order based upon tolerance. Yet the settler colonialists of New England made up highly orthodox religious communities, most of them devoted to pursuing and policing religious and moral truths as fiercely as any cult might today, even as individual conscience was for many of them a critical principle.[15] Hence, while tolerance of, first, conflicting religious practices and, then, dissident ideas or speech of other kinds is certainly at the heart of the political tradition of tolerance in the United States, this heart is not without its own paradox: tolerance is a principle coined of necessity, a necessity produced by a collision of absolutist principles, and it is in this sense something of an antiprinciple. Tolerating other zealots was required so that one's own zealotry would be tolerated, and there were, of course, all kinds of limits to toleration in the founding period.[16] Moreover, tolerance was initially an intercommunal principle—granting the autonomy of religious communities vis-à-vis the state and other communities—rather than an intracommunal one, as the haunting figure of Hester Prynne affirms.

These absolutist and authoritarian strains in the ostensibly tolerant New World suggest yet another tension at the heart of the American tradition of tolerance, one captured in the present by Will Kymlicka's distinction between what he calls a liberal model of tolerance based on individual liberty and a hypercommunitarian model based on group rights.[17] Kymlicka largely associates the second model with the Ottoman Empire's "millet system," in which Jewish and Christian communities were permitted both religious freedom and a degree of political self-governance by the Muslim Turks. But this model is not exclusively non-Western; it describes as well the various edicts of tolerance (governing minority religious communities, mainly those of Protestants and Jews) episodically promulgated in various European nations from the end of the sixteenth century well into the nineteenth. These edicts were explicit acts of tolerance that permitted the existence of a minority religious community but hedged such permission with restrictions and other markers of the community's unequal and sub-ordinate status. This kind of tolerance was not based on individual freedom of worship or liberty of conscience; rather, it was crafted as an expedient amid a process of modern state consolidation heavily marked by bloody religious conflict.

Though tolerance of subcommunities by a hegemonic one is a crucial part of the story of tolerance in the West, the Lockean version of tolerance that radically individualizes and privatizes religion, and therefore is also most closely fitted to Protestantism, tends to overshadow it, just as the history of tolerance across various orthodox religious communities in early America is overshadowed by the history of tolerance rooted in the notion of individual conscience or moral autonomy. The existence of the former was especially repressed in the past century, surfacing mainly in law and policy concerned with explicitly marginal and often closed communities—Mennonites, the Amish, Native Americans. But with the revival of tolerance by multi-culturalist discourse, the notion of tolerating the group rather than the individual—or, more precisely, of tolerating individuals as representatives of particular groups—has returned to the fore. This practice flags an interesting moment of anxiety and potential incoherence within liberalism. Tolerance rooted in respect for moral autonomy is addressed to individuals as bearers of such autonomy. When tolerance is proffered for practices, beliefs, or behaviors associated with attributes tied to race, ethnicity, or sexual practice, tolerance is at risk of enshrining that which cancels what it claims to value: ascription or attribute triumphs over choice. This is one reason that liberals, when considering group rights and other ways of legally or politically accommodating culture, are always so anxious to establish that individuals must have their autonomy signaled by "exit" options.

But more is at stake in this anxiety and incoherence than a conceptual shuttling between individual and group, between moral autonomy and essentialized cultural or ethnic belonging. Rather, as the succeeding chapters will argue in greater detail, this difficulty emerges today because the objects, subjects, and place of tolerance in liberal governance have undergone significant transmogrifications since the early modern origins of tolerance. Coined in early modern Europe to deal with religious dissent and the eruption of individual claims of conscience against church and state authority, tolerance now takes as its object a wide array of differences, including sexuality, ethnicity, race, nationality, and subnationality, as well as religious affiliation. Indeed, if you were to ask an American public school child today what tolerance is about, she would be far more likely to talk to you about racism or homophobia than religion, and might well be surprised to learn that our use of the term is rooted in a history of crises and civil wars concerning authority of church and of state. But more has transpired than changes in or multiplication of the objects of tolerance. Tolerance addressed to religious beliefs, themselves taken to express individual moral understanding and potentially invoking deliberation as well as personal revelation, has a different mechanics and produces different effects than tolerance addressed to attributes or identities taken to be given, saturating, and immutable. Tolerance of dissident beliefs is—or ought to be—on a different ontological chessboard from tolerance of sexual or ethnic "difference"; belief, desire, and ascriptive identity are not equivalent problematics, either from the perspective of individual freedom or from the perspective of governmentality. Moreover, while tolerance in the West arose in response to the governance and legitimacy crises produced by the emerging individuation and sovereignty of subjects in the context of entwined political and religious authority, today's range of tolerance objects means that tolerance pertains to the relation not only of state and religion but also state and ethnicity, state and culture, state and sexuality. As the executive of a tolerant regime, the liberal state adopts a formal (but disingenuous) posture of secularism or neutrality in relation to each of these markers of power and stratification.[18]

These shifts in the objects of tolerance alter the relationship between tolerance and liberal equality. When tolerance is primarily about religious belief or other matters of conscience, and aims at consolidating state power by privatizing belief, it is more or less coterminus with a formulation of equality rooted in equal rights to freedom of conscience or worship. Thus, religious freedom and tolerance are relatively interchangeable terms in many historical accounts of early modern Europe. Tolerance is not equivalent to equality and does not promote substantive equality among religions or their devotees, although it does converge fairly unproblematically with the moral autonomy formulated by early liberals as the substructure of political equality. However, when objects of tolerance are persons of certain attributes viewed as inherent, or of certain public social identities considered intractably different from the mainstream, tolerance takes shape as a complex *supplement* to liberal equality, making up for and covering over limitations in liberal practices of equality, completing what presents itself as complete but is not.[19] At one level, this supplementary relationship is rather straightforward: Liberal equality is premised upon sameness; it consists in our being regarded as the same or seen in terms of our sameness by the state, and hence being treated the same way by the law. But tolerance is premised upon and pertains to difference; it is deployed to handle the differences that liberal equality cannot reduce, eliminate, or address. Tolerance arises to cope with social, cultural, and theological material that cannot be finessed by the relatively formal operations of liberal equality and especially by liberal legalism's disavowal of involvement with social, cultural, or religious life. At another level, the operation of tolerance as supplement to equality is complex and indirect: as chapter 3, on Jewish and female subordination, and chapter 5, on the tolerant and intolerable subject, both argue, the emergence of tolerance at particular moments and for particular groups, where formal equality is also present, manages the demands of marginal groups in ways that incorporate them without disturbing the hegemony of the norms that marginalize them. This is an impressive feat, and one that is uniquely performed by tolerance within liberal discourse. Tolerance also often emerges when formal egalitarianism is retrenched or limited in some way, when the liberties of a particular group are restricted (as in the rounding up of Arab Americans after 9/11), or when a group is marked as ineligible for full equality (as in prohibitions against same-sex marriage). Here tolerance appears as a *dynamic* supplement in liberal formulations of equality and citizenship. It produces new subject formations and actively addresses political exigencies to contain potential crises for the legitimacy of liberalism, crises that threaten to reveal the shallow reach of liberal equality and the partiality of liberal universality.

While the objects of tolerance have changed significantly over three centuries of liberalism, so too have the sources and agents of tolerance. Once limited to edicts or policies administered by church and state, tolerance now circulates through a multitude of sites in civil society—schools, museums, neighborhood associations, secular civic groups, and religious organizations. Tolerance is routinely promulgated by liberal democratic states in nondoctrinal ways; and as an element of international human rights doctrine, tolerance is now also figured as something to which people around the globe are entitled, irrespective of the regime under which they live. The dissemination of tolerance across substate and suprastate sites and its circulation as a generic principle linking incommensurate features of civil society are consonant with its shift from the domain of belief to the domain of identity, and with its shift from an element in the arsenal of sovereign power to a mode of governmentality.

There is one other feature of contemporary tolerance discourse that veers sharply from its Renaissance and Reformation origins. Though today tolerance is generally associated with cosmopolitanism, it has not always carried this connotation; and tolerance embraced as political expedient, as it often was in the early period, does not require it. Only recently has tolerance become an emblem of Western civilization, an emblem that identifies the West exclusively with modernity, and with liberal democracy in particular, while also disavowing the West's savagely intolerant history, which includes the Crusades, the Inquisition, witch burnings, centuries of anti-Semitism, slavery, lynching, genocidal and other violent practices of imperialism and colonialism, Naziism, and brutal responses to decolonization. But even more than an emblem, tolerance has become a discursive token of Western legitimacy in international affairs. As chapters 5 and 6 will discuss in detail, the identification of liberal democracies with tolerance and of nonliberal regimes with fundamentalism discursively articulates the global moral superiority of the West and legitimates Western violence toward the non-West. That is, the exclusive identification of the West with tolerance, and of tolerance with civilization, makes the West into the broker of the civilized, delimiting what is "intolerable" and therefore legitimate for imperial conquest cloaked as liberation. Tolerance thus becomes a critical term in the legitimation of Western empire in the twenty-first century.

If the contemporary referents, agents, dynamics, effects, objects, and related discourses of tolerance differ from those of seventeenth-century England, nineteenth-century Austria, or even 1950s America, this does not mean that we are conscious of these differences as we deploy the term or navigate its effects. And the vocabulary of tolerance, like other political vocabularies that have metamorphosed and migrated significantly over the period called modernity, leans on its dispersed heritage for a good deal of its power and legitimacy in the present. Thus, even as it may be deployed for different purposes in the present, tolerance carries its historical glory of liberating individuals from church and state persecution, and its identification of modest freedom of religious belief with freedom *tout court*.[20] Consideration of this historically mottled feature of political terms reminds us that their etymologies, genealogies, and political histories are necessary but insufficient for understanding how they operate in present-day political and social life.

This past-in-the-present feature of liberal political terms is part of what sustains a certain blindness to the heightened regulation of subjects that tolerance discourse now performs, part of what makes tolerance such an effective instrument of contemporary biopower while appearing only as a genial neighborly value. The state-limiting, freedom-maximizing, "live and let live" heritage of tolerance is a critical element of its potency *as* governmentality in the present; to draw on a different theoretical lexicon, this heritage works as part of the contemporary ideology of tolerance. The remainder of this chapter explores this territory by returning to the difference between tolerating beliefs and tolerating identity; it considers the cloaking of the production and regulation of identity by the emancipatory and progressive aura of tolerance talk related to its protection of belief.

TRUTH, IDENTITY, AND BELIEF IN OBJECTS OF TOLERANCE

As suggested earlier, the Lockean argument for religious tolerance involves situating moral and theological truth at the individual, private, nonpolitical level and divesting the state—the formal site of political community in liberalism—of matters of collective belief beyond the most abstract constitutional principles. This move inevitably overbuilds local sites of truth, intensifying their significance as moral and religious truth is eliminated from the formal political domain. Subnational communities of truth are fostered that may be radically antagonistic toward one another and that can avoid hostile clashes only through the principle of tolerance *combined with* formal and informal prohibitions against re-politicizing these truths, making them into bids for public policy. And the more secular, technocratic, and bureaucratic the state becomes, the more powerful is this overbuilding of local sites of moral-religious truth and conviction. This tendency is expressed not only in those persistently difficult policy issues that the secular state tries to finesse—in contemporary American life, abortion, homosexuality, and capital punishment are some of the most highly articulated— but also as a social formation of marked subjects. The overbuilding of local sites of truth thus contributes to civil society increasingly organized by local identities based on ethnicity, religion, sexuality, or culture and expressed through differing belief structures or values that putatively correspond to these identities.

As tolerance discourse contributes to the production of strong local and private truths and excessively thin collective and public ones, it abets a developing relativism in the domain of moral truth.[21] Paradoxically, it simultaneously presents such truth as the deepest and most important feature of human existence yet as that which must be lived and practiced in a contained, private fashion. This argument was at the heart of Locke's brief for toleration: precisely because saving one's own soul was so important, it had to be a private, individual matter and could not be politically or publicly imposed. In a similar fashion, the 1997 "world report" titled *Freedom of Religion and Belief* calls "the capacity for belief . . . a defining feature of human personality" and declares that "religion or belief, for anyone who professes either, is one of the fundamental elements in his conception of life."[22] Yet tolerance requires that such beliefs, so fundamental, so definitive of our humanness, must not be held or acted upon as moral absolutes or as sites of moral superiority. Tolerance also requires a public acceptance of beliefs and values at odds with our own, beliefs and values that we may consider wrongheaded and even immoral. Thus, in its peculiarly modern formulation, tolerance necessitates that a constitutive element of our humanness, belief, be cultivated and practiced privately, individually, and without public effect or public life. A thoroughgoing civic tolerance permits moral absolutes only among private individuals and in private places; publicly, religious and moral truths must be affirmed as individual and nonauthoritative. In this context, a morally passionate citizen becomes strangely intolerable.

If civic tolerance both fosters a withdrawal from a common morality and demands a modest epistemological and moral relativism in public life, the effect of these requirements on political life is particularly significant. Politics necessarily becomes amoral or anti-moral to degrees never dreamed of by Machiavelli and becomes inherently relativist about truth. Symptoms of this condition appear in the past several decades of incessant American talk about the importance of moral values and religious conviction, neither of which can be featured concretely in political discourse without violating the spirit of tolerance. Meanwhile, in keeping with the overbuilt sites of local truth produced by tolerance, moral absolutism seethes below the surface of politics, making public tolerance appear as little more than a détente strategy for conflicts among private moral or religious absolutes. But tolerance also forces the displacement of religious belief and ethical conviction into rhetorically strategic political claims, giving political debate about value-laden policy a deeply disingenuous character and intensifying the rationalization of political life that Weber forecast even as he rooted it in other causes.

This story of politics stripped of moral and religious ground, and of religion stripped of public truth value and public purchase, is, of course, the story of liberalism we have told ourselves for several centuries. The compromises it entails are variously celebrated and decried by theologians, constitutional scholars, political theorists, citizens, and political actors. However, a peculiar formation of identity and difference in recent decades has added a new fillip to these troubling tensions between community and truth, public life and belief, local enmity and universal tolerance. It is to that formation that we now turn.

One contribution made by Michel Foucault to understanding contemporary political life pertains to his tracing of the formation and regulation of the modern subject through a discursive equation of certain beliefs and practices with essential truth of a given subject. This order of subject formation, in which behaviors or beliefs are traced back to inner (hidden) truths that are in turn regulated by the sciences of these behaviors and beliefs, is understood by Foucault as a means of ordering, classifying, and regulating individuals in the age of mass society. Individuality is in this way organized as a basis of knowledge that can be deployed as an instrument of regulation.

Foucault's best-known example of this kind of subject formation is the construction of the homosexual in modernity through the convergence of various scientific, administrative, and religious discourses. According to Foucault, what was regarded prior to the eighteenth century as a contingent act becomes—through nineteenth-century medicine, psychiatry, pedagogy, religion, and sexology—increasingly constitutive of identity such that homosexual *acts* come to be seen as expressions of the homosexual *subject*. Homosexual acts become signs of the core truth of this subject, which is now also reduced to its desires; its sexual desires are the truth of this subject. No longer is one defined by being of this village or that family, this language group or that vocation, but rather by a particular and fundamental sexual or other persona—an identity rooted in desire and behavior. Here is the oft-quoted passage from the *History of Sexuality* in which Foucault summarizes this historical transition:

> As defined by the ancient civil or canonical codes, sodomy was a category of forbidden acts; their perpetrator was nothing more than the juridical subject of them. The nineteenth-century homosexual became a personage, a past, a case history, and a childhood, in addition to being a type of life, a life form, and a morphology. . . . Nothing that went into his total composition was unaffected by his sexuality. It was everywhere present in him: at the root of all his actions because it was their insidious and indefinitely active principle. . . . Homosexuality appeared as one of the forms of sexuality when it was transposed from the practice of sodomy onto a kind of interior androgyny, a hermaphrodism of the soul.

The sodomite had been a temporary aberration; the homosexual was now a species.[23]

Foucault makes a similar claim in *Discipline and Punish*: what was once regarded as a criminal act, a singular event, becomes the sign of the criminal soul or psyche.[24] In the nineteenth century, the prisoner becomes a type, a case, a total personality, as she or he becomes the subject and object of criminology, psychology, sociology, and medicine.

If Foucault is right about this dimension of subject production in modernity, and about its fairly steady expansion as a form of biopower concomitant with a decline in corporal and other kinds of juridical power, this adds another worrisome dimension to the tolerance problem. Marked identities, ranging from "black" to "lesbian" to "Jew," are understood to issue from a core truth that generates certain beliefs, practices, and experiences of the world. The practice or attribute is seen as issuing from the identity and as constitutive of certain kinds of experiences, and the combination of the identity and the experiences is treated as the fount of certain views or beliefs. (Only from this construction is it possible to make sense of the claim that a particular woman "does not really understand that she's a woman" or that a black person is "not really very black," claims that presume to issue from a radical critical position on race and gender but are, according to this analysis, actually complicit in the dominant view.) And, if tolerance designates the right to mutual existence possessed by these identities representing nodes of belief, experience, and practices, it also designates them as existing in a potentially or even inherently hostile relationship to one another. Built as sites of identitarian truth that differ fundamentally from the truth of others, respective identities cancel out one another's truths, threatening or canceling one another's orthodoxies or absolutes—and thus, in the case of identity, threatening one another as persons. In other words, the enmity or cancellation occurs not simply at the level of belief or experience but rather, since the person and the belief are conflated and indexed through attribute or practice, at the level of persons as well. Moral relativism pertaining to belief, coined through an undecidable discord among beliefs, is now conveyed to identity based in body and soul.

From this perspective, it would appear that the incorporation of a language of tolerance into the contemporary ethos of cultural pluralism is no mere accidental slide from a discourse concerned with free speech and religion to a discourse concerned with persons, ethnicity, sexuality, gender, or race. Instead, it seems to express a historical formation in which subjects are identified with and reduced to certain attributes or practices, which in turn are held to be generative of certain beliefs and consciousness. These beliefs and this consciousness is presumed to issue from the essence or inner truth of the person or, at minimum, from his or her culture, ethnicity, or sexuality. In this peculiarly modern discourse of the subject, opinions, belief, and practices are cast not as matters of conscience, education, or revelation but as the material of the person of which certain attributes (racial, sexual, gendered, or ethnic) are an index: hence, the notions of "black consciousness," "women's morality," "cultural viewpoint," or "queer sensibility." In each case, one's race, sexuality, culture, or gender is considered to generate the consciousness, beliefs, or practice—the difference—that must be protected or tolerated. This formulation stands in significant contrast to the Lockean notion that beliefs are matters of personal revelation or deliberation in which our agentic individuality is the expression of our fundamental humanness. In its place, this order of subject formation expresses our humanness as a cultural, ethnic, or sexual being and not as a choosing or thinking—free—individual.

There is an additional paradox here. In *Discipline and Punish*, Foucault argues that disciplinary power marks a moment in what he calls "the reversal of the political axis of individualization."[25] Unlike in feudal and other nondisciplinary societies, in which "individualization is greatest where sovereignty is exercised and in the higher echelons of power," Foucault proposes that in the disciplinary regimes of modernity, "individualization is 'descending': as power becomes more anonymous and more functional, those on whom it is exercised tend to be more strongly individualized." In disciplinary societies, the normal subject is less subject to individuating mechanisms than is someone who deviates from the norm. Thus,

> in a system of discipline, the child is more individualized than the adult, the patient more than the healthy man, the madman and the delinquent

more than the normal and the non-delinquent. In each case, it is towards
the first of these pairs that all the individualizing mechanisms are turned
in our civilization; and when one wishes to individualize the healthy, normal and law-abiding adult, it is always by asking him how much of the
child he has in him, what secret madness lies within him, what fundamental crime he has dreamt of committing.[26]

This regulatory individuation of the deviant, the abject, the other, suggests a further implication of the normalizing work of contemporary
tolerance discourse. Tolerated individuals will always be those who deviate from the norm, never those who uphold it, but they will also be
further articulated as (deviant) individuals through the very discourse
of tolerance. Tolerance can thus work as a disciplinary strategy of liberal individualism to the extent that it tacitly schematizes the social
order into the tolerated, who are individuated through their deviance
from social norms and whose truth is expressed in this individuation,
and those doing the tolerating, who are less individuated by these
norms. To be sure, it is not only members of socially marked groups
who are tolerated according to this schema: the bigot, the refusenik,
the atheist, the street poet, the stereotypical nonconformist—all of
these are individuals establishing the classical justification for tolerance
in the American discourse of individualism. But these figures—and in
some ways they stand as a single figure in American lore—are romantic distractions from the particular story of individualization that Foucault is telling, a story in which disciplinary knowledge and power,
rather than self-fashioning and idiosyncratic belief, are at work in the
organization of populations and construction of subjects.

Now consider the way in which this formation of subjects converges
with what Kymlicka identified as the tolerance model associated with
the Ottoman millet system and what I suggested was an important, if
suppressed, element of both the European and American traditions of
tolerance, in which the existence of a marginal, relatively homogenous
community is regulated by a political or religious regime. If, as Foucault's formulation suggests, minority sexualities, ethnicities, races,
and religions are discursively treated as nearly exhaustive of subjectivity and identity, then the contemporary practice of "teaching toler-

ance" oriented toward these markers tacitly draws on this strain of tolerance. Yet the object of tolerance is not the group but individual marked subjects who carry the group identity. What children are "taught" to tolerate is neither groups nor precisely individuals but, rather, subjects carrying what the sociologists call ascriptive identities. But these are ascriptive identities of a very particular sort: they harbor orders of belief, practices, or desire cast as significant enough to provoke the rejection or hostility that makes tolerance necessary. Thus, advocacy of tolerance toward others who are "different" intensifies the totalizing features of the subject and identity formation described by Foucault. It reifies and exaggerates the "otherness" of a tolerated subject by construing it as the product of a group identity representing, in the words of a docent at the Simon Wiesenthal Center Museum of Tolerance, a set of "practices and beliefs different from ours."[27] That is, the tolerated subject is not just disliked but disliked because it is different, and different by virtue of its practices and beliefs. On the one hand, this logic essentializes race, ethnicity, and sexuality as cultural, as "practices and beliefs." Exactly as Foucault's theory of the modern subject would suggest, racialized being or "sexual preference" is treated as intrinsic and as generating certain beliefs and practices that are "different," and therefore as producing an inherent and permanent condition for which tolerance becomes the solution. Nowhere is race or sexual preference recognized as produced by the essentializing of difference that the discourse of tolerance itself reiterates; that is, nowhere is tolerance recognized as reproducing racialization or sexual identity. On the other hand, the invocation of tolerance inflects these "practices and beliefs" with a religious quality and reaffirms the conceit that the tolerating body—whether the state or an unmarked identity—is neutral or secular. All otherness is deposited in that which is tolerated, thereby reinscribing the marginalization of the already marginal by reifying and opposing their difference to the normal, the secular, or the neutral.

This is one way in which contemporary tolerance takes shape as a normative discourse that reinforces rather than attenuates the effects of stratification and inequality, a reinforcement achieved by casting the religious shadow of early modern tolerance over the disciplinary identitarian formation of the late modern subject. Religiously inflected tolerance discourse oriented toward ascriptive identity simultaneously (1) intensifies the regulatory effects of essentialized identity accounted by Foucault, (2) ideologically constitutes a "difference" out of an effect of subordination or inequality, and (3) strengthens the hegemony of dominant or unmarked identity. Moreover, since (as chapters 3 and 5 will argue) tolerance requires that the tolerated refrain from demands or incursions on public or political life that issue from their "difference," the subject of tolerance is tolerated only so long as it does not make a political claim, that is, so long as it lives and practices its "difference" in a depoliticized or private fashion. In addition to being at odds with the epistemological and political stance to which many politicized identities aspire, this requirement also results in the discursive suppression of the social powers that constitute "difference" as well as in the strengthening of the hegemony of unmarked cultures, ethnicities, races, or sexualities; together these outcomes constitute the signature move of universal or abstract political rights and principles in inegalitarian and normatively striated social orders. Yet, as suggested in the earlier discussion of tolerance as supplement, there is also an important breakdown of universalism signaled by this deployment of tolerance, a breakdown occasioned by the very developments in subject formation that Foucault identifies. That is, the move from tolerating *opinion* and *belief* to tolerating *persons* would appear to correspond to a historical shift from a universal subject imagined to arrive at particular beliefs or values through revelation or deliberation to a particular subject (of sexuality, ethnicity, etc.) who is thought to have these beliefs or values by virtue of who he or she is, *and to continue to be inscribed by a difference even if the beliefs that are the sign of this difference are given up.* At this point, the project of tolerance becomes fully inverted from its original aim to license diverse belief in private while maintaining a common public order and becomes instead a mode of inscribing essential otherness within the common.

We have now come to a quite insidious edge in contemporary tolerance discourse. By converting the effects of inequality—for example, institutionalized racism—into a matter of "different practices and beliefs," this discourse masks the working of inequality and hegemonic culture as that which produces the differences it seeks to protect. As it essentializes difference and reifies sexuality, race, and ethnicity at the level of ideas and practices, contemporary tolerance discourse covers over the workings of power and the importance of history in *producing* the differences *called* sexuality, race, and ethnicity. It casts those culturally produced differences as innate or given, as matters of nature that divide the human species rather than as sites of inequality or domination. This result becomes most apparent when we consider that of all the "differences" addressed by the "teaching tolerance" rhetoric, the one that is routinely missing is class, and the one that is sometimes present but fits most awkwardly is gender. Presumably class is the one social identity in contemporary liberal discourse that is widely viewed neither as rooted in an inner nature nor as manifest in external bodily attributes, although there are certainly elements of bourgeois discourse that make these moves. Within liberal discourse, especially American liberal discourse, class is the one marker of difference that, when mentioned at all, is seen as produced rather than innate, an assumption reinforced by the phenomenon and ideology of class mobility in twentieth-century capitalist societies. If class is not regarded as an inner essence or attribute, then it is also presumed not to exhaust the definition of the person or to be accompanied by a certain set of beliefs; hence it is not a subject for "tolerance." Race, ethnicity, nationality, and sexuality, by contrast, are all cast as distributions of difference that must be accommodated by tolerance.

Gender is another matter. It is routinely essentialized and is often included on *lists* of differences toward which tolerance is to be practiced. However, when focused on by itself, gender is rarely cast as a matter of tolerance. Men as a group are not generally thought of as tolerating women as group, and, for the most part, gender inequality and even gender violence are not represented as redressable by tolerance. What, then, is the anomaly of gender difference in multicultural formulations of difference, and what does the inconsistent and ill-fitting inclusion of gender in contemporary tolerance discourse reveal about that discourse? To these questions we now turn.

THREE

TOLERANCE AS SUPPLEMENT: THE "JEWISH QUESTION" AND THE "WOMAN QUESTION"

> Tolerance is intolerant and demands assimilation.
> —Herman Broch, quoted in the Jewish
> Museum, Vienna, Austria

> The very being, or legal existence of the woman is sus-
> pended during the marriage, or at least is incorporated
> and consolidated into that of the husband.
> —Sir William Blackstone

Why is the condition of women, or relations among the sexes, so rarely framed in terms of a discourse of tolerance? Why did the "Woman Question" in the eighteenth and nineteenth centuries not emerge as a question of tolerance? Certainly, there are occasions when gender inclusion engages this discourse—when, for example, women seek access to ostentatiously male homosocial venues such as exclusive social clubs, military schools, and sports teams or their locker rooms. But equality, not tolerance, is our conventional rubric for speaking about gender desegregation and gender equity. Moreover, while women's "difference," whether identified as sexual, reproductive, or affective, may be an object of tolerance in workplaces, space missions, or combat zones, it is not women as such who are said to be tolerated in these instances; rather, their *difference* becomes a matter for practical accommodation through separate facilities or for special arrangements related to pregnancy and the demands of early maternity. Why? Why is it that today minority religions, minority ethnicities or races, minority sexualities are all treated as subjects for tolerance but women are not? Is the key in the word "minority"? That is, does tolerance always signify a majoritarian response to an outlying or minoritarian element in its midst? Is it simply the case that majorities can never be subjects for tolerance? What, then, of the place of tolerance in the colonial-native relation or in a postcolonial ethos? Isn't cultural or political hegemony rather than proportionalist demographics what tills the field for tolerance?

This chapter approaches these questions through a comparative problematic: why was the "Jewish Question" often framed as a matter of tolerance in eighteenth- and nineteenth-century Europe, while the "Woman Question," from the beginning, emerged through the language of subordination and equality? (Or the contemporary version: why was the 1988 Democratic vice presidential candidacy of Geraldine Ferraro heralded as a victory for feminist "equality struggles," while the nomination of an orthodox Jew, Joseph Lieberman, to that position twelve years later was cast by political pundits as a "triumph of tolerance"?) It is insufficient to respond that Jews were historically ostracized while women were straightforwardly subordinated by law and by individual men, or that Jews were a religious group while women were excluded on the basis of their bodies.[1] Such responses at best open up rather than answer the question. For whatever the difference in the mechanisms and putative bases of disenfranchisement, both exclusions were justified by an imagined difference from the figure of universal man at the heart of the emerging European constitutional political orders. And both exclusions provoked a common desire and goal: political membership, political and civil rights, and access to public institutions, education, and a range of vocations—in a word, indeed, in the word that was most often used in the nineteenth century, *emancipation*. Why did one emancipation movement, then, remain within the rubric of tolerance and conditional inclusion while the other took shape as a project of political equality? How and why did emancipation efforts fork in this way, and what light does this historical phenomenon shed on the metamorphosing relationship of equality and tolerance in liberalism? More precisely, what transformation of the relationship between equality and tolerance in nine-

teenth-century liberalism can be discerned in the particular politicization of identity entailed in these respective emancipation efforts and
in their divergence from each other? In liberal discourse, equality presumes sameness; tolerance is employed to manage difference. So why
did "sex difference" become thinkable and politicizable through the
terms of sameness while Jewishness did not?

The answers to these questions will be found in the imbrication of
several different discourses in the nineteenth century: those construct-
ing gender and Jewishness respectively, on the one hand, and those organizing the terms of liberal tolerance, equality, and emancipation on
the other. Scrutiny of the way in which the discursive construction of
Jewishness framed the politicization of the Jewish question will enable
us to see how the discourse of tolerance shifted its object from conscience and belief to racialized identity and soul, all the while appearing to broker religious difference. And scrutiny of the discursive construction of gender that made possible certain arguments about
women's equality and foreclosed others, while retaining a strong notion of sex difference, will illuminate important features of nineteenth-
century liberal notions of emancipation and equality.

THE JEWS

In considering the formation of the "Jewish Question" in relation to
the discursive construction of Jews in the nineteenth century, and in
connecting this formation and this construction to the establishment
of Jews as subjects of tolerance, we will focus initially on post-revo-
lutionary France. This approach may seem counterintuitive at first
blush, given that from 1791 until the Dreyfus affair at the turn of the
century, France understood itself to have preempted the Jewish Question raging elsewhere on the Continent with straightforward emancipation and enfranchisement. In fact, as students of this period know
well, the picture is more complex. Precisely because "emancipation"
was the standard for the civic and political inclusion of Jews across
Europe in the nineteenth century, and because the French revolutionary commitment to universal equality and liberty was so explicit and
yet so compromised on the question of Jews (and women), France

stands as a kind of paradigm, or even parable, of modernity in the story it harbors of Jewish emancipation, assimilation, and tolerance.[2]

In December 1789, the French National Assembly conducted an intense debate on the question of Jewish emancipation. The debate turned on whether Jews were Frenchmen—and, if not, whether they could become citizens in a newly born regime in which the republic and its members were held to be mutually constitutive.[3] In the context of the consensus in favor of secularizing the state and diminishing the public force of religion, no one in the Assembly argued straightforwardly for tolerance of practicing Jews; that argument would have implied a hegemonic and public religion at odds with the pervasive antireligious sentiment of the time. There was, however, heated argument about whether Jews constituted a nation apart and, if so, whether such a constitution inherently debarred Jews from membership in the republic. For those, such as Abbé Maury, who insisted that the very term *Jew* "denotes a nation," it followed that Jews should be protected but not enfranchised—they could not simultaneously belong to two nations.[4] But for those who understood the Revolution itself as encompassing the project of French nation-building, the clear task was to dismantle rather than honor the remnants of Jewish nationhood.

Here is the case put by Count Stanislaw de Clermont-Tonnerre, the lead speaker on behalf of Jewish emancipation in the December 1789 Assembly session: "As a nation the Jews must be denied everything, as individuals they must be granted everything; their judges can no longer be recognized; their recourse must be to our own exclusively; legal protection for the doubtful laws by which Jewish corporate existence is maintained must end; they cannot be allowed to create a political body or a separate order within the state; it is necessary that they be citizens individually."[5] Entwining Hobbes and Foucault in a single sentence, Clermont-Tonnerre specifies the requirements for carving the new citizen-subject out of the old corporate body: individuation, adherence to general rules and to a single legal and social norm, undivided state authority. Even as conventional tolerance arguments were spurned by the Assembly, Clermont-Tonnerre's reasoning makes clear the tacit toleration deal undergirding emancipation, a deal that submits the tolerated subject to state administration at the very moment of emancipation and enfranchisement. His formulation precisely expresses the twin processes of individuation and privatization of subnational filiations and beliefs entailed in belonging to the new universal state, processes that required what might be termed the Protestantization of the Jew. To be compatible with membership in the French republic, Jews had to be individuated, denationalized, decorporatized as Jews. To cohabit with Frenchness, Jewishness could no longer consist in belonging to a distinct community bound by religious law, ritualized practices, and generational continuity; rather, it would consist at most in privately held and conducted belief.

In the 1789 debate, the French Assembly stalemated on the question of rights for Jews. However, two years later, when debating the issue of Jews inhabiting the eastern provinces, the Assembly voted to rescind all decrees, prohibitions, and privileges relating to Jews.[6] Without resolving the question of whether Jews were French, of whether they constituted a nation apart, Jews were formally enfranchised as citizens. Why? Though the question of Jewish Frenchness could not be easily settled, the matter of incorporating outlying elements of the population into the state was pressing. According to the historian Salo Baron, "Jewish emancipation was as much a historic necessity for the modern state as it was for the Jews."[7] Jews were but one node in the "untidy complex of estates, guilds, classes and corporations, all quite loosely supervised from above, if at all, none totally devoid of autonomy and the capacity to go its own way";[8] this untidiness and attendant subnational freedom and autonomy had to be overcome for the consolidation of state power. Thus, the formulation of and the answer to the Jewish Question was framed as much by *raison d'état* as by political principle or considerations of Jewish welfare, though the latter sometimes figured importantly in the justification and legitimization of emancipation.[9] Put another way, retrospectively the stumbling, stuttering approach to Jewish emancipation in the French Revolution can be explained by the cross tides of immediate concern with membership criteria in building republican France and the longer-term process of consolidating state sovereignty. French revolutionary incorporation of Jews appears inevitable as the logical extension of principles of universal equality and liberty, but it is also fundamentally consistent with the tendency of all European states, starting in the late eighteenth century, to centralize, rationalize, and regularize their power and reach. The anomalous status of Jews in Europe during the medieval and early modern periods—"in" but not "of" various European nations—had to be resolved. And to that end, Jews had to be brought within the ambit and orbit of the state, a process that involved incorporation into a nation increasingly defined through abstract, universal citizenship.

However, to be brought into the nation, Jews had to be made to fit, and for that they needed to be transformed, cleaned up, and normalized, even as they were still marked as Jews. These triple forces of recognition, remaking, and marking—of emancipation, assimilation, and subjection; of decorporatization as Jews, incorporation as nation-state citizens, and identification as different—are what characterize the relation of the state to Jews in nineteenth-century Europe and constitute the tacit regime of tolerance governing Jewish emancipation.

What did it mean for French Jews to become citizens? Insofar as citizenship in republican France was not a formal category extended to an individual with rights but, rather, involved membership in the republic, identification with the state, and participation in French national culture, the process of making Jews citizens meant making them French—that is, modulating any distinctively Jewish sense of community and fealty along with distinctively Jewish public practices and habits. Becoming part of the French nation in this deep sociological way supplied yet another impetus for severing attachment to the dispersed Jewish nation, and it was ideologically framed as well by an Enlightenment rationalism. Assimilation, the thinking went, would make Jews more modern, more European, and more free; Jews shedding archaic and tribal Jewish practices and beliefs in favor of becoming French signified all three outcomes insofar as the French nation stood for all three. Emblematic in this regard is the nineteenth-century assimilationist Jewish historiography that cast the Revolution of 1789 as the "modern Passover," the second flight from Egypt.[10] In this historical metanarrative, the Revolution that emancipated French Jews conferred upon the French nation a hallowed place in Jewish history and in so doing established France as a nation especially worthy of Jewish attachment and loyalty.[11]

As assimilation proceeded over the course of the nineteenth century, what kept Jews themselves from disappearing? This question pertains not only to Jews who abandoned religious belief but to those who, in accord with the formulation of tolerance delivered by the Reformation, persisted in some semblance of religious practice as a private activity.[12] How could Jewish law and ritual practice, rabbinic authority, belief, and attachment to the Jewish nation decline or vanish altogether without taking the Jew with it? "Judaism . . . is not a religion: it is a race," declared Tourasse in 1895, encapsulating the half-century-long process by which a definition of Jews as a physiological *race* came to supplant a definition of Jews rooted in common language, beliefs, practices, and above all nationhood.[13] Since, according to nineteenth-century race discourse, race was inscribed in every element of the body and soul, mind and sexuality, temperament and ability, it could endure after the constituent elements of nation—elements that had to be *performed*, and were not (discursively inscribed) attributes—had been reduced or eliminated.[14] Race enabled (indeed required) the Jew to be a Jew no matter how fully assimilated, no matter how secular. By marking Jewishness as a set of physically distinguishable attributes—skin color and health; specified characteristics of the nose, genitals, and feet—and at the same time casting it as that which saturated every aspect of the being of the Jew, race sustained Jewishness through the process of assimilation in ways that definitions rooted in nationhood or religious belief could not.

Racialization also produced a new subject of tolerance in Christian culture: defined neither by belief nor filiation, the racialized Jew became highly individuated as well as physiologically, intellectually, and emotionally saturated by Jewishness. This new Jewish subject in turn became a crucial site for (1) a new semiotics of tolerance in which Otherness was carried on and in the racialized body; (2) a new administrative subject of tolerance in which the racialized body rather than practices, beliefs, or filiation would be decisive, or at least in which bodily being was presumed to carry the morphological code for all else such that difference was ontologized, hence cast as permanent; and (3) new and ambiguous sources for the conferral of tolerance, dispersed through civil society rather than concentrated in the state and the church.[15]

The racialization of the Jew during the nineteenth century was produced by discourses ranging from anthropological and biological to philological and literary. All of these built on the nineteenth-century zeal, both scholarly and popular, for typology, classification, and measurement and drew for evidence on everything from brain size and survival capacity to the origins of languages and language groups. The developing body of racial theory was not internally coherent or systematic, nor was it radically distinct from cultural theory and historical claims. Biological theories were mixed with historical analyses of oppression to explain how, for example, Jews had survived despite oppression and persecution, how certain physical atrophies in the Jewish body might have resulted from oppression, or why Jews came to look more like their gentile brethren in certain European nations than in others, indeed, why Jews varied so much in their appearance across Europe.[16]

What these notably unsystematic and unscientific theories provided to Jews, Gentiles, leftists, liberals, and anti-Semites alike was a means of establishing the enduring fact of Jewishness independently of belief or ritual. Particularly in the context of French Catholicism, but also in a more general context of tolerance discourse concerned with Protestant sects, the racialization of the Jew circumvented the difficulties in submitting Jewishness to a construal of religion as a belief community. Rather, treating Jewishness as a racial formation enabled Jewish belief and the Jewish nation to fade while the Jew lived. Neither God nor Torah nor Jewish corporate community nor ritual practices were relevant to the identification of Jewishness once race had taken hold. Defined racially, Jewishness was something one carried individually, everywhere and always. Again, this meant that tolerance would change the definition and circumscription of its object: Jews might still be thought of as a group, but the structure of affinity so rendering them was race rather than the nation. Race conjured putatively objective traits rather than subjective attachment or matters of consciousness; but since these traits are carried individually, racialization constituted Jews as individuals incorporable by the nation-state rather than as a community of believers potentially alien to or alien within the nation-state. Yet racialization also established the Jewish difference as permanent, deep, and impossible to overcome. Even after the dismantling of Jewish nationhood and the enfranchising of Jews, even after assimilation, racialization constituted Jews as a permanent difference within the imaginary of a homogeneous nation-state.

Despite the anti-Semitic uses to which it could be and was put, the discourse of racialization was generally taken up by nineteenth-century European Jews with equanimity and even zeal.[17] However awkwardly, this discourse allowed Jews to retain and comprehend a Jewish identity, one that established a modicum of community and connection across generations even as they assimilated; it guaranteed that Jewishness itself would not perish through assimilation.[18] Nor did accounts of Jews as a racial type run in a purely pejorative direction— Jewish superiority as well as inferiority was inferred from it by Jews and non-Jews alike. And in the context of French nationalism, the racial discourse offered the peculiar potential for establishing a certain affinity between Jewishness and Frenchness, in which superior moral characteristics attributed to each were understood as carrying the potential for mutual enrichment as Jews assimilated and intermarried. If both Jews and the French, as racial types, were figured as sharing a bourgeois orientation toward family, work, money, and the future, and if both the Revolution of 1789 and ancient Israel were figured as historical episodes expressing a collective aspiration to liberty, equality, and fraternity, then not only were the French and the Jews each an elect people, they were also compatible elects. This line of thinking produced yet another argument for assimilation, one having utility for the French bourgeoisie as well as for Jews: Jewish blood coursing through France was conceived as strengthening French society and improving the overall stock of a nation already at the forefront of world history. According to one historian, by the time of the Dreyfus affair at the turn of the century, this theoretical association of the messianic projects of Judaism and modern France had become the official doctrine of French Jewish community, challenged by none.[19]

Assimilation, of course, came with various kinds of subtle tolls, which themselves reveal important features of the governmentality of tolerance. As bourgeois French Jews devoted themselves to becoming French and to identifying with Frenchness, not only was their connection to and identification with Jews in other lands necessarily attenuated but Jews also had to moderate their own responses to domestic anti-Semitism if they were not to seem excessively Jewish rather than French. To move from the margins to the mainstream of French society, French Judaism became increasingly politically and socially conservative during the second half of the nineteenth century. In particular, assimilated French Jews drew back sharply from the new Jewish immigrants fleeing the eastern European and Russian pogroms. These newcomers were an embarrassment—they were too poor, too unmannered, and, above all, too Jewish.[20] Thus, the process of trying to become French while racially marked as Other involved not just disavowing Jewish belief, practice, or the nation but disidentifying with one's most victimized brethren and politically radical brethren, as well as abandoning political enmity (e.g., toward Russia) where it was not shared by the French state. Altogether, the price of tolerance was considerable: compromise of religious and political belief, repudiation of fellow Jews, and fealty to a state that did not return it.

To this point, the term *tolerance* has been used in two different senses to analyze Jewish emancipation in the nineteenth century. First, there is the tolerance held out to Jews in exchange for assimilation, a tolerance administered simultaneously by the state and by Jews themselves. This practice was not named tolerance in France—that is, it was not framed as the orientation of the state or the church toward a minoritized religion by a dominant religion. Rather, it was a project directed toward producing a unified nation, a homogeneous and manageable citizenry, and aimed as well at ending the clash of nations represented by the Jewish presence in France. Not named tolerance but tolerance it was, as Clermont-Tonnerre made clear in delineating its strenuous conditions: the disaggregation of the Jewish nation, the decorporatization of Jews, the attachment of Jews to the French nation, the making of Jews into modern French republicans, the dissociation of French Jews from Jews elsewhere. The binding force of the Jewish nation was replaced by the regulating discourses of racialization on one side and of Frenchness on the other; toleration of assimilating Jews was administered through the normative powers of these mutually constitutive discourses. Nor was the effect of these powers slight: assimilated French Jews became politically moderate, religiously closeted, and disinclined to affiliate with radical or Jewish causes. Yet as a racially marked and often racially disparaged people, Jews lived in fear of their vulnerability to tides of anti-Semitism (such as that inciting and buoying the Dreyfus affair), a fear that is itself a sign of the regulatory work of tolerance, even if this work is increasingly located in civil society rather than church or state.

Such anti-Semitic tides evoke a second sense of tolerance, a sense that also brings us closer to the histories of Jews in other European nations. These histories were not always structured by early formal emancipation or liberal republicanism but did share the managed assimilation and racialization of the French case. Whether ghettoized or educated, heavily regulated or simply forced to adopt Christian surnames, serve in the military, or conduct business in German, the various approaches to Jews across Europe in the nineteenth century converged in the construal of Jews as a distinctive people who nevertheless had to be fitted into the consolidating and centralizing nation-states—and thus reformed as well as tolerated. Tolerance in this sense involved a state and civil administrative practice toward a people who had to be incorporated into the nation, but whose racial distinctiveness limited their participation in an emerging universalistic formulation of man. Moreover, because Jewishness was racialized, and because racialization implicated every aspect of being—body, gait, sexuality, gesture, soul, mental capacity, disposition—the object of tolerance was discursively relocated from belief to *ontoi*. Indeed, belief itself was now separable from yet also derivable from the ontics of race, a separability and derivability critical in formulating subjects of tolerance today.

WOMEN

Alongside the distinctive requirements of state consolidation and distinctive discourses of racialization configuring Jewish emancipation in the nineteenth century, certain parallel forces were configuring the emancipation of women. There was, of course, no historically prior subnational or transnational community of women that had to be broken apart to produce women as citizen-subjects, nor did women present the explicit governance problem posed by Jewish communities. However, women were emerging from their submersion in the corporate world of kinship to claim entitlements as individuals, and women were being individuated as subjects through emerging discourses of science, medicine, social work, pedagogy, and sexology. At the same time, new discourses of gender were developing and circulating, discourses that bound women exhaustively to sexed being, much as racialization came to define the Jew. This racialization, which occurred as Jews were emancipated, was deployed in part to mark the limits of emancipation; it is also true that amid the debates about women's emancipation, sexual difference was being drawn more radically and inscribed on the body more deeply than in prior centuries.

As Thomas Laqueur tells the story, in the ancien régime, being female was a status related to activity and venue; through the new biological, anthropological, literary, medical, and psychological discourses, it was reconfigured as a matter of human sexual nature.[21] Like race, this sexed nature was held to saturate the being.[22] Writing in 1803, the anthropologist Jacques-Louis Moreau went beyond insisting on the distinctiveness of the sexes to argue that "they are different in every conceivable aspect of body and soul, in every physical and moral aspect."[23] Or, in the words of J. L. Brachet, a mid-nineteenth-century physician and the author of *Traité de l'hystérie*: "All parts of her body present the same differences: all express woman; the brow, the nose, the eyes, the mouth, the ears, the chin, the cheeks. If we shift our view to the inside, and with the help of the scalpel, lay bare the organs, the tissues, the fibers, we encounter everywhere . . . the same difference."[24]

But discourses about sex difference are hardly the only forces organizing gender and reconstituting the meaning of women during this time. The decline of feudal and petit bourgeois economies and the full onslaught of industrial capitalism wrought enormous changes in the sexual divisions of labor inside and outside the family and in the sexed ownership of trades and means of local production. The sexual division of labor and especially the heterosexually based economic partnerships of agricultural economies gave way to an order in which women's and men's laboring hands were often—not always and not completely—interchangeable and in which women lost control of trades such as dairy and brewing that had heretofore secured them small beachheads of economic and social power. Thus, while Laqueur argues that the new sexual dimorphism emerges in response to "politics[, . . . the] endless new struggles for power and position in the enormously enlarged public sphere of the eighteenth and particularly the postrevolutionary nineteenth centuries,"[25] surely of equal if not greater importance are the breakdown of an ideologically naturalized sexual division of labor in many domains and the severely reduced productivity of the household in the transition from agrarian to industrial economies. Sexed bodily being is articulated as decisive at the very historical moment when practical activity and venue become less so. As household production decreases, as proletarianization amasses women in the factory, and as a growing class of bourgeois women are increasingly shorn of any productive economic function at all, the incitements for demanding women's emancipation are stoked alongside new discourses of female sexual difference that repel those demands.

In sum, the extraordinary ability of capital to, in Marx's phrase, "batte[r] down all Chinese walls"[26] included a powerful capacity to erase gendered social distinctions and transform gendered social spaces heretofore reproduced by sexual divisions of labor in agricultural economies. But in the place of these modalities of making and organizing gender arose a pervasively sexed body, a body that produced a new foundation for subordination rooted in putative difference, a body whose meanings would be interminably debated for their implications about women's candidacy for political and social equality. In the same pattern seen in the racialization of the Jew, there were first-wave feminists who embraced the radical saturation of women by their sex, and there were others who tried to parse and contain it. None wholly rejected it.

EQUALITY AND TOLERANCE

To return to our original question: How did the Woman Question and the Jewish Question take shape within a common rubric of emancipation and at the same time split into respective projects of equality and tolerance? Nineteenth-century European nations faced the problem of fitting two historically subordinated or excluded groups, Jews and (Christian) women, into an emerging universalist humanist rhetoric and liberal political ideology within which human sameness—underspecified but fraught with tacit norms—is taken to be the basis of equality. The discourses of subordination and exclusion producing Jewishness and gender were themselves in transition, and these discourses were both an effect of and contributors to the formulation of the problem of political membership for Jews and women. The growing racialization of the Jew and the relentless gendering of sexed being framed the debates about emancipation and were themselves configured by these debates.

Prior to the emergence of the Jewish Question and the Woman Question, and prior to the political discourses of equality and the social discourses of racialization and gender shaping those questions, Jews and women were cast not simply as different from Christian men but as bearing a difference in status and social location that sharply distinguished them from Christian men and from their privileges. Jews were a nation outside the nation; women were subsumed in the household—underneath the nation, as it were. Yet as each is carried by the new formulations of abstract citizenship and by the new discourses of race and gender toward eligibility for that citizenship, difference is not simply retained but is relocated from status and location to ontology. There were parallels in the construction of difference for each, especially in the extent to which the difference was understood to saturate the respective body, mind, and soul of Jews and women—that is, to exhaustively define their respective identities, subjectivities, and potential public personae. But parallel is not identity. Counterintuitively, perhaps, European feminist emancipation movements were able to cast women's difference as potentially less saturating of women's existence than Jewish emancipation movements could achieve for Jewishness. Let us see how this happened.

Mary Wollstonecraft in the late eighteenth century and John Stuart Mill in the late nineteenth century both root their arguments for women's equality in a strong Cartesianism. "There is no sex in souls,"

Wollstonecraft proclaims, and from this premise she develops her insistence that women are first and foremost human beings, not sexed beings. Since "virtue has no sex," and the highest virtue is the rational use of the mental faculties, then as Poullain de la Barre, following Descartes, declared in 1673, "mind has no sex."[27] In Wollstonecraft's analysis, if women and men share the same moral nature, they ought to share the same moral status and rights. The fact that most women "act as creatures of sensation and feeling rather than as rational beings" is simply the consequence of a faulty education, one that makes women into "plumed and feathered birds" rather than morally upright beings.[28]

Women and men both have the capacity for "educated understanding," a capacity that includes worldly knowledge and a knowledge of God's scheme to direct and temper the passions. Wollstonecraft toys with the idea that the two sexes may have different amounts of such understanding as a consequence of their differences in strength, but it is the same in kind—virtue is androgynous because mind and soul are.[29] Liberty and education, which together produce autonomous reasoning capacity, are the mothers of virtue and therefore must be equally available to women and men. In short, when they are engaged in mental deliberation and other practices of moral virtue, women are not women at all but simply reasoning beings. But what of the sex difference from which Wollstonecraft abstracts in order to make this argument? Where does that sex difference live and what are the implications of its designated habitat for women's civic and political equality? We will return to this matter shortly.

John Stuart Mill makes remarkably little reference to women's bodies in On the Subjection of Women, save for the terrible degradation he imagines women to suffer when they must have sex with men (husbands) they do not like or respect.[30] Mill's argument for women's freedom is pinned entirely on their intellectual potential, even as he argues that their institutionalized subordination originated historically from their physical weakness. What allows him to work both sides of the argument about women's bodies (weaker) and women's minds (potentially equal) is not only a Cartesian metaphysics but a progressivist insistence that the age of bodies and physicality as determinants of merit and place is finished, as far in the past as the age of blind adherence to custom, tradition, and rule by despotic monarchs. What makes women's subordination a historical relic, hence wholly illegitimate, is its basis in a physical difference at a time when other social and political practices—from the abolition of slavery to the repudiation of social rank as a criteria for rights or suffrage—signify a popular and political rejection of stratification by physical difference or circumstances of birth.[31] In the modern age, according to Mill, what brokers legitimate distinction is mind, talent, capacity, and ambition, all set loose in an open field of competition. This age, too, knows the supreme importance to the individual and the species of choosing one's own life course and one's own governors.[32]

Taken together, Mill and Wollstonecraft can be seen to argue for a feminine subjectivity that is at once androgynous and different: androgynous in the rational, civic, and public order of things where mind alone matters, and saturated with its sex difference in the private realm where bodies, temperaments, emotional bearing, and "instinct" are thought to prevail. Neither rejects the sexualization of gender prevalent in the age; rather, each contests only the totalizing reach of this sexualization and draws on Enlightenment rationalism and (as we will see) a certain Cartesian and bourgeois splitting of the modern subject to argue for the androgyny of public sphere existence. Indeed, the reassurance that both Wollstonecraft and Mill offer to those potentially alarmed by the specter of emancipated women lies in their confirmation of women's heterosexual and maternal identity in the domestic sphere, an identity that is treated as natural even if not exhaustive of women's existence. Although both Wollstonecraft and Mill advance the possibility that women ought to be able to choose whether to marry, neither can tarry long with the figure of the unmarried woman; both return incessantly to the assumption of women's married and maternal state. Moreover, both spill a great deal of ink describing the ways that improvements in woman's education and liberty will improve her wifely and maternal capacities: she will be more enlightened, less shrewish, more straightforward, less conniving, a better model for the children, less of an embarrassment to them. All of these advantages, however, are to one side of the central point: women will not cease to be wives and mothers by virtue of their emancipation. Through the division of mind and body, of virtue and daily existence upon which both premise their arguments, women can be women in private, humans in public.

Of course, the counterargument to Mill and Wollstonecraft's position, ubiquitous in the age and against which both are working, is that the sexual or reproductive functions of women's bodies *do* fully saturate women's nature; this is exactly what the strong version of the new sex difference discourse establishes. At the extreme is Rousseau's contention that every element of woman's existence is conditioned by her sexuality—from her inherent lack of authenticity and *amour de soi-meme* to the natural strategic deployment of her sexuality to capture, hold, and even domestically govern men.[33] Similarly, Hegel's reduction of women to creatures of pure immanence is rooted in their reproductive capacities, while his argument that woman is ethically fulfilled in the family pertains to what he characterizes as her natural passivity in love, her unique capacity to both lose and achieve her individuality in and through a male subject.[34] For both Hegel and Rousseau, not simply women's activities and proper venue but women's minds and virtue differ radically from those of men. Indeed, what otherwise diverse late-eighteenth- and nineteenth-century antifeminist arguments share is the notion that woman's nature and the activities and entitlements appropriate to it are fully determined by sexual difference, that woman is fully saturated by this difference.[35] This is precisely the saturation that the Enlightenment feminists resisted. As Joan W. Scott recounts in her study of nineteenth-century French feminists, "they argued that there was neither a logical nor an empirical connection between the sex of one's body and one's ability to engage in politics, that sexual difference was not an indicator of social, intellectual, or political capacity."[36]

Nineteenth-century Europe, then, debated the Woman Question from a roughly common and strikingly new ontology of gender, one in which elaborate sex difference was taken to be a fact while the reach and significance of this difference was contested, particularly from a Cartesian perspective that permits of the separability of mind and body—a separability that, like abstract rights and liberties themselves, was difficult to elaborate for men while it was being refused to women. But it is not Cartesianism alone that permits this splitting off of the androgynous mind from the otherwise wholly sexed being. And it is not the abstract character of liberal personhood alone that creates a wedge for feminism in the new formulation of citizenship. Rather, if sex difference always recurs to the body in some way, then exactly this seemingly obstinate fact makes possible a humanist feminism in a liberal idiom that both disunifies the female subject and brackets the body to make its claims for women's equality. This disunification operates by literally splitting female ontology, parceling it out for different social spaces in which different activities and duties occur. Thus, the feminism of Wollstonecraft and Mill both privatizes the sexed female body—leaving it to individual men, as it were—*and* abstracts from women's embodied existence to make claims on behalf of women's capacity for public life, a capacity that makes women eligible for education, rights, and above all citizenship.

These moves to divide and abstract the subject from its embodied dwelling are typical of the age and by no means unique to the category of gender. The divided subject born with modernity and intensified by liberal ideological and capitalist political-economic constructions—particular/universal, subjective/objective, private/public, civic/political, religious/secular, *bourgeois/citoyen*—is the very subject that can be gathered under a universalizing political rubric such as "equality, liberty, fraternity" while subsisting in a civic and economic order organized by inequality, constraint, and individualism. The subject represented as free, equal, and solidaristic in state and legal discourse is abstracted from its concrete existence where it is limited, socially stratified, atomized, and alienated. In short, the figure of man to which Wollstonecraft and Mill make recourse in their arguments about women—man split in his activities and consciousness, and man abstracted from his everyday embodied existence as he is represented by the state—is the dominant figure of the age. If citizenship and rights are premised upon this abstract, disembodied figure, then it is also the basis on which women's enfranchisement can be claimed. If man has no body in public but exists only abstractly, discursively, through mediated voicing and representation, then woman need not have a body in public either and the sexualization of gender ceases to be an impediment to public sphere equality claims. In other words, that which is understood to make women women need not accompany them into public life where we are all disembodied abstractions, where we are all split off from our private, economic, or civil existence. Women's difference is not, according to this kind of feminism, a public difference.[37]

But why do we not see the same argument made on behalf of Jews? What is the casting of the "Jewish difference" that permits the slide from "emancipation" to tolerance—with the latter's implications of a permanent, insoluble difference—rather than equality? If modern citizenship is predicated upon man as man, not as he actually lives and works but as a potentially divisible and abstract being, why cannot the Jew be split off from or abstracted from her or his Judaism to become a rights-bearing citizen with the same relative conceptual ease displayed in late-eighteenth- and nineteenth-century feminism? To be sure, there were those (e.g., the left Hegelian Bruno Bauer, Marx's famous foil in "On the Jewish Question") who argued that Jews could be dealt with in precisely this fashion. From this perspective, racialization of the Jew was no more determining than sexualization of the woman: Jews could be and were enfranchised on the condition of assimilation, on the condition that they shed identifying and constitutive Jewish practices, or at least on the condition that these practices became completely private.

But it is already telling that there is a qualifier here: namely, that emancipation was tacitly or expressly dependent on assimilation, which is to say on transformation of the Jew. Such a move was never made in the debates about the Woman Question; though at times cajoled to "ascend to reason," women were not asked to give up anything in order to become candidates for emancipation. What could women be pressed to surrender in order to become more acceptable members of the nation, in order to become more like men, in order to gain proximity to, if not inclusion within, the universal? Any effort to desex women would be seen as making them monstrous, exactly what antifeminists accused feminism of doing. Here, emancipation itself already means something different for Jews and for women, for even with emancipation, the tolerance "deal" was already in place for Jews in a way that it was not for women, where a different set of social powers will be seen to sustain women's difference and their subordination through it.

For nonassimilated Jews, the arguments against enfranchisement emerging from the mid-nineteenth-century German debates on this question can be divided into three: (1) the Jew has fealty to another (higher) god, and another (higher) legal order, which preempts his or her fealty to the Christian or secular state; (2) the Jew lives a "partial" (Jewish) life, conceives of him- or herself not as part of universal humanity but rather as belonging to the Jewish portion of humanity, and hence does not participate in the universality the modern state is held to embody; and (3) the Jewish religion cannot easily be rendered a wholly private affair—Sabbath and holiday requirements, as well as public worship and prayer, contour the daily civic life of the Jew and so prevent Judaism from the eligibility for tolerance available to Protestant sects, in which religion can be rendered a purely individual and private order of belief. Judaism as practice combines with Jewishness as a racial difference to remove the possibility of containing the Jewishness of the Jew in the private sphere; to the extent that Jewishness and Judaism saturate the being and daily practices of the Jew, and subtend the Jew through Jewish community, law, or ethnic affiliation, they leak into the domain where the abstract and universal equality, liberty, and community of man are held to reign.[38]

But if these are the arguments against emancipating or enfranchising nonassimilated Jews, arguments that all amount to refusing the incorporation of a nation within a nation, how is it that assimilated Jews could be offered forms of "emancipation" that nonetheless left them vulnerable to anti-Semitic state as well as civil practices (signaling that this emancipation opened onto a regulatory regime of tolerance rather than equality)? To be sure, this regime of tolerance was a different creature from that administered by the seventeenth- and eighteenth-century Edicts of Tolerance in Austria and elsewhere; it had begun its migration from the state to the social as the site of its emanation, and it also was beginning to attach to individuals rather than to subnational groups. But tolerance rather than equality it was, as became clear in ensuing episodes of state and civic "intolerance" in which Jews could lose privileges, be stripped of rights, or be (re)ghettoized, exiled, or exterminated.

What is the relationship between this vulnerability, experienced by Jews as subjects of tolerance but not by women as subjects of equality, and the respective nineteenth-century discourses of racialization and sexualization we have considered? How does each of these discourses position its subjects vis-à-vis the emerging state discourses of universality that organize and confer citizenship? One way these questions may be addressed is through a consideration of Foucault's discussion, in *The Order of Things*, of the epistemic shift between early and classical modernism. In the former, Foucault argues, the truth of an object or relation is based on manifest or visible signs; in the latter (the period we are considering), it comes to be rooted in the presumption of a generally invisible organic structure of things.[39] If Foucault is right about the classical modern episteme, then only in the nineteenth century does it become possible to argue that the female body, for all its putative visible difference, does *not* carry the complete code for women's nature and capacities—or, more precisely, that the visibly sexed body is not the hermeneutic key to the mind or soul of the woman. Rather, feminists asserted, the body is precisely that which must be seen past or seen through for women's soul and mental capacities to be grasped—the mirror image of antifeminists' insistence that the gendering of the female sex, determined by its reproductive function, was carried in every dimension of this being. No one in the feminist debates, in other words, argued directly from bodily appearances to soul and mind; rather, appearances were as likely to belie as to express a comprehensive ontology, and if it could be rhetorically established that souls and minds were ungendered, then the question of women's bodies could be rendered largely irrelevant to public sphere feminist aims. Racialization, however, was another story. If, in a racialized discourse, blood was the index of the Jew, soul was the essence of the Jew, and a people apart was the historical origin of the Jew, then racialization is already a discourse working from the inside (organic structure) out (appearances) and from history (hidden) to the present (manifest). In accord with what Foucault insists is the dominant episteme of the age, racialization is achieved genealogically and metaphorically rather than deduced directly from visible codes, even as it also produces and interprets these visible codes. As Gustave Le Bon formulated the racialization thesis at the end of the nineteenth century, "The life of each people, its institutions, its beliefs, and its arts, are only the visible traces of its invisible soul."[40] In the nineteenth-century episteme, abstracting from bodily appearance to arrive at an ungendered mind or soul is a possibility; abstracting from blood and soul to arrive at the nature of a being is an oxymoron.

As we have seen, the sustained marking of Jews as racially distinctive even as they were emancipated was critical to the contradictory state imperative of simultaneously incorporating and regulating Jews, an imperative that Foucault identifies more broadly as the twin modern forces of "totalization and individuation," though he rarely considers their contradictory nature.[41] Racialization facilitated the coexistence of pressure to assimilate, on the one hand, and the marking of Jews as an object of surveillance to ensure conformity with the terms of their emancipation on the other. The political theorist Patchen Markell argues that "such a surveillance requires that Jews be recognizable. The imperative of emancipation becomes, paradoxically, that *the state must see at all times that each Jew has ceased to be Jewish.*"[42] For Markell, incorporation of an alien element in its Christian midst required a peculiar form of state recognition in which Jewishness never ceased to be identified and never ceased to be targeted for reduction or erasure. This form of recognition is itself paradoxically achieved by the assimilated Jewish embrace of a racialization discourse *and* refusal of solidarity with Eastern Jewry figured as a lower, less cultured, less modern form of life.

The difference between discourses of racialization and sexualization is not limited to the ways in which Jewishness and femininity are inscribed on and in individual bodies; each discourse also posits distinctive forms of association (or lack of it) among these bodies. While racialization, in contrast with nationhood, potentially renders Jews in the image of sovereign individuals and hence as subjects ripe for nation-state incorporation, even decorporatized Jews may still be conceived as a solidaristic people. Even as the decorporatization entailed in the pressures to assimilate, and required for the first order of formal emancipation and toleration, met its limit in the racialization of Jews, this racialization also links them naturally to one another and conjures their natural association. The gendered sexualization of women, by contrast, casts women as individual complements or opposites of individual men. Any essential similarity in women does not imply their political or social relatedness, their intragroup affinity or solidarity. To the contrary, this gendered sexualization establishes women's natural place in the heterosexual family; it produces them as different from men but not as a solidaristic people or nation.

Both of these aspects of modern subject formation—that which ontologizes certain kinds of marked subjects and that which specifies the relation of marked subjects to other similarly marked subjects—remind us that during nation-state consolidation, the discourse of abstract universal citizenship was crosscut with other subject-producing discourses, discourses that facilitated the classification and regulation of citizens who deviated from the Christian, bourgeois, white, heterosexual norm at the heart of these orders. Incorporation of the historically excluded through a discourse of abstract citizenship, a process that threatened to erase the subnormative status of the excluded, itself provoked intensified forms of marking and regulation to reinscribe that status. Tolerance, coined originally to incorporate differences in belief while regulating them, was an available vehicle for this incorporation: it simultaneously permitted individual and group regulation, facilitating the marking of a difference through which both the incorporation and the individuation required for regulation could be sustained.

As tolerance begins to attach to identity rather than belief (as it does in the figure of the Jew), it responds to the moment in liberalism when individualism combined with abstract citizenship falters as a principle of demarcation, when equality-as-sameness falters as a justice principle, when the depoliticization of difference is either incompletely achievable or incompletely desirable on the part of either the subject or the state. Tolerance emerges at this point as a *supplement* to equality rather than a mere extension of it: as a supplement, it is variously a substitute, an alternative, and, above all, that which finesses the incompleteness of equality—making equality "true" when it cannot become so on its own terms. Political and civic tolerance, then, emerges when a group difference that poses a challenge to the definition or binding features of the whole must be incorporated but also must be sustained as a difference: regulated, managed, controlled. In their dispersal and in the sexualization of their identity, women do not represent such a problem; they are not perceived as a solidaristic group, nor does their manifest difference threaten to disappear. But in their association and in the racialization of their identity, Jews do pose such a threat; tolerance is the mantle cast over their emancipation to contain it.

One account, then, of the emergence of a discourse of equality for (Christian) women, and of tolerance for Jews, reveals tolerance to be the sign of a discursively established, obstinate, and pervasive difference that cannot be assimilated in public life without disturbing the norms at the heart of that life; it signals a difference that cannot be abstracted from and that forms the basis for a community—imagined or literalized, minimal or substantial—apart from the nation-state. There is not only the question of the lingering Jewish nation, raised by the continued presence in cities as well as in the countryside of unassimilated Jews; white supremacy combined with Christian hegemony in Euro-Atlantic states means that even assimilated Jews cannot be fully abstracted from their difference to participate in a universal order, whereas (Christian) women can be. In a bodiless public saturated with Christian norms, (Christian) women can achieve a formal legal equality, while Jews, even when enfranchised and accorded rights, are still tolerated (or not) in their difference. Tolerance marks inassimilability to a hypostasized universal, and Jewishness—as a nation or as a race—is figured as such inassimilability.

But we cannot be completely satisfied with this formulation. On the one hand, it overstates the assimilability of women into a humanist universalism and especially into the public and economic life of modern constitutional orders. We know that deep anxieties about sexual difference persist in these domains, and we know that sexual difference is often a far greater barrier than religion (even religious orthodoxy) or ethnicity or race to participation in normatively masculine

regimes. On the other hand, this argument also understates what assimilation *and* racialization make possible by way of privatizing or
eliminating Jewish practice and belief and by way of detaching the individual Jew from a community of Jews. Even if it was not completely
successful, the project of detaching the Jew from a transnational identity and fealty, and of producing the Jew as a European citizen-subject, should have largely neutered political concern with Jewish difference; all that should have been left was scattered social prejudice.
So I want to till different ground now.

If, according to Kant and Blackstone, women are naturally "concluded by their husbands," if husband and wife are "one person in the
law,"[43] what is it that makes woman so incorporable, so available to
being concluded or represented by individual men? There would appear to be only two possibilities here: similitude or natural subordination within an ontological hierarchy. Woman cannot be incorporated by man, cannot be represented by him, as a true opposite; she
can only be that which is either similar or naturally subordinate to
him. If Laqueur is right about the shift, during the eighteenth century,
from a one-sex to a two-sex model of gender, then we are not dealing
with similitude. As we have seen, the similitude asserted even by feminists in this period pertains only to the realm of mind, virtue, and abstract citizenship—the argument is not that women are the same as
men *tout court* but that rationality, virtue, and citizenship have no sex,
are not embodied. Thus, woman's difference—as body, as maternity,
as sexuality, as subject and sign of the household—remains outside the
language and purview of equality, thereby leaving open the possibility
of naturalization and subordination. Female difference, within a presumed heterosexual sexual order, is incorporable by men to the extent
that it is cast as a difference of inherent subjection, exactly the casting
that Kant's and Blackstone's remarks imply. Moreover, within a heterosexual matrix, individual women can be claimed, "concluded," or
represented by individual men, and their alterity within liberalism can
in this way be secured at the same time it is politically resolved.[44] By
contrast, the Jewish difference, however saturated with signs of inferiority within a Christian hegemonic order, cannot be assimilated or

managed in this fashion. Counterintuitively, it remains more unruly precisely because it directly mediates men's relations with one another (notwithstanding Judaism's matrilineal descent structure). Though it first appeared that racialization was a more powerfully determining discourse than sexualization in establishing limits to nation-state incorporation, it would now seem that sexualization functions as a more relentlessly subordinating discourse and is therefore precisely what permits women's enfranchisement as political equals without the risk of substantive equality—and, more importantly, without the risk of a challenge to the masculinist, heterosexual, and Christian norms at the heart of the putative universality of the state.

Another way to see this point involves turning slightly from the public/private axis as the vehicle of subordination and focusing instead on the sexual division of labor left intact by formal emancipation. As critics of liberal feminism have often pointed out, when women are made candidates for political equality, a heterosocial division of labor and association is by no means called into question. Indeed, both Wollstonecraft and Mill anxiously reassured their readers that legal gender neutrality—women's acquisition of economic, civil, and political rights—is not a ticket to gender integration in most of the substantive domains of life. With legal equality, social and economic sex segregation persists and so literally domesticates the effects of women's enfranchisement as citizens. An official policy of complete religious neutrality and racial equality, however, does promise and promote such integration and its attendant ramifications: once Jewish men are fully enfranchised and are full bearers of rights, the "Jewish difference" lives on institutionally only in an epiphenomenal fashion. There is potentially no limit to the political, social, and economic domains that Jews and gentiles will cohabit, even as informal enclaves for each may persist—from commercial enterprises to neighborhoods to country clubs to academic departments. Thus, the language of tolerance, which always signals the undesirable proximity of the Other in the midst of the Same, becomes an index of this very capacity for mixing and of the perceived threat to a social norm that it portends. If the language of tolerance is invoked for women only when they are knocking at the doors of expressly male or masculine venues, then to the extent that women stay in their sexually assigned places and to the extent that the feminine body is heterosexually appropriated and privatized, the need for tolerance does not arise.[45] Women's formal political equality is neither the sign nor the vehicle of their integration; to the contrary, such equality is founded in a presumption of difference, organized by a heterosexual division of labor, and underpinned by a heterosexual familial structure, all of which attenuate the need for tolerance and at the same time underscore the difference between formal and substantive equality.

What this means is familiar from several decades of feminist theorizing about the effort to obtain gender equality in a liberal political frame: precisely because this effort abstracts from women's condition and activities in the private realm (the condition and activities that implicate women's sexuality and women's designation through maternity) and yet reifies the subject, woman, rather than apprehending the discourses constituting that subject, women's social equality within liberalism always remains incomplete. A subjection is presupposed and institutionalized, a subjection that turns on women's privatized and unemancipated heterosexual difference, a subjection that licenses everything from marital rape to the feminization of poverty to an inegalitarian sexual division of labor in both the family and the market. It is because and insofar as women are subordinated by a sexual-social division of labor devolving on their bodies that they can be rendered equals in the public; it is the capacity to split their existence in this fashion that makes them candidates for equality rather than tolerance, or, more precisely, that means their attainment of political equality does not require the supplement of tolerance for male superordination to be maintained.

The rhetoric of tolerance would thus seem to function as one diagnostic key for relations of subordination in liberalism. It is summoned to redress histories of subordination or exclusion where a more thoroughgoing equality is immediately at stake, where maintenance of an abjected or subjected Other is possible neither through a mechanism such as privatization of this subordination nor through sustained institutionalization of this subordination in the economy. Tolerance is invoked in liberal democratic societies when a hegemonic norm cannot colonize or incorporate its Other with ease, when that norm maintains or regroups its strength through a new technique of marginalization and regulation rather than through incorporation and direct relations of subordination. Hence today, popular political discourse treats heterosexual women as candidates for equality, while lesbian women are candidates for tolerance; the subordinating difference of the former is secured by a heterosexual social and familial order while the latter cannot be. More generally, while gender conceived heterosexually is not a subject for tolerance, gender detached from a heterosexual matrix—not only gay but transgendered and transsexual bodies—immediately convenes the discourse of tolerance, confirming that it is the heterosexual family, the family-economy relation, and the sexual division of labor that secure a gender regime in which male superordination is achieved by means other than an expressly normative discourse excluding or abjecting women. In this regard, the invocation of tolerance functions as a critical index of the limited reach of liberal equality claims. Practices of tolerance are tacit acknowledgments that the Other remains politically outside a norm of citizenship, that the Other remains politically other, that it has not been fully incorporated by a liberal discourse of equality and cannot be managed through a division of labor suffused with the terms of its subordination.

This is not to argue that identity crafted from race, sexuality, ethnicity, Judaism, or Islam is crafted from material that inherently makes an individual eligible for tolerance. It is not to claim that these are primarily normative powers of subordination, producing claims for recognition, while gender and class are materially organized powers, eligible for redistribution claims.[46] To the contrary, that one order of power is assigned to norms and the other to materiality is itself symptomatic of the discursive mystification of certain forms of inequality reinforced by tolerance discourse and the powers of subordination in tolerance discourse. Tolerance *appears* as a discourse of pure normativity, of pure recognition and its limits; what this appearance hides is the inequality and the regulation (achieved through the governmentality of tolerance dispersed in society), and not simply the normative marginalization organizing its subjects. Norms of gender subordination can be entrenched through the privatization of one crucial aspect of them: the laboring, sexualized, reproductive, often-but-not-always heterosexual feminine body. The fashion in which the gendered body can be split and domesticated is echoed in a homosexual, Jewish, or other racialized body only through the practice of passing.

If tolerance discourse is triggered when subordination at the site of a difference cannot be maintained through privatization of that difference, it would seem that gender subordination, but not the Jewish difference figured as masculine and racialized, could be almost completely privatized. If tolerance discourse is triggered when a historical practice of social marking and exclusion can be sustained while its subordinating effects are somewhat attenuated, then a sociofamilial division of labor allows male superordination to be sustained amid a discourse of formal equality, but there is no parallel institutional instantiation for white and Christian superordination. If tolerance discourse is triggered when incorporation of a given subcommunity threatens the unity and homogeneity as well as the formal and informal norms of the nation, sex difference construed heterosexually does not figure such a subcommunity or such a threat, while Jews as a nation, and Jews as a race, do. If tolerance discourse is triggered when a marked group is simultaneously incorporated by the nation yet, in order not to disturb a governing norm, is at the same time denoted as Other, then such a discourse is not needed for a group whose incorporation does not erase the visible sign of difference.

But if tolerance entails privatization of a difference that matters, a privatization that always threatens to leak into the public, why doesn't women's situation elicit it? Privatization of a difference is not equivalent to subordination through difference in the private sphere; the former is an expressly political and discursive achievement, while the latter can occur inarticulately and independently of the law and independently of other discourses of governmentality. Women do not need to be tolerated, because the discourse of their difference remains the site and vehicle of a subordination achieved through a division of labor working across, and itself articulating, a set of public/private distinctions.

Both Jews and women, formally emancipated in nineteenth- and twentieth-century Europe, gain political equality without fully shedding the stigma of their difference. But for Jews, emancipation is accompanied by the governmentality of tolerance because once the legal strictures are removed, the discursive construction of the Jewish difference ceases to be systematically subordinating as a state or economic operation—and this very loss constitutes a threat to a crucial Euro-Atlantic nation-state norm. In this regard, tolerance iterates differences whose significance may be fading but, in so doing, veils its own role in activating these differences and hence its own work of subordination. This veiling is enhanced by the dispersion of the rationality of tolerance, its steady governmentalization over the nineteenth and twentieth centuries. As tolerance comes to emanate from a growing range of civil sites—from schools and police forces to neighborhood associations and individuals—and comes to target ever more and diverse objects, from sexual minorities to Muslims, it appears as nothing more than a simple and benign strategy of peaceful social cohabitation.

■ ■ ■ ■

TOLERANCE AS GOVERNMENTALITY: FALTERING UNIVERSALISM, STATE LEGITIMACY, AND STATE VIOLENCE

> We need to understand how fortunate we are to live in
> freedom. We need to understand that living in liberty is
> such a precious thing that generations of men and women
> have been willing to sacrifice everything for it. We need to
> know, in a war, exactly what is at stake.
> —Lynne V. Cheney

What is the relation of contemporary tolerance discourse to formulations of citizenship and the state? And what is the relationship of this discourse to state legitimacy and state violence? This chapter poses these questions against the backdrop of nineteenth- and twentieth-century changes in the objects, agents, and project of tolerance discussed in chapter 3. There, we witnessed a shift from the tolerance of beliefs or opinions (religion and other matters of "conscience"), which are generally considered subjective, to the tolerance of identities rooted in ideologically naturalized differences (race, ethnicity, sexuality), which are generally considered objective. There is also a shift in the agents and vehicles of tolerance: in the twentieth century, tolerance no longer emanates only from state and church but is promulgated from a variety of sites in civil society.

This chapter will develop the argument that together these changes are part of what configure tolerance today in the form of what Foucault terms "governmentality." As an order of policy discourse that is largely nonlegal without being extralegal, as a state speech act that is only occasionally an enforceable rule, and as a popular discourse that circulates in and among schools, churches, civic associations, museums, and street conversation, tolerance will be seen to exemplify Foucault's unorthodox account of government: "not a matter of imposing laws on men, but rather of disposing things, that is to say, to employ tactics rather than laws, and if need be to use the laws themselves as tactics."[1] Moreover, as a discourse that peregrinates between state, civil society, and citizens, that produces and organizes subjects, and that is used by subjects to govern themselves, tolerance will also be seen to embody what Foucault formulated as a distinctive feature of modern governmentality: The state is not the wellspring or agent of all governing power, nor does it monopolize political power; rather, the powers and rationalities governing individual subjects and the populace as a whole operate through a range of formally nonpolitical knowledges and institutions. The ensemble of legal and nonlegal, pedagogical, religious, and social discourses of tolerance together produce what Foucault understands as the signature of modern governmentality, its effect of *omnes et singulatim* ("all and each," the title of one of Foucault's lectures and a constant referent for him in conceptualizing the nature of modern political power). Simultaneously totalizing and individualizing, amassing and distinguishing, and achieving each effect through its seeming opposite, tolerance emerges as one technique in an arsenal for organizing and managing large and potentially unruly populations. As such, it is a strand of biopower, that modality of power so named by Foucault because it operates through the orchestration and regulation of life rather than the threat of death.[2]

Suggestive as Foucault's analysis is, however, it is also insufficient for the analysis I want to pursue here. To begin with, his formulation of governmentality is notably thin, conceived mainly in terms of the genealogy of its emergence in the eighteenth century in Europe, when population becomes the critical object of political power and political economy becomes a principal form of political knowledge. Foucault's formulation of governmentality is also problematically inflected by some of his relatively local theoretical skirmishes; in Foucault's rendering, governmentality perhaps stands to state sovereignty as genealogy stands to dialectical critique and as discourse stands to structuralist accounts of ideology. Each is mounted as a critique of the other, is intended to correct the perceived conceptual flaws of the other, and thus is somewhat overdrawn in its opposition to the claims and premises of the other.

Before we rework Foucault's account of governmentality to free it slightly from the parochialisms enabling and constraining its theorization, it may be useful to consider what Foucault was trying to achieve through his recuperation of the old-fashioned term *government*, and through his coinage of the strange cognate terms *governmentality* and *governmentalization of the state*. With the notion of governmentality, Foucault was striving to integrate a set of concerns that preoccupied him during the 1970s: the critique of sovereignty (state and individual); the decentering of the state and of capital as the organizing powers of modern history (and a corollary decentering of state theory and political economy as dominant frameworks for conceiving power); the elaboration of norms, regulation, and discipline as crucial vehicles and organizations of power; and the development of analyses that illuminate the production of the modern subject rather than chart its repression. Foucault's governmentality thesis not only integrates these concerns, it gathers them into a project that moves from critiques of inadequate models and conceptualizations toward the development of a framework for apprehending the operations of modern political power and organization.

The questions of modern governance, according to Foucault, are "how to govern oneself, how to be governed, how to govern others, by whom the people will accept to be governed, and how to become the best possible governor?"[3] Government in this broad sense includes but is not reducible to questions of rule, legitimacy, and state institutions. And governmentality, a term that explicitly fuses government and rationality, is designed to capture the uniquely modern combination of governance by institutions *and* by knowledges, to stress the dispersed nature of modern governance, and to grasp the circulation of political rationalities as rivaling Weber's classic "monopoly of violence" in defining political power.

Governmentality as Foucault elaborates it has several crucial features. First, governing involves the harnessing and organizing of energies in any body—individual, mass, international—that might otherwise be anarchic, self-destructive, or simply unproductive. And not only energies but needs, capacities, and desires are harnessed, ordered, managed, and directed by governmentality. Governing thus concerns what Foucault calls "the conduct of conduct"—it orchestrates the conduct of the body individual, the body social, and the body politic. Second, as the conduct of conduct, governmentality has multiple points of operation and application, from individuals to mass populations, and from particular parts of the body and psyche to appetites and ethics, work and citizenship practices. Third, far from being restricted to rule, law, or other visible and accountable power, governmentality works through a range of invisible and nonaccountable social powers, of which Foucault's best example is pastoral power.[4] And fourth, governmentality both employs *and* infiltrates a number of discourses ordinarily conceived as unrelated to political power, governance, or the state. These include scientific discourses (among them medicine, criminology, pedagogy, psychology, psychiatry, and demography), religious discourses, and popular discourses. Governmentality, then, draws on without unifying, centralizing, or rendering systematic or even consistent a range of powers and knowledges dispersed across modern societies.

Within the problematic of government and governmentality, Foucault's interest in the state is largely limited to the way in which it is "governmentalized" today—both internally reconfigured by the project of administration and externally linked to knowledges, discourses, and institutions that govern outside the rubric and purview of the state. The "governmentalization" of the state connects "the constitutional, fiscal, organizational, and judicial powers of the state . . . with endeavors to manage the economic life, the health and habits of the population, the civility of the masses, and so forth."[5] While governmentality in general includes the organization and deployment of space, time, intelligibility, thought, bodies, and technologies to produce governable subjects, the governmentalization of the state both incorporates these tactical concerns into state operations and articulates with them in other, nonstate domains.

Foucault's de-centering of the state in formulating modern governmentality corresponds with the contrast between governing and the state that introduces his discussion of governance. Even as he acknowledges that the state may be "no more than a composite reality and a mythicized abstraction,"[6] Foucault takes the state to signify powers of containment and negation, a signification that does not capture the ways in which modern subjects and citizens are produced, positioned, classified, organized, and, above all, mobilized by an array of governing sites and capacities. Government, as Foucault uses it, also contrasts with rule; as monarchy ended and the homology between family and polity dissolved, rule ceased to be the dominant modality of governance. However, Foucault is not arguing that governmentality chronologically supersedes or fully replaces sovereignty and rule. In his own words, "we need to see things not in terms of the replacement of a society of sovereignty by a disciplinary society and the subsequent replacement of a disciplinary society by a society of government; in reality one has a triangle, sovereignty-discipline-government, which has as its primary target the population and its essential mechanism the apparatuses of security."[7]

Yet as already indicated, however promising governmentality is for tracking tolerance as a discourse that circulates between a variety of pedagogical, religious, legal, political, and cultural sites, and that produces and positions citizens and subjects, Foucault's account is also problematic here precisely because of its strategic diminution of the state in theorizing modern political power. For tolerance discourse not only governs subjects, it not only quiets potential civic conflict or social unrest, it also shores up the legitimacy of the state and in so doing shores up and expands state power. As we will see, both state and nonstate deployments of tolerance serve important strengthening and legitimating functions for states suffering from weakened sovereignty occasioned by globalization and crises of universalism related to exposed investments in certain hegemonic powers, groups, and status categories. Tolerance discourse will also turn out to be paradoxically important in legitimating certain kinds of state violence.

So here is the corrective I would offer to Foucault's account: Although the state may be a minor apparatus of governmentality, although it is itself governmentalized and survives only to the degree that it is governmentalized, the state remains the fulcrum of political legitimacy in late modern nations.[8] But political legitimacy, especially the political legitimacy of institutions conferred by those subject to them, is not a matter in which Foucault was much interested.[9] And legitimacy is largely excluded from his formulation of governmentality (though it does make an appearance in his discussions of specifically neoliberal governmentality).[10] Yet even as governmentality captures both the unboundedness of the state and the insufficiency of the state as a signifier of how modern societies are governed, it fails to convey the extent to which the state remains a unique and hence vulnerable object of political accountability. If state legitimacy needs determine at least some portion of political life, then this is a fact with which a theory of the imperatives conditioning and organizing governance ought to reckon—and Foucault's theory does not.[11] We can think about this another way: modern political power not only manages populations and produces certain sorts of subjects, it also reproduces and enlarges itself. Because such reproduction and enlargement at times fall among political power's primary aims, they cannot be treated independently of the project of governing populations and individuals. A full account of governmentality, then, would attend not only to the production, organization, and mobilization of subjects by a variety of powers but also to the problem of legitimizing these operations by the singularly accountable object in the field of political power: the state. These two functions may be analytically separable, and at times they may appear at cross purposes, but they do not occur separately in practice; an account of contemporary governance therefore must capture both. This is not to say that the state is the only source of governance, or even always the most important one; but where it is involved (and this includes privatization schemes in which the state's connection with the enterprises to which it turns over certain functions is still visible), the question of legitimacy is immediately at issue.

In this vein, I will be arguing that the deployment of tolerance by the state is in part a response to a legitimacy deficit and, in particular, to its historically diminished capacity to embody universal representation. Tolerance discourse masks the role of the state in reproducing the dominance of certain groups and norms, and it does so at a historical moment when popular sensitivity to this role and this dominance is high, when those who have been historically excluded by norms of sex, race, ethnicity, and religion are vocal about such exclusion. State tolerance talk both softens and deflects these tensions. So, for example, in the context of the national security crisis precipitated by 9/11, the American state not only guaranteed equality across ethnicity and subnationality, it also expressly called for civic tolerance of what is conjured as threatening Americans in the post-9/11 period: "Middle Eastern types" in "our" midst. The state's guarantee of equality expresses its powers to fulfill the social contract, while the state's call for tolerance seeks to incite a modality of citizen behavior that rejects stereotyping, prejudice, and above all vigilantism. Yet at the same time that the state represents itself as securing social equality and rhetorically enjoins the citizenry from prejudice and persecution, the state engages in extralegal and persecutorial actions toward the very group that it calls upon the citizenry to be tolerant toward. From roundups of illegal aliens by the Immigration and Naturalization Service (now Immigration and Customs Enforcement, within the Department of Homeland Security) to detention and deportation of one ethnic subcategory of illegal residents to racial profiling in airport security searches to police and FBI interrogations that abrogate civil rights, the state has busily vilified and persecuted Arab Americans and Arab foreign residents, constituting them as potential threats to national security and as a suspect, hence vulnerable and tenuous, population.[12] These apparently Janus-faced actions are not mere hypocrisy or subterfuge but are, rather, precisely what tolerance—as both a subject-regulating and state-legitimating discourse—makes possible.

To understand how tolerance may have acquired this complex contemporary governing function (where governmentality includes the amassing and legitimating of state power), we need to return to the question of how tolerance came to have a late modern renaissance in the first place—how it came to be a justice discourse in our time and what kind of justice discourse it is. Tolerance is popularly framed as one phase of a steady progress toward civil and political enfranchisement of historically excluded populations—a frame in which candidates for tolerance always eventually become candidates for political equality—but it has surged back into popular and state discourse at the very historical moment that Western democracies ought to have moved "beyond tolerance." Why has it emerged as a justice discourse at this particular juncture, when, according to the progressivist account, it should have largely disappeared? And what is the significance of its new features? That which was in an earlier time a state practice of managing dissent from settled truths and deviance from settled norms, and took the form of express edicts and other laws stipulating the conditions under which tolerance would be offered, is now promulgated as a group and individual practice for negotiating entrenched differences and social identities. What are the implications for tolerance, as a regulatory discourse, of these shifts in its locale, agents, and aims?

Beginning with the conventional story of why tolerance has lately had such a renaissance may help loosen its grip on our intellectual imaginations. On this account, the combined effects of globalization, the aftermath of the cold war, and the aftermath of colonialism have led to the world's erupting in a hundred scenes of local and internecine conflict, roughly rooted in identity clashes, and tolerance is an appropriate balm for soothing these conflicts. The explanations offered for the eruptions themselves are several, including the following: (1) In the Soviet bloc, the end of the cold war lifted the lid repressing ancient blood feuds and the tensions between unlike peoples forced to cohabit by artificially drawn nation-state boundaries. The volatility of this sudden de-repression is compounded by new power vacuums in which identity conflicts fester and bids for hegemony are waged. (2) Late modernity features the rise of fundamentalisms—ethnic, religious, national—that are by nature intolerant and must be countered with an array of cosmopolitan values and conflict-reduction techniques, including tolerance. (3) Globalization's historically unprecedented mixing of the world's peoples—migrations and settlements incited by late modern capitalism and violent postcolonial political legacies—leads, especially in the North Atlantic nations, to ethnically and religiously diverse people living cheek by jowl, often in economically precarious and socially deracinated circumstances. In the absence of the comforting affirmation of long-standing homogeneous communities, anxiety arises about "difference," thereby intensifying identity claims and identity conflicts which the learning of tolerance can soften. Or, ethnicized others become scapegoats for economic hardships, and teaching tolerance is a means of reducing the violence if not attenuating the projection that this scapegoating entails.

In short, the story derivable from each of these accounts or any combination of them is that tolerance discourse is ubiquitous today—indeed, is urgently needed today—because the steady process of secularization and universalization promised by an Enlightenment metanarrative has been displaced by a backwash into tribalisms, localism, raging nationalisms, and fundamentalisms. Since tolerance was coined to manage eruptions of the particular against the imagined universal, the marginal against the mainstream, the outsiders against the insiders, it is little wonder that tolerance has made a *revenu* as the Enlightenment narrative of history has faltered. The universal lies in tatters, the normal is under constant challenge, the outsiders are all inside now but without cosmopolitan sophistication or aspirations the result is hardly harmonious.[13]

Commonsensical and ubiquitous as it may be, this answer to the question of how tolerance has come to be such an important justice discourse in our time is inadequate because it presumes the creature it needs to explain: it presumes that tolerance ameliorates conflicts rooted in intrinsic differences, it presumes that these conflicts took their shape prior to the discourse called on to broker them, and it presumes that tolerance is a natural and benign remedy for such conflicts. It does not explain how these conflicts come to be framed as problems of intolerance rather than something else. It does not explain why the proposed remedy for these conflicts is tolerance rather than emancipation, tolerance rather than equality, tolerance rather than autonomy or sovereignty, tolerance rather than armed struggle, tolerance rather than repression, pathologization, or criminalization. Or, as Foucault argued in his studies of power, the question *why* often presumes to know in advance the nature of *what* we are analyzing, thereby inadvertently ontologizing the discursive organization of the present and naturalizing the very terms we need to subject to genealogical disruption if, for example, we want to understand what kind of social order and subject tolerance brings into being or stabilizes.[14] This line of reasoning suggests that instead of asking why we need tolerance so badly today, we might more productively ask, What produces the conviction that we need it badly, what kind of tolerance is being called for, who or what is doing the calling, who is called on to enact it, what is tolerance being invoked to achieve, what kind of subjects and objects is it producing, and what ramifications does it have beyond its surface aim of conflict resolution?[15] Such questions allow us to consider how tolerance discourse itself frames and organizes the conflicts it is summoned to solve.

To relocate the ground of inquiry, then, and to grasp tolerance as a technology of domestic governmentality, we need historically attuned accounts of the late-twentieth-century emergence of tolerance as a discourse of domestic justice and as a means of obtaining civil peace.[16] Here, speculatively, are two historical tributaries potentially contributing to this emergence.

First, the *popular* promulgation of tolerance, as it issues from civil rights groups, schools, religious organizations, and neighborhood associations, would appear to be part of a general retreat from the more ambitious liberal and left political agendas of the mid–twentieth century, a retreat that signifies dashed hopes for realizing such agendas and lost faith in the worth of justice projects bound to the elimination or radical reduction of social, political, or economic inequality. Framed thus, the contemporary embrace of tolerance appears to emanate from not merely a compromised but a despairing political ethos. Nor does a new valorization of tolerance underscore a retreat only from equality or emancipation projects. The promotion of tolerance also abandons participatory models of civic and political life. Rodney King offers a plaintive epigram—"Can't we all just get along?"—for the terribly thin vision of membership, participation, and social transformation heralded by tolerance. (Contrast this with the epigram offered by the other King, which was emblematic of a mid–century political vision: "I have a dream . . ."[17]) Tolerance as a primary civic virtue and dominant political value entails a view of citizenship as passive and of social life as reduced to relatively isolated individuals or groups barely containing their aversions toward one another. And insofar as cultivating tolerance is frequently figured as the best means of preventing what have come to be called "hate crimes," tolerance is countenanced not to dissolve the hatred but only to forestall the crime.

This depiction of citizenship stands in sharp contrast to a politically interested and mobilized citizenry, one that has certain solidarities, is capable of acting on its own behalf, and anticipates a future of ever-greater social equality across lines of race, gender, and class. Tolerance as a social ideal figures a citizenry necessarily leashed against the pull of its own instincts; it embodies a fear of citizen sentiments and energies, which it implicitly casts as inherently xenophobic, racist, or otherwise socially hostile and in need of restraint. In its bid to keep us from activating or acting out our dislikes and diffidence, the ubiquitous call for tolerance today casts human society as a crowded late modern Hobbesian universe in which difference rather than sameness is the source and site of our enmity, in which bonds fashioned from mutual recognition are radically diminished, and in which both the heavy hand of the state and the constraining forces of necessity are frighteningly absent.

We can go further here. Through its routine privatization of sites of difference (discussed in chapter 1), the call for tolerance aims to reduce encounters with difference in the public sphere—that is, to reduce public engagement with difference and, by this means, to reduce the very problem of difference as an expressly political problem, referring it instead to "culture" or "nature" and thereby depoliticizing its sources and solutions. As the political theorist Anne Phillips suggests, on the one hand these reductions sacrifice the possibility of politically transforming "differences" lived as both effects and vehicles of inequality or domination. On the other hand, they sacrifice the possibility of developing deep knowledge of others in their "difference" and hence the possibility of substituting such engaged understanding for moralistic distance from or denunciation of difference.[18] In short, tolerance as a dominant political ethos and ideal abandons not only equality projects but also the project of connection across differences, let alone solidarity or community in a world of differences. It aims to separate and disperse us, and then naturalizes this social isolation as both a necessity (produced by difference) and a good (achieved by tolerance).

The retreat from more substantive visions of justice heralded by the promulgation of tolerance today is part of a more general depoliticization of citizenship and power and retreat from political life itself. The cultivation of tolerance as a political end implicitly constitutes a rejection of politics as a domain in which conflict can be productively articulated and addressed, a domain in which citizens can be transformed by their participation, a domain in which differences are understood as created and negotiated politically, indeed a domain in which "difference" makes up much of the subject matter. To the contrary, as it casts the political and the social as places where individuals with fixed identities, interests, and ideas chafe and bargain, tolerance discourse attempts to remove from the political table as much of our putatively "natural" enmity as it can. This formulation undercuts the cultivation both of shared citizen power and of a substantive public sphere devoted to the fashioning of democratic political culture and community. Moreover, the retreat from a political encounter with difference exacerbates the problem imagined to occasion it. The thinner that public life and citizens' experience with power and difference grows, the more citizens withdraw into private identities and a perception of fellow citizens as tools or obstacles to their private aims, and the more we appear in need of tolerance as a solution to our differences—a solution that intensifies our estrangement from one another and from public life as a field of engagement with difference.

Nor does the anti-political thrust of contemporary tolerance discourse end here. As previous chapters argued, in its privatization and naturalization of difference, tolerance discursively buries the social powers constitutive of difference. When heterosexuals are urged to tolerate homosexuals, when schoolchildren are instructed to tolerate one another's race or ethnicity, the powers producing these "differences," marking them as significant and organizing them as sites of inequality, exclusion, deviance, or marginalization, are ideologically vanquished. Indeed, in its move to individualize, to decorporatize, and to solve conflict through individuation and privatization, tolerance would appear to carry a certain fear of the political. Perhaps the contemporary embrace of tolerance carries as well an anxiety about the contiguity of politics and violence, an anxiety that identity conflict must either be suppressed or be fought to the death, an anxiety itself fomented by the contemporary retrenchment of a discursive public space—a domain of relatively nonviolent political contestation—that would teach otherwise.

Though tolerance discourse may represent the retrenchment of more thoroughgoing justice projects and a generalized retreat from robust formulations of political life, it also represents, and indeed is incited by, a retreat from the Enlightenment notion that Man is a universal creature and is only contingently and epiphenomenally divided by language, culture, nation, or ethnicity.[19] Those halcyon days are over: today, we hear from every corner, differences matter. If not intrinsic and permanent—which is what much popular and scientific discourse holds—they are at least considered highly intractable. And tolerance is required because they are intractable. Indeed, as the homosexuality-is-curable advocates make clear, differences eligible for transformation do not require tolerance. Tolerance arises at the dusk of Enlightenment Man not to relieve us of the problem of difference but to inscribe its power and permanence.

This first approach to a historically minded account of the resurgence of tolerance talk emphasizes a generalized post-1960s retreat from far-reaching justice projects and efforts at cultivating robust participatory democracy. But in focusing primarily on tolerance in popular and civic life, it ignores the state's deployment and exploitation of tolerance discourse. Moreover, the account dwells on the intellectual climate and the *mentalité* that undergirds eruptions of tolerance discourse while eliding the relevant historical-material formations that incite this discourse. These two elisions compel a host of questions connected with the other historical tributary. With regard to the first elision—the multiple locations and addressees of tolerance discourse—what are the routes through which tolerance discourse circulates between citizenry and state, and between civil society and state? What is the difference—

in object, in aim, in moral and political valences—between state and civic discourses of tolerance? What kind of governmentality is forged from the movement of tolerance between civil sites and the state? And with regard to the second elision, which concerns the historical-material conditions fomenting the current circulation of tolerance discourse, what is the place of globalization in producing and organizing this circulation? In particular, what of the unprecedented migrations of the world's populations that have brought about the end of even the faintest conceit of the homogeneous nation-state?[20] And what of the tensions between state sovereignty and the eruption of nationalisms and other fundamentalisms in the postcolonial and especially post–cold war period that make tolerance seem so necessary? After considering the second set of questions, about the nation-state and globalization, we will be positioned to address the first set of questions regarding the circulation of tolerance discourse between state and civil society, a circulation that signals the presence of governmentality.

To grasp how and why tolerance discourse is employed in conflicts engendered by the challenges to state sovereignty posed by the rise of nationalist, transnationalist, and other sovereignty and identity claims, we need to return to the breaking up of subnational communities attendant upon the consolidation of the modern nation-state, discussed in chapter 3. That discussion suggested that events such as the 1782 Edict of Tolerance for Jews in Austria and the declaration of Jewish emancipation by the French National Assembly in 1791 offered Jews a straightforward choice: either embrace a particular form of assimilation in which Jews still remained marked as Jews or accept near-total exclusion from the premises and promises of modernity.[21] This marked a turning point for European Jewry: the shift from the self-regulating, if persecuted, Jewish communities of medieval Europe to the individuation of Jews as citizen-subjects in modern European states. The Jewish nation, and primary identification with it, had to be dismantled as Jews became citizens of European nation-states. Further, and most crucially for understanding the effect of tolerance on the development of the public sphere itself, though Jews might continue to behave collectively, the public aspect of this behavior occurred within a liberal discourse in which Jewishness itself had no place. Thus, the development of the modern public sphere is revealed as premised not simply upon the destruction of prior corporate structures but upon a complicated formula of inclusion entailing the exclusion of rich, sub- ject-constituting, ethical, moral, and religious discourses.[22] As reli- gious and other minorities were incorporated into the state, minority communities were disaggregated *and* minority discourses were ex- cluded from legitimate public and especially political discourse. This particular economy of disaggregation, individuation, incorporation, and discursive exclusion continues to structure productive and espe- cially regulatory dimensions of tolerance in the present. However, as we will see, this economy is no longer primarily driven by law and pol- icy emanating from state institutions; rather, it is fueled by a variety of sites of civic discourse, state pronouncements, and citizen interpel- lation—in short, by governmentality, in which the state figures but is not the only figure.

Premodern corporate communities created certain zones of collec- tive self-determination and self-regulation vis-à-vis formal feudal gov- ernance and the emerging nation-state, zones that disappeared as these corporate structures were disaggregated. Such zones of modest local sovereignty, earlier undermined by the various forms of "enclosure" entailed by nation-state consolidation, are further reduced by the gov- ernmentality of tolerance, as (1) an outlying or anomalous culture or community is submitted to state and especially liberal norms; and (2) the individual carved away from these communities is fashioned (at the subjective level) and positioned (in the social order) by homoge- nizing forces such as Christianity, liberal political discourse, and the market. Corporate bonds are thus broken *from within* as the individ- ual is excised from the corporate community and broken *from with- out* as the community is brought into hegemonic political, economic, and cultural orbits, and as the protection from the nation afforded the community by spatial separation and discursive autonomy is thereby diminished.[23] Concretely, the state becomes a formal administrator of the community, but so also do other hegemonic forces—for example, Christianity and the market—which have informal but powerful transformative effects on the newly tolerated and enfranchised com- munity. The philosopher Joseph Raz offers uncritical, indeed approving, support for this process in his account of how multicultural societies, even when they are not dominated by a privileged cultural majority, avoid high levels of social and political fragmentation precisely because a single (capitalist) economy and a single (liberal democratic) political order have felicitous homogenizing effects.[24] These forced involvements with common culture, in Raz's view, usefully restrict the meaning and reach of differences in a multicultural population.[25]

It is through these triple mechanisms—excision of the individual from the corporate community, loss of protection for communal norms and practices in a homogenizing cultural and political-economic context, and incorporation/inclusion of the community in a state discourse—that what begins as a project of freedom or inclusion acquires an edge of subjection and regulation. As communities, dug out of their ghettoized or otherwise anomalous political spaces, are brought under the jurisdiction of the state and into the orbit of mainstream economy and culture, individuals abstracted from ethnic, religious, or other subnational orders are converted into citizens on the condition that the belief world from which they hail be excluded from legitimate public discourse. After working moderately well from the middle of the nineteenth through the third quarter of the twentieth century, this tacit bargain has begun to reveal its limitations and contradictions as a practice of governmentality. For the more that rich cultural norms are eradicated from public discourse, the more vulnerable this discourse becomes to fundamentalist and other counterhegemonic social movements. A public sphere formally devoid of all nonsecular sources of moral and ethical judgment is quite defenseless against substantive ethics claims; it has only proceduralism to fall back on, and thus cannot deliver compelling judgments about, or even interpret the meanings of, a polity's thorniest ethical or political dilemmas. Once nation-state sovereignty itself begins to fray—with damaging consequences, among others, for the presumed cultural neutrality and universalism legitimating the liberal nation-state—public discourse becomes more vulnerable to subnational or transnational identity claims (ethnic, racial, sexual, religious) that compete with state-based nationalism. As the nation-state loses its embeddedness in cultural hegemony—indeed, as it must loosen itself from explicit involvement with reproducing white, Christian, male, heterosexual norms—a range of social movements fill the public sphere with noisy demands and complaints, including reactionary, anti-modernist ones. The commitment of liberalism to a public sphere uncontaminated by nonliberal moral discourses, whether explicitly religious or not, paradoxically makes it vulnerable to challenges to its imbrication with norm-based inequalities as well as to the claims of fundamentalist or essentialist identity-based social movements.

But we need to back up here. While contemporary objects of tolerance are conventionally conceived in terms of "subnational" identities or groups, these objects also generally possess a transnational element, however variable in degree. The very decorporatization of community—Jewish, sexual, Islamic, or ethnic—that is frequently a condition of tolerance seeks to lessen if not eliminate the transnational dimension of the identity at issue. As chapter 3 argued, the Jewish nation must recede for the Jew to be enfranchised, just as the good (tolerable) homosexual shuns a life revolving around the bars and baths—a sexual community—in favor of family and corporate values, and the good American Catholic listens more closely to the president than the pope and sides with British *raison d'état* against the IRA. Consider, in this regard, Bush's account of American Muslims following the September 11 attacks on the World Trade Center and Pentagon: "there are millions of good Americans who practice the Muslim faith who love their country as much as I love the country, who salute the flag as strongly as I salute the flag."[26] Muslims who love the American flag, who salute it "strongly," are the polar opposite of "religious extremists" bound to Allah or Osama bin Ladin and interpellated by calls to jihad.[27] America can tolerate Islam in its midst to the extent that Muslims have fealty to the (American) nation-state over transnational Islam. This transfer of loyalty is paradoxically literalized through love of a symbol—the flag, a literalization that Arab business owners and cab drivers in New York understood perfectly as they plastered their windows with American flags in the aftermath of the attacks.

Tolerance responds to transnationalist forces and formations, which themselves threaten or at least haunt the integrity and sovereignty of the nation-state, by countering them with an acceptable nationalism, by making national citizens out of transnational subjects. This process is evident in the eighteenth- and nineteenth-century production of French Jews as French cultural subjects and as French republicans, rather than as mere individuals with rights. Similarly, in twentieth-century state discourses of tolerance oriented toward multicultural populations, tolerance produces a new national citizen on the ground of a deracinated culture of origin. Tolerance is offered on the condition that the individual shifts *public* attachments and fealty from the old object to the new, and potentially from one nationalism to another. This conditionality is not always easy to see, because the old attachment may be retained but privatized (and often renamed as cultural), while the new attachment is performed in public (and identified as civic or political). Thus, in the weeks after September 11, Muslims in New York could be found praying to Allah in the basement of shops whose upstairs windows were adorned with those American flags.

But here is the paradox that arises when tolerance as governmentality demands this shift in fealty objects, a paradox brought into view by correcting for Foucault's inattention to the specific needs and powers of the state in theorizing governmentality: The state places itself in a hostile relationship with the community being tolerated even while representing itself as that which confers emancipation and tolerance, that which offers protection to minorities. This is the political face of tolerance's requirement of decorporatization: the state promises to protect and tolerate individuals, not groups whose fealty is to some higher or lower god, to some other national formation, to some elsewhere. Tolerance discourse thus appears both as a disciplinary strategy to control a motley, potentially ungovernable and growing number of transnational affiliations in a time of weakening nation-states and dramatic international population migration, and as a restorative strategy to legitimate weakening nation-state sovereignty and thinning notions of nation-state citizenship. That is, not only is tolerance a tactical political response aimed at quelling the disturbances of the peace wrought by erupting fundamentalisms and other identity-based demands, it is also a technique for relegitimating liberal universalism and restoring the notion of the culturally unified nation at a moment when both are faltering. Even as globalization has, among other things, eroded both nation-state sovereignty and nation-state fealty, tolerance emerges as a civic disciplinary technique—not quite a state or juridical practice—for rejuvenating both. Moreover, if, consequent to both late modern material and ideological developments, the liberal state itself can no longer promise universal representation, if it can no longer pretend to a norm-free cultural standing, and if liberal values of assimilation, secularism, or formal equality are being called into question as a basis for nation-state belonging and as the best means of solving problems rooted in "difference," then state promotion of tolerance can serve simultaneously to distract from these losses, to resurrect the neutral status of the state on a post-universal footing, and to expand state power to pursue "intolerant" and even violent domestic and foreign policies. And to the extent that "freedom" remains the primordial term through which liberal regimes obtain their legitimacy, tolerance shores up this legitimacy in the face of curtailed freedoms or exposures of the limited efficacy of liberal freedom. Finally, as certain demands for equality by marginal or socially subordinate groups are negotiated by the state, the function of tolerance as a supplement to—and at times a substitute for—liberal equality is activated. State speech about tolerance grows more vociferous as the state falters in its commitment to equal treatment, when it focuses on difference rather than equality.

These multiple dimensions of tolerance as governmentality, and the range of its venues, agents, and functions, appear in two recent policy episodes in American politics: the same-sex marriage debate and the Bush administration's discourse in the immediate aftermath of the September 11 terrorist attacks. In both cases, we can track the circuitry of tolerance discourse from state to civil society to individual and back to the state. This is the circuitry that contains the simultaneously state-legitimating and civic-disciplinary effects of tolerance and is part of what organizes the governmentality of tolerance.

SAME-SEX MARRIAGE

Both the campaigns for and against same-sex marriage can be situated in the genealogy of liberal inclusion practices and development of the public sphere briefly recounted above. The very possibility of arguing for state recognition of same-sex unions on a par with heterosexual unions is premised upon the prior existence of a politically intelligible challenge to a social order of male dominance and heteronormativity historically certified and reinforced by the state. In other words, a campaign for same-sex marriage becomes intelligible only when a wedge has already been driven between state proclamations of universal representation and orders of exclusion that the state has heretofore endorsed and supported. To the degree that rich cultural norms, including those of religion, are formally excluded from legitimate public discourse, and to the degree that laws rooted in those norms thus become vulnerable to challenge, counterhegemonic social movements can access a wide port of entry into public debate.

The campaign to legalize gay marriage is, in short, a campaign for inclusion that depends on there being a political-cultural hearing for a critique of state codification of masculinist and heterosexual norms in existing marriage law. Such a hearing is possible only when universal equality and inclusion have triumphed over other moral discourses constitutive of public life and the state, when the commitment to juridical equality is the dominant chord in liberal public life. However, as chapter 1 argued, it is not just that equality has triumphed but that those other discourses have been delegitimated as *public* discourses by the very commitments that brought religious tolerance into being in the first place: the commitment to the privatization of moral and religious belief, the commitment to dethroning the state as a site of moral authority. Thus, the campaign against same-sex marriage is part of this same story insofar as it represents a reaction to the emptying out of religious or cultural norms from state and public discourse. Indeed, this campaign insists on the importance of the state embodying and upholding certain norms that stand to one side of formal liberal principles, such as those that consecrate and privilege heterosexual marriage.

Now let us consider, within this context, George W. Bush's position on the question of gay marriage as he formulated it in a preelection debate with Al Gore in 2000: "I'm not for gay marriage. I think marriage is a sacred institution between a man and a woman. . . . I'm going to be respectful for [sic] people who may disagree with me. . . .

I'm a person who respects other people. I respect their—I respect—
. . . I will be a tolerant person. I've been a tolerant person all my life.
I just happen to believe strongly that marriage is between a man and
a woman."[28] Bush's stance, which has remained consistent throughout his presidency and which undergirded his 2004 press for a constitutional amendment to ban same-sex marriage while tacitly endorsing
civil unions, couples a rejection of the petition for same-sex marriage
with the advocacy of tolerance for people who disagree with him *and*
for homosexuals (his syntax, or lack of it, implicitly equates the two).

On one level, this formulation attempts to position the state as con-
querable neither by the gay marriage campaign nor by those who oppose homosexuality *tout court*. It even constitutes the state as the potential peacemaker between the gay marriage advocates and the
homophobes: it advocates tolerance of homosexuals as individuals
while protecting the institution of marriage from the debasement
feared in letting its gender economy slide. But this positioning is not
achieved by the state actually taking a middle position. Rather, Bush
commits the state to actively shoring up the family values and marriage form that its own secularization has weakened, while advocating that the general public be tolerant of "alternative lifestyles."[29] As
the protector of heterosexual marriage and prerogative, the state itself
does not and cannot stand for equality in the sexual field; and the tolerance it urges is not its own but is carried out *by* individuals *toward*
individuals in the realm of the social, not the legal. Importantly,
though, only by urging tolerance can the state resecure legitimacy (its
commitment to universalism having been challenged by the revelation
of its investment in hegemonic cultural norms) while taking a position
at odds with equality, and while taking a position that sides with one
counterhegemonic movement against another. Thus, as tolerance substitutes for equal rights, this substitution is masked by its being performed by the citizenry rather than the state.

The state, as protector of heterosexual marriage and of heterosexual privilege more generally, beholds gender difference and confers
marital rights and sexual legitimacy on the basis of what it sees. But
in calling for tolerance, the state urges citizens not to look, not to see
what it sees. The tolerance the state urges on the citizenry is secured

through our averted glance, by a kind of visual privatization that is a ghostly repetition of the actual privatization of sexuality required if homosexuals are to be tolerated at all. This complex economy of seeing and not seeing, in which state and citizenry have opposite assignments—the state sees and enjoins homosexuals from marrying, the (heterosexual) citizenry averts its glance and tolerates homosexuality in its midst—means that tolerance in this domain can only be a civil and individual rather than a state practice. The state does not do the tolerating, citizens do. Yet the state's advocacy of tolerance and the citizenry's interpellation as tolerant are crucial to state legitimacy at the moment that the state is taking a religious and inegalitarian stand on marriage. Viewed from another angle, the state's advocacy of tolerance conjoined with fundamentalist policy implicates the citizenry in a complex ruse that disciplines increasingly unruly kinship practices at the same time that it relegitimates a state whose cultural norms are showing.[30]

TOLERATING ISLAM

In the immediate aftermath of the September 11 terrorist episodes, George W. Bush surprised many Americans with his frequent remarks about the importance of treating Arab Americans with respect, his effort to distinguish Islamic belief and practices from the violence of the perpetrators, and his warnings against scapegoating and stereotyping as well as abuse and vigilantism. His efforts in this direction were sometimes fumbling—he spoke of "women of cover" when expressing his dismay about intimidation of Islamic Americans wearing religiously sanctioned clothing and he stuttered over the formulation of an American "we" that was not normatively Christian: "Our nation must be mindful that there are thousands of Arab Americans . . . who love their flag just as much as . . . [we] do. And we must be mindful that as we seek to win the war that we treat Arab Americans and Muslims with the respect they deserve."[31] Following a meeting with American Islamic leaders in Washington, D.C., on September 17, he declared, "It is my honor to be meeting with leaders who feel just the same way I do. They're outraged, they're sad. They love America just as much as I do."[32] Multiculturalist talk does not come easily or naturally to Bush: he reinstalls a "we" and a "they" at the very moment he is trying to dispel the distinction; he tacitly represents Muslims as outsiders to America; and he can establish belonging only by asserting subjective identicality—"they feel exactly the way I do." Still, the very earnestness and the repetition of these efforts to staunch bigotry and racial violence took many by surprise.

But while Bush continuously urged citizen regard for the rich diversity of the American population, while he preached respect and tolerance as model citizen behavior, this was hardly the state's bearing either in prosecuting the war in Afghanistan or in "fighting terrorism" on the domestic front. Even as the populace was suborned to civility and tolerance, state practice was immediately and flagrantly extralegal, violent, race-conscious, and religion-conscious. The prosecution of the war on Afghanistan involved substantial "collateral damage"— that is, civilian Afghan casualties at rates that would have been flatly unacceptable if suffered by Europeans or Americans.[33] The state detained thousands of Arabs and Arab Americans after the September 11 attacks, several hundred of whom remain in custody without being charged, despite subsequent revelations that evidence linking them to any illegal, let alone terrorist, activity is nonexistent.[34] During these detentions, near relatives of the detainees were not informed of the names or whereabouts of the detainees, nor were the detainees permitted legal counsel.[35] Interrogation at their residences of another 5,000 young men on student, tourist, or business visas who were reputed to "have come to the U.S. from countries with suspected terrorist links" began in December 2001; Miranda rights were not read to these men, and those questioned who had expired visas joined the growing numbers of individuals from the Middle East targeted by the Immigration and Naturalization Service for immediate deportation or indefinite detention.[36] At the same time, the state was rapidly creating an increasingly wide domain of unaccountable power for itself. The first USA Patriot Act, signed into law shortly after September 11, licensed not only unprecedented levels of surveillance of the citizenry but also "court stripping"—removing authority from the judiciary in times of crisis and, in particular, circumventing judicial powers that protect civil liberties. In early October 2001, Attorney General John Ashcroft also instructed all federal agencies to resist Freedom of Information Act requests made by American citizens whenever "institutional, commercial, and personal privacy interests could be implicated by disclosure of the information";[37] in effect, he single-handedly overturned the FOIA in the name of national security. Meanwhile, federal investigators began to chafe against civil and criminal rights provisions protecting detainees who refuse to speak. In November 2001, the FBI and the Justice Department raised the possibility of using truth serums or torture to extract information, or of sending detainees to countries where such means of interrogation are legal or routine.[38] (Four years later it has come to light that many of the torture techniques involving sexual humiliation and religious desecration performed at Abu Ghraib were also used on Arab detainees in domestic custody, and were directly sanctioned by Secretary of Defense Donald Rumsfeld.)[39] Then came Bush's mandate that terrorists be tried in military tribunals rather than federal courts and his refusal to abide by Geneva Convention standards, coupled with images of Afghan prisoners of war in Guantánamo Bay—shackled, blindfolded, shaved, gagged, caged in the open air—and in crowded prisons in Afghanistan, starving, sometimes to death.

Thus, in the months after 9/11, the state's own vigilantism, violence, and racial profiling, at home and abroad, did not simply stand in contrast with the state's proscription of citizen vigilantism and calls for tolerance. Rather, it was legitimated by this proscription and these calls; as long as the state implores its subjects to be peaceful, law-abiding, and without prejudice, it can use its prerogative power—and even mobilize the citizenry—for the opposite practices. The state can abrogate its commitments to upholding civil liberties and to egalitarian enjoyment of these liberties by substituting a discourse of tolerance for a practice of equal protection or equal treatment. Moreover, the state issues calls for tolerance not because it is or can be tolerant, but so that we will be and it does not have to be—so that it can act like a state. This is not to say that the state is forthrightly intolerant, but that neither equality nor tolerance nor protection of civil rights is within the ambit of *raison d'état*.

On one level this is obvious enough and old news: throughout modernity, *raison d'état*, especially in the international sphere, has always enjoyed modest independence of liberal institutions and values, an independence justified within liberalism by the state's security function rather than its equality function. However, particularly as a globalized economy and transnational social and political forces erode state sovereignty and the efficacy of state action in the international sphere, thereby attenuating the state's capacity to fulfill its security function, state legitimacy depends on a sustained identification of the state with liberal principles of equality and liberty; it depends as well on the capacity of the state to maintain an unrestive citizenry, one that does not turn against itself or turn against the state. Tolerance talk is, among other things, a vehicle for producing this quietude, passivity, even submission. Tolerance calls out a docile, individuated, deactivated citizenry in the context of a volatile multicultural order striated with potent transnational alliances—Afghan, Islamic, Jewish, Iraqi, Arab. Tolerance, combined with the post-9/11 injunction to "shop, spend, buy" to boost a war economy, figured a somnambulant population—unified by the culture of commerce—that stood in sharp contrast to the vigilant, violent, and divisive posture of the state and in sharp contrast as well to the potential mobilization of sub- and transnational identity among the citizenry that such a crisis could engender.

But in addition to mutual respect and tolerance, and the newfound patriotism of shopping, the state hailed its subjects in yet another way in the immediate aftermath of 9/11, one that initially seems at odds with the above analysis. In the domestic war against terrorism, Americans were asked to become the "eyes and ears of the government," and to heighten vigilance about strange people and strange behaviors: we were to be wary of mail we didn't recognize, people we didn't know, actions that seemed out of place.[40] This need for wariness, of course, justified racial profiling undertaken by the citizenry—for example, suspiciousness toward an Arab man sitting in an office reception area with a package on his lap or toward a "foreigner" on an airplane who was nervous and fidgety. Indeed, such "intolerant perspectives" were not only justified but patriotic, insofar as they constituted the suspicious citizen as a member of a citizen militia in the war on terrorism. Patriotic, too, as the very name of the congressional act licensing it indicates, was the embrace of curtailed civil liberties and thus *our* tolerance of racial profiling in airport security stations, reductions or loss of access to public buildings, searches and seizures without warrants, detainments without cause and without Miranda rights, wiretaps on phone conversations, surveillance of book buying and library habits, and interceptions of mail between prison inmates and their lawyers. In this interpellation, we are no longer distant and passive subjects of the state but rather its agents and mirror image, appendages of a nonliberal *raison d'état*.

Both interpellations—as passive and docile subjects organized by tolerance and by shopping, and as agents of the state organized by xenophobic fear—are essential to a complex project of legitimating the state in late modernity. On the one hand, citizens, like the state, must embrace a multicultural rather than homogeneous figure of the nation. On the other hand, citizens, like the state, must incarnate some strong notion of a national "we" to sustain the identity of nation and state, respectively, as well as the relationship between them. On the one hand, citizens, like the state, must express through their behavior the "Americanness" of equal treatment, mutual respect, tolerance, and freedom of belief and association.[41] On the other hand, citizens, like the state, must be hyperalert to the dangers in their midst; in this way, they become the state's everyday foot soldiers against terrorism.[42] But here is how the legitimating logic goes: defined against the unfree, intolerant peoples who menace us, a tolerant citizenry is a virtuous and free citizenry; and it is precisely this virtue and freedom that licenses the violation of principles of tolerance and freedom in the name of our security. This virtue and liberty contrast with the direct racialized violence of the state; however, in conferring the virtue of tolerance upon the people, in calling for tolerance, the state allies itself with virtue, regardless of what it actually does or incites. The state must be the source of the call for tolerance; it must dress itself in citizen virtue (as well as patriotism) in order to pursue actions often in violation of domestic law and international accords, independently of international organizations and alliances, and often with indifference to the principles of justice it feigns to embody. Thus, for example, Assistant Attorney

General Ralph Boyd wrote just two days after 9/11: "Any threats of violence or discrimination against Arab or Muslim Americans or Americans of South Asian descents [sic] are not just wrong and un-American, but also are unlawful." And Bush himself remarked, "Those who feel like they can intimidate our fellow citizens to take out their anger don't represent the best of America. They represent the worst of humankind."[43]

The logic unfolding here is not simply one of state hypocrisy or manipulation. Instead, the governmentality of tolerance makes the citizenry less a puppet of *raison d'état* than a crucial vehicle of it, and hence a vehicle of its own subjugation as a citizenry. Another episode from the immediate post-9/11 period makes clear how this aspect of the governmentality of tolerance works: On 30 September 2001, the Anti-Defamation League, which describes itself as a "not-for-profit civil rights/human relations organization dedicated to combating anti-Semitism and bigotry of all kinds, defending democratic ideals and safeguarding civil rights," bought a full-page ad in the *New York Times*. Headlined "Empowering Children in the Aftermath of Hate: A Guide for Educators and Parents" and packed with didactic small print, the page detailed activities for schoolchildren of various ages designed to teach the damage done by "stereotypes, prejudice, and discrimination." "Intolerance of difference," the ad opined, "is at the root of most violence"; therefore, it is our task as parents or teachers to "give our children the tools they need to confront hate effectively in the aftermath of the frightening and violent events of September 11, 2001."[44] There are several strategic agendas one could ascribe to this ad, but the intentional ones are less interesting here than how its message represents the citizen task of tolerance and casts the relationship between this citizen task and a legitimation of state violence. Here is how this goes:

The Anti-Defamation League is unequivocal in its support for Israel's occupation of Palestine and in its defense of all the state violence this occupation entails.[45] It was unqualified in its support for Bush's invasion of Afghanistan, and later of Iraq. What is the connection between the call for tolerance and the legitimation of Israeli and American state violence? How might the former even serve to legitimate the latter? In the wake of the September 11 attacks, those Americans who qualified their support for Israel, and for America's support of Israel, were cast by the ADL as inherently anti-Semitic; ergo, intolerant.[46] Similarly, Americans who blame Israel in the Israeli-Palestinian conflict are inherently anti-Semitic; ergo, intolerant. Initially counterintuitive, the logic works perfectly once you enter it: If lack of support for Israel equals anti-Semitism equals intolerance, then tolerance does not just permit but requires both state violence and American support for it. The language of tolerance is part of what sanctions the state violence that itself reproduces and mobilizes the "difference" that becomes the occasion for tolerance in the first place. But tolerance is not merely a cover for ethnicized or racialized state violence; it is not only a cloak for the state's dagger. Rather, tolerance mobilizes a discourse of essentialized differences through which state violence is legitimated; at the same time, the need for tolerance is activated by state violence— indeed, it is produced by the violence, even as it appears as its idealistic antidote or alternative.[47] So, while tolerance connotes the opposite of domination and violence, Israel's practice of both is supported by the ADL under the very mantle of tolerance. And increased Israeli violence amplifies the demand for tolerance, where tolerance of this violence is equated with tolerance of the Jewish difference. The violence produces the demand or need for tolerance ("don't blame Israel because that would be anti-Semitic"); gratification of this demand ("Israel/Jews are not to be blamed in the conflict—to do so would be anti-Semitic") in turn legitimates the violence.

Even tolerance discourse concerned with free speech and dissent can be turned into a tactic of citizen subjection and technology of increased state power in a crisis such as the current war on terrorism. Free speech is subverted through a reversal of the state-citizen circuitry described above; this time, the state does the tolerating/protecting, while turning civil society into the scene for intolerant vigilantism. The state promises to protect free speech and dissent, while declaring at the same time that "if you're not for us, you're with the terrorists," thereby allying dissent with support for the enemy. Dissent becomes equated with un-Americanness and cannot be tolerated; indeed, as we have seen, the limit condition of tolerance is fealty to the nation, expressed through identification with and loyalty to the nation-state. Within the logic of "if you're not with us, you're against us," dissenters are not eligible for tolerance; moreover, if they are giving "aid and comfort to the enemy," there is every reason not to tolerate them.[48] So, even as they are formally protected by the state in their right to dissent, when the equation of dissent with un-Americanness is taken up by corporations, the media, and other powers in civil society, dissenters can be pulled from the airwaves, from the pages of magazines, from educational forums, and occasionally from academic and other positions at what appears to be the behest of the citizenry, not the orders of the state. The combination of popular and commercial power in constraining or filtering dissent (mainly by limiting its venues) leaves the state appearing as a protector of free speech, even as it has provided the rationale for curtailing it. The state remains a tolerant state—and stands for a tolerant and free civilization against an intolerant and unfree one—even as the people are rallied around a certain intolerance of dissent in the name of displaying patriotism at home and extending democracy abroad. Again, tolerance becomes both a tool of state power, this time as a set of exclusions required for building a national consensus behind state violence, and a vehicle of citizen subjugation. This is tolerance as governmentality, "not a matter of imposing laws on men, but rather of disposing things, that is to say, to employ tactics rather than laws, and if need be to use the laws themselves as tactics."

■ ■ ■ ■

TOLERANCE AS MUSEUM OBJECT: THE SIMON WIESENTHAL CENTER MUSEUM OF TOLERANCE

Founded in 1993 by the Simon Wiesenthal Center, the Los Angeles Museum of Tolerance (MOT) declares that its mission is "to challenge visitors to confront bigotry and racism, and to understand the Holocaust in both historic and contemporary contexts."[1] There are a few Holocaust artifacts displayed in its Multimedia Center, but collecting and exhibiting artifacts is not the museum's main focus; it is thus not a museum in the usual sense of the word. Describing itself as "the teaching arm of the Simon Wiesenthal Center," the MOT makes extensive use of contemporary design and media technology to stage absorbing presentations on prejudice; ethnic, racial, gendered, and sexual violence; anti-Semitism; and the Holocaust. This dazzling ensemble of sound-and-light shows and interactive computer sites is gathered under the hallowed moral value of tolerance and the hallowed epistemological status of a museum.

In addition to its devotion to remembering the Holocaust and combating anti-Semitism, the Simon Wiesenthal Center is also a fierce and active defender of Israel.[2] More recently, the Wiesenthal Center has supported the United States' invasions of Afghanistan and Iraq as cornerstones in a war waged against terrorism and on behalf of democracy in the Middle East. The museum itself reflects these positions in its inclusion of American troops in Afghanistan as heroes of tolerance, its easy reference to pre-1948 Palestine as "the Jewish homeland," and its occluded mention of any other peoples living on that land then or now. For a time, one of its exhibits featured the widely disseminated footage of Palestinians falsely reputed to be gleefully celebrating the events of 9/11. At this writing, there are two brief representations of Palestinians in the whole of the MOT: a glimpse of the famous 1993 handshake on the White House lawn between Yitzhak Rabin and Yasir Arafat appears in the opening of one film, and a dubbed clip of angry Palestinian children crying out "We, the children, will go to kill them, murder them . . . we won't leave a single Jew" appears in another.[3]

This chapter does not examine the limitations of the Museum of Tolerance that result from its preoccupation with the Holocaust and investment in the unqualified defense of Israel. It instead asks, What makes tolerance a rubric relevant to this preoccupation and this investment, and how is tolerance appropriated for these purposes? How does tolerance become available to the construction and legitimation of a certain political positioning, and how does tolerance also mask this positioning? How are Palestinians made to appear as enemies of tolerance while Jews are only ever victims of intolerance? How is Israel depicted such that it is not a problem for tolerance? How is tolerance constructed such that Israel is not a problem for it? That is, how is Israel identified with tolerance? And how are Jews figured as sages of tolerance, teachers of tolerance, and paragons of tolerance?

The Museum of Tolerance is an enterprise that many regard as a beacon of light in a world darkened by bigotry, hatred, and violence. It offers an emotionally powerful account of how damaging, indeed how deadly, social hatred can be. It may move some of its visitors, especially the more than 100,000 schoolchildren who visit every year, to be more internally—and perhaps externally—vigilant against social prejudice and stereotyping.[4] It is possible that connecting contemporary instances of sexism, racism, homophobia, and religious and cultural prejudice with the Holocaust produces an understanding of the seriousness of all these issues, a recognition of their capacity to escalate to murderous, even mass murderous, proportions.[5] And certainly many of the young people who visit are introduced to episodes of history—including, but not only, the Holocaust—that they had not previously known much about or regarded very seriously.

So, while critical, this analysis is not a round rejection of the Museum of Tolerance. Nor is it an argument that the museum is thoroughly or deliberately nefarious. Rather, one purpose of this chapter is to track the uses and deployments of tolerance for the Zionist political agenda of the Wiesenthal Center. A second purpose is to continue the consideration, developed in earlier chapters, of tolerance as a contemporary discourse of depoliticization in which power and history make little or no appearance in representations or accounts of ethnicized hostility or conflict, in which ethnicity, culture, religion, race, and belief are often confused and conflated, and in which historically produced antagonisms are reified as essential, the results of a natural enmity regarded as inherent in "difference."

HISTORY

The *Beit Hashoah: Museum of Tolerance*, as it was originally called, was the brainchild of Rabbi Marvin Hier, an orthodox rabbi who left Vancouver in the mid-1970s to found a yeshiva in Los Angeles. A brilliant fund-raiser, Hier quickly established the school (the Nagel Family Campus, run by orthodox rabbis, is now located next door to the MOT); soon thereafter, Hier convinced the famed Nazi-hunter Simon Wiesenthal to lend his name to a small Holocaust museum within it. From this base, Hier began to build membership in the Wiesenthal Center, develop political connections, and raise astonishing sums from Hollywood glitterati.[6] The Wiesenthal Center grew exponentially and today claims to be the largest Jewish organization in the world.

The yeshiva remained the home of the Wiesenthal Center until the mid-1980s, when Hier incorporated the center as a separate nonprofit institution. This move came at the suggestion of California lawmakers who were considering Hier's bid for state funding to add to the substantial private funds he had raised to build his grand new museum.[7] But by all accounts, the separation was on paper only: the

Wiesenthal Center and the Yeshiva University of Los Angeles share not just a director but a board of trustees, and the Wiesenthal Center fully owns and operates the Museum of Tolerance.[8]

As a consequence of these vague lines of demarcation, Hier's bids for state funds to help build the MOT and federal funds to supplement its educational programs were plagued with controversy. The American Civil Liberties Union as well as prominent Jewish organizations, including the American Jewish Committee and several chapters of the Anti-Defamation League of B'nai B'rith, objected strenuously to the reach for public funding as a breach of the separation between church and state.[9] The Jewish Federation Council of Greater Los Angeles, which had developed a Holocaust museum of its own in a different location, was officially silent during the debate, but individual members of the federation spoke out furiously, suggesting strong resentment of Hier's overwhelming success in building his empire on territory that had been the provenance of various local Jewish leaders. In addition, the combination of Hier's high-rolling entertainment industry fundraising and Likud leanings produced nervousness among large swaths of the secular Jewish population in Los Angeles.[10] Even members of the 1939 Club, a group of concentration camp survivors, were angered by what they took to be Hier's plans to monopolize and sensationalize representation of the Holocaust, and to exploit its survivors for political and financial purposes extrinsic to Holocaust remembrance.[11]

Nor did Hier's first Holocaust museum, the small basement collection of World War II artifacts and Judaica in the yeshiva, bode well for what was to come. It was, in the words of *Commentary* writer Edward Norden, "a low-tech affair fashioned by and for Jews and holding nothing against the Gentiles back—an outsized portrait of Pius XII was given a prominent place among pictures of those who 'didn't care.' The message was that Jews have enemies, murderous enemies, and should look out. When Rabbi Hier first announced his plan for a much grander museum, some assumed it would merely enlarge on this theme . . . one reason why his announcement was not greeted with universal joy."[12]

Notwithstanding the wide-ranging opposition to his bids for state and federal monies for projects openly involving religious institutions and personnel, Hier won out. There were several reasons for this triumph. Hier was immensely successful at private fund-raising and at collecting endorsements in powerful corners: the Wiesenthal Board of Trustees was peopled with leading lights from Hollywood (Elizabeth Taylor, Frank Sinatra) as well as Wall Street (Ivan Boesky). Hier also knew how to build an organization at the base: the Wiesenthal Center's membership had grown to almost 300,000 before ground was broken for the new MOT. And Hier and his partners knew exactly how to say "yes, of course" at the right moment: to curry favor from then-California governor George Deukmejian (of Armenian descent), an exhibit on the Armenian genocide was promised, and this pledge also garnered support from the Armenian National Committee and the Armenian Committee of America.[13] Such an exhibit is nowhere to be found in the MOT today. Similarly, at federal hearings before a subcommittee of the House Committee on Education and Labor, representatives queried whether genocides other than the Shoah would be featured and, in particular, whether the "early treatment of American Indians" would have a significant place.[14] Again, assurances were given, and again, other than an appearance on the Tolerance Dateline—a wall listing hundreds of events, laws, court decisions, personages, books, and speeches marking watershed moments in the history of tolerance and intolerance in the United States—there is no mention of Native Americans, let alone Native American genocide, in the current MOT installations. Instead, as one docent made explicit in introducing the various parts of the Museum, "the Tolerancenter is about prejudice, and Beit Hashoah is about the Holocaust."[15] That is, there are many varieties and targets of prejudice, but there is only one holocaust, one significant attempt at genocide. This position is reinforced by the MOT educational materials designed for high school students, in which "genocide" is identified as the correct word to match up with the statement "Nazis try to kill all the Jews," but "discrimination" or "racism" is the correct correlative to "Thousands of Native Americans are forced off their land."[16] Thus, even as the name change and some of the newer exhibits of the MOT would seem to be part of a continuing attempt to widen and adapt its scope and appeal, other changes, such as the removal of the film on other genocides, ensure that the

Holocaust is recentered, that this episode of "man's inhumanity to man" has no rival and no parallel.[17]

In addition to explaining its awkward effort to both center and decenter the Holocaust, the fund-raising and political history of the MOT is relevant to understanding several other of its features. First, the wealth and involvement of Hollywood are partly behind the high-tech infotainment design and style of its installations, though these also converge with its goal of conveying the memory and meaning of the Holocaust to young people from diverse backgrounds.[18] Second, the bid for public funding required more representation of non-Jews and non-Jewish issues than would have otherwise been the case and even today often brings the Tolerancenter close to incoherence in themes and content. And yet, as already suggested, these representations are not a mere sop to funders. From the beginning, the museum was designed to tap into the preoccupations, styles, references, technological habits, attention spans, and rhythms of a wide range of contemporary youth, especially the Los Angeles area's Asian, black, and Latino population, something most Holocaust museums do not do. To gain wide cross-cultural appeal, the museum's planners had to foresake a viewpoint (manifest in the backroom yeshiva Holocaust museum) of "everyone hates us, we can only be for ourselves" for a different construal of Jewish experience: "having been its most severe victims, we are in a unique position to represent the woes of intolerance, ethnoreligious hatred, and prejudice and to advance the alternative." Not only did this shift require repackaging the Holocaust for outsiders, it also entailed exchanging an inward, parochial, and xenophobic sensibility produced by centuries of persecution for a bearing of cosmopolitan concern and even leadership in a global campaign against ethnic and religious hatred, persecution, and violence.[19] In other words, a Likud mentality had to give way to one of American Jewish liberalism; an outlook rooted in bitter survival of the Nazi genocide had to metamorphose into thoughtful deployment of the memory of the Holocaust for the purpose of universal teachings. If successful in making this shift, or at least in presenting the appearance of it, the MOT would be able to link Jewish experience with that of other oppressed groups more effectively, and could also claim a place for Jews as seers and leaders in the present. More than being recognized as having suffered the most, Jews could become the master teachers of tolerance. This status, in turn, could give Jews broad authority on matters of social and political justice and attenuate their identification with a narrow and particular interest. This is exactly the authority and the attenuation that the Museum of Tolerance conveys and performs.

What may be most striking about the MOT's history, even to its founders, is the raw success of the enterprise. In little more than a dozen years, the museum has hosted 4 million guests. Some 350,000 people visit annually, including more than 110,000 children, figures that are all the more impressive given that the museum is closed on Saturdays, the Jewish Sabbath, typically the biggest day for museum attendance in the United States. The MOT is a destination for hundreds of school field trips every year and has also become a "training site" for police and others considered in need of tolerance training. (On one of my visits, a large group of young men from the Army-Navy Academy was being guided through the museum.) And it has spawned two sister institutions. One is the New York Tolerance Center, "a professional development multi-media training facility targeting educators, law enforcement officials, and state/local government practitioners" that opened in 2003.[20] The other is the Jerusalem Museum of Tolerance, under construction at this writing and designed for completion in 2009.[21]

VISITING THE MUSEUM OF TOLERANCE

The four parts of the Museum of Tolerance are all housed within a large, imposing, and tightly secured eight-story building on the corner of Pico and Roxbury boulevards in Los Angeles. The most prominent and heavily visited sections are the Tolerancenter and the Beit Hashoah. On other floors of the building are the Multimedia Learning Center, which contains information on the Holocaust and World War II, and the newest multimedia installation, "Finding Our Families, Finding Ourselves." There are also several small and large auditoriums for special events, films, and lectures, as well as for daily testimonials by Holocaust survivors.

To gain entrance to the building, one must show picture identification to a security guard outside. After purchasing a ticket that indicates a set time for entering the various sections (even on days when there are only a dozen or so visitors in the museum), one walks through an airport security–style metal detector and then puts one's belongings through an X-ray screening device. No cameras, laptops, or recording devices are permitted anywhere in the building. The heavily screened and regulated admission to the museum conveys a sense of potentially violent enmity toward the enterprise and the need for constant vigilance in relationship to this risk. What the visitor gleans is that the passwords of tolerance are not openness or trust but watchfulness, security, surveillance, and regulation.[22]

Admittance to the Tolerancenter and Beit Hashoah is staggered at ten-minute intervals, the approximate length of the audiovisual presentation offered by each diorama in the Beit Hashoah. Docents invite guests to use the restrooms in the lobby while waiting to enter, an invitation most visitors accept after learning that there are no facilities in the Tolerancenter or Beit Hashoah, where the next several hours will be spent. No bathrooms . . . is this a replication of an experience of dehumanization, a subtle tool of total surveillance, or a minor inconvenience in the name of maintaining security against the enemies of tolerance?[23] Or, given the number of middle and high schoolers who visit the museum and the propensity of this age group to express itself through bathroom graffiti, is it perhaps a way to eliminate one particular forum for responding to the museum experience?[24] There is yet another possibility: once inside the Tolerancenter and Beit Hashoah, there is literally nothing that permits visitors a return to a pre- or extramuseum subjectivity put in abeyance by the completely organized and radically saturating experience of the museum. Bathrooms not only would remove visitors from the constant and watchful eyes of the docents but would constitute a break in the total experience of the museum and would, however briefly, allow a return to another social-emotional world.

With the exception of the Multimedia Center, all sections of the museum are introduced by docents. And the docents retreat only when their technological replacements—videos, recorded voices greeting or directing visitors, speaking manikins, darkening rooms, or automatically opening doors—take over as guides and narrators. In fact, the visitor's first clue that this is no ordinary museum is the lack of any museum map, or any need for a map. Though one might not know precisely where in the museum one is at any particular moment—indeed, the sense of descending into a space wholly organized and controlled by others is either intended to convey the space-time experience of the Holocaust or unconsciously mimics its techniques—certainly one never fears missing something or getting lost. In addition, unlike most museums, no guided tour or rented audio tour is available; again, there is no need for such an offer, since guidance is built into the installations themselves.[25] More than being guided, the visitor's very experience of the museum is orchestrated by the media installations; so, too, almost all thinking about tolerance, bigotry, and prejudice is undertaken by the museum, notwithstanding the frequent injunction to the visitor to "think."

At the appointed time of entry, guests gather at a podium and the docent wordlessly leads them down a large Guggenheim-like spiral ramp in the center of the building. The docent waits for the group to gather at the bottom and then devotes anywhere from a few seconds to a few minutes to describing the different parts of the Museum. On one of my visits, the docent, who later identified herself as a Holocaust survivor, stated simply, "There is a tolerance section and a Holocaust section. The tolerance section deals with prejudice, and the Holocaust section deals with the rise of Hitler and the Holocaust."[26] This division can be interpreted several ways: the two subjects are separate, or the former leads to the latter, or the former is relatively mild compared to the latter. But it is also tellingly inaccurate, since "prejudice" does not actually capture the range of identity-based violence included in the Tolerancenter—violence against women, slavery and genocide in American history, terrorism, and mass killing in Rwanda and Bosnia. Categorized as "prejudice," however, these things appear less significant, and less horrible, than what the docent then describes as the "ultimate example of man's inhumanity to man." It avoids the "relativizing" of the Holocaust that distresses the Holocaust scholar Alvin Rosenfeld and others who worry that its uniqueness is diluted by connecting it to "human rights abuses, social inequalities suffered by racial and ethnic minorities and women, environmental disasters, AIDS, and a whole host of other things."[27]

The docent also informs guests of when Holocaust survivors will be speaking (usually twice daily), the length of time needed for the Holocaust section (seventy minutes), and the inadvisability of leaving that section midcourse. Then, we are ushered to the entrance of the Tolerancenter through a wide corridor of projected black-and-white images of "happy multiculturalism," scenes of groups and families having good times. As we walk through the corridor, our silhouettes are projected into the scenes as well, "to indicate that each of us affects and changes the world," one docent explained. At the entrance to the Tolerancenter, the docent may or may not define prejudice ("judgments—not necessarily negative—about people based on how they look") but routinely defines tolerance: "the acceptance of practices and beliefs different from our own." The lack of convergence between the lay definitions of prejudice and tolerance is noteworthy: tolerance is about beliefs and practices, while prejudice is about looks. Presumably this means that the elimination, or even the attenuation, of prejudice is not a precondition of becoming tolerant; rather, tolerance is a matter of managing one's prejudices. In fact, we will soon learn that because we are all prejudiced and always will be, the museum attempts not to correct prejudice via tolerance but to reduce some of its most damaging effects. We may keep our prejudices, but a commitment to tolerance will prevent us from voicing them publicly or otherwise enacting them in dangerous or damaging ways.

This curious account of the museum's driving purpose—"the acceptance of practices and beliefs different from our own"—reminds us how thoroughly governed by the specifics of anti-Semitism this purpose is. Although we are about to be exposed to sufferings attached to racism, homophobia, and misogyny, as well as ethnic and religious hatreds, all of these are reduced to the problem of accepting others' "practices and beliefs." In this way, race, gender, sexuality, and ethnicity—every vector of social injury or inequality—are all "culturalized," that is, taken to consist in practices and beliefs. Here, Judaism in Christian Europe becomes the model for the problem of tolerance, and tolerance itself is depicted as operating outside the politics of identity production, apart from power or inequality; it is simply a matter of responding to "difference." Before we even have set foot inside the Tolerancenter, tolerance has already performed the classic essentializing and depoliticizing moves described at length in chapter 1.

After the docent defines tolerance, a computerized "host provocateur" takes over, hailing new visitors as "above average" for visiting a museum, and then, having flattered us with a positive stereotype, traffics in a series of negative innuendos about "certain people," thereby reminding us that felt superiority to and open denigration of others are part of the same problem. The docent next points to two doors, respectively marked "prejudiced" and "unprejudiced," and asks us to choose one. After a few moments or after someone tries to walk through the "unprejudiced" door, the docent explains that it is permanently locked—in almost a figurative inversion of an eternal flame—because "none of us is completely unprejudiced." Following this staged event, apparently intended to induce or humiliate visitors into identifying with the perpetrators of intolerance, and making us all equals in the problem of prejudice, we are now ready to learn about the consequences of this fallen state of the species and how to keep prejudice from becoming injurious and even murderous intolerance.[28]

Our first stop is in front of a video montage, "The Power of Words," in which words are depicted as having the capacity to inspire, incite, terrify, hurt, or intimidate. The depiction suggests an unsettled quality or a hermeneutic difficulty inherent in this form of power, but the substance of the video subverts the potential for intellectual vertigo or critical deliberation that such openness of meaning entails. No thought is needed to determine which words are inspiring ("I have a dream . . .") and which are hateful and intimidating ("Matthew Shepherd will enter hell. . . ." ". . . we will kill all the Jews . . ."). Moreover, despite the initial insistence on our collective implication in prejudice, and despite the putatively moral and political ambiguity of the power of words, the video depicts a world divided into friends and enemies of prejudice, purveyors of brotherly love and purveyors of hatred. We see Churchill, Kennedy, and King on one side, and Le Pen, Stalin, angry Palestinian children, and unnamed members of hate groups on the other. The lesson that we are all prejudiced is already being diluted by the Manicheanism that also courses through the MOT, a tension that is characteristic of contemporary tolerance discourse, which simultaneously casts tolerance as mutual conduct (accepting differences) and as that which distinguishes the good from the bad, the allies from the foes of civilization.

The docent, still with us, leads visitors from the video over to a wall titled "Confronting Hate in America," which features pictures of hate crimes and hate groups; below them are mounted computer stations for Hate.com, a museum installation that catalogs descriptions of websites for hate groups around the world.[29] Visitors are invited to look up predigested information on the more than 500 hate websites now on the Internet, and a few do so. The docent then moves the group to the "Point of View Diner," a facsimile of a 1950s diner replete with counters and booths for viewing and electronically responding to a video, or toward the "Millennium Machine," a large room also arranged into clusters of seated sites for watching and responding to a video presentation.[30] The overt aim of each installation is to present contemporary controversies or problems, provide some basic information and viewpoints, and solicit the visitors' own opinions about the controversies and views on the problems' causes and solutions.

In the Point of View Diner, the issue of the day on one of my visits was "gang injunctions"—laws that limit the wearing or showing of gang colors and insignia. The dilemma was presented as (not much of) a choice between maximized "freedom" or "safe neighborhoods," opponents of the injunctions being aligned with freedom and proponents with safety. The respective "points of view" were offered in one-minute accounts by public officials; we were asked to vote our own position before and after hearing the arguments on either side. We were also asked to vote on questions such as whether having a father in the household, improving after-school programs, or having ex-gang members speak at school assemblies would deter gang membership and gang violence. The arguments were not deep, the tension between "freedom" (itself never defined) and "security" was never elaborated, and no detail was offered about whose freedom and whose security might be at stake. As for the voting, since results are tallied and presented for the whole room, its main purpose appeared to be to discover how close (or far) one's "views" are from the majority opinion, or how much one minute of argument from an attorney in public office affects one's viewpoint.

On another day, the Point of View videos were devoted, respectively, to the questions of who is most responsible in a drunk driving accident—the under-age driver, his parents, the liquor store owner, or the girlfriend who obtained the fake ID—and who bears responsibility for the effects of "hate speech" in a society that cherishes free speech. The vignettes are extremely dramatic; the first video contains enough blood, agony, death, and sorrow that it could easily be a high school driver education film, and the second ends with the accidental killing of an innocent bystander by an enraged black security guard. Following each, the characters are interviewed by a narrator about who they think is responsible or how to take responsibility. Again, viewers are asked to vote their own opinions both before and after these "interviews."

These videos have several striking features. First, in their crosscutting pedagogic purposes they are characteristic of the rhetoric of the Museum of Tolerance. On the one hand, they emphasize individual agency, thoughtfulness, and responsibility. On the other hand, they are highly didactic and moralistic. Through this combination, the videos press strong moral-political positions, which are supplemented by emotionally powerful dramatizations, at the same time that they stress the value of individual thoughtfulness and difference of opinion. The fierce and moralistic positions (under-age drinking is dangerous, permissive parenting is wrong, everyone has a responsibility to stop a crime or a potential danger, hate speech ignites violence, we are all responsible for effects of our actions regardless of our intentions) may correspond to the social values and moral code that the MOT wants to promote, but they do not embody the respect for moral and deliberative autonomy on which tolerance as a value is founded. The finessing of this contradiction through "interactive participation" will be discussed shortly.

A second feature of these videos is that like so many of the MOT installations, including aspects of the Holocaust Museum, the line between reality and fiction is extremely blurry. Both the drunk driving video and the hate speech video are fictional, yet the "interviews" conducted with the characters following the drama conflate reality and fiction. As each character explains his or her point of view, they are clearly meant to represent reality—just as Hate.com impersonates a real website, the actors who read the letters and diaries of the Holocaust survivors in the Beit Hashoah are meant to seem authentic, and the unnamed figures at a Berlin café in the early 1930s, whose trajectory is then traced into the Nazi era, are meant to seem like people who really said these things at the café one sunny afternoon. Why the incessant blurring of the real and the fictional, especially when Holocaust historiographers have staked so much on facticity and veracity? Here we circle back to the first point, where the pedagogical aims of the museum come into conflict with both the murkiness of reality and its inadequacy for catchy and dramatic instruction. This conflict does not arise simply because the audience is incapable of navigating ambiguity, subtlety, and complexity, though such incapacity certainly appears to be an operating assumption of the entire museum. More importantly, under the rubric of tolerance the MOT aims to teach respect for the other and to demonize bad behavior—from expressing bigotry to shirking individual responsibility. Because of this combined commitment to simple "take-home messages" and a moral Manicheanism, the museum cannot deploy reality in anything other than small and manipulable slices. For something like the Point of View Diner, it has to fictionalize its scenes and present interviews with fictional characters—that is, with those who will stay fully in character (completely good or completely bad) throughout the "interview." If its moral didacticism is to succeed, it must stage scenarios, and conversations about those scenarios, that are shorn of all the unpredictability and complexity of real life and real conversation. But it must cover this moral didacticism by presenting multiple points of view along with the conceit of thoughtful probing and reflection carried by the idea of the interview.

The irony of this fictionalization, however, appears in the third feature of the videos: their extensive trafficking in stereotypes and clichés. These fictional characters are really cartoon figures—a preoccupied and permissive single mother, stupid and irresponsible teenagers, a sleazy working-class liquor store owner, a thoughtful black owner of a diner, a bombastic group of stupid white guys listening to Rush Limbaugh, an otherwise temperate black security officer who draws his gun in rage when he's pushed to the edge by racist talk. One doesn't really need to "interview" any of them to know what they will say about the issue of responsibility; the stereotypes have already made their views easy to predict. The irony, of course, is that although stereotyping is one of the things that the museum ostensibly aims to disrupt, it is also something produced by its essentialization of differences and required by its didacticism.

While the Point of View Diner engages controversy superficially, divides it neatly into positions that rarely correspond with the complexity of the real world, traffics in stereotypes, and gratuitously solicits the opinions of museum visitors on relative nonissues, in the Millennium Machine these weaknesses grow to insidious proportions. Here, too, one enters a large room and chooses a seat at a booth with three or four others; in front of each seat is a multiple-choice console that connects to a monitor at the booth. As the room darkens, one of four videos begins on a large screen in the middle of the room. Regardless of the specific presentation—on the exploitation of women, the exploitation of children, refugees and political prisoners, or terrorism—each video begins the same way. "Throughout time," we are told, "people have had the choice between good or evil, knowledge or ignorance, tolerance or hatred, compassion or indifference—choices we also face today. All of us have the power to shape the world, to address injustice, crimes against humanity, human rights abuses." Then the topic of the day is introduced.

The video on violence against women features five instances of such violence: discussions of honor killings, genital mutilation, and sexual slavery in the Third World are followed by a focus on rape and finally on domestic violence in the United States. Each segment, early in its presentation, poses a question about a factual matter—such as how little one could pay for a sexual slave, or what the frequency of rape is—and viewers select from multiple-choice answers by pushing a button at their console. The combined results for each table of viewers are indicated with a bar graph at the local monitor, and the correct answer is then provided. Following the informational presentation, the narrator of the video asks, "Why so much violence against women?" This question is immediately followed by a second: "Does the media contribute to it?" Astonishingly, we are asked to take a full minute to discuss this hypothesis with our neighbors, because "here at the Millennium Machine, your opinion matters to us." Since the "us" of the Millennium Machine is a video display terminal, this claim becomes a perfect parody of contemporary participatory democracy—as meaningless as it is slick, and solicitous in its capacity to personalize the names and addresses of mass mailings—yet visitors earnestly turn to one another to discuss the question. And when they are told to vote "yes" or "no" at the end of the elapsed minute, they obediently do so. Despite the esteem in which our opinions are supposedly held, however, the Millennium Machine presumes an answer in the affirmative, because the next questions are "Should the media be forced to limit violent content?" and "Should media producers be held culpable for acts of violence against women?" One guesses that the answers to these questions must be "yes" as well, given the presumption of the media's responsibility for the problem. But we are never sure, because after our responses are tabulated, the video concludes with the statement that there are two crucial ways we can all help solve this problem. The first is to "stay informed" and let our political representatives know our views; the second is to get involved with nongovernmental organizations (NGOs) such as the Wiesenthal Center that are concerned with the problem. In short, if you oppose violence against women and favor regulating the media as a means of curtailing this violence, you should support the Wiesenthal Center. Such support, apparently, is what was meant by the opening statement that we each hold in our hands the power to shape the future. The individual power to choose between good and evil, and to address injustice and crimes against humanity, boils down to writing e-mails to one's political representatives and writing checks to the Wiesenthal Center.

The Millennium Machine video on terrorism is even more of an explicit political polemic. After the opening, in which we are reminded that the choice between good and evil in the world belongs to each of us, September 11 is introduced. The events of that day are described as having cast us into a new world, one saturated with fear, but also as continuous with several decades of terrorist attacks in Israel, Indonesia, Britain, and elsewhere. The link between these is that on September 11, Americans ceased to be immune from what these other countries experience and, as a consequence, "our complacency died." Yet what also distinguishes 9/11 is that in contrast to terrorist events that have explicit political goals (never named) and that limit their bloodletting to what is necessary to achieve those goals, the attacks of 9/11 "aimed to destroy as much and kill as many as possible." Moreover, the target was not our government but "our way of life, our civilization." How the latter is ascertained, the video does not explain.

But neither are these distinctions pursued. Instead, as the video quickly tours other episodes of terrorism, it lumps them all together as a single phenomenon, as simultaneously threats to security and attacks on civility. No political conflicts—between Catholics and Protestants in northern Ireland, between Palestinians and Jews in the Middle East, or between Chechnya and Russia—are ever mentioned. It is as if terrorism is its own cause, a cause that could be promulgated only by barbarians, those who hate the ways of life of others, or simply hate others for having a way of life. Terrorism is thus reduced to an extreme expression of intolerance—the failure to "accept practices and beliefs different from [one's] own" carried to murderous proportions.

We then learn that Israel suffers more from terrorism and suicide bombing than any other nation, although, again, this fact is given no political context. Rather, the utterance appears aimed at drawing post-9/11 American suffering and fear into identification and solidarity with Israel. And, after viewers are queried on what international body has outlawed suicide bombing, we learn that it has never been internationally or institutionally outlawed or condemned, and that, unbelievably, suicide bombing has actually been defended as a legitimate tool of war. Now the line from Israel's suffering to 9/11 is complete: there are suicide bombers and their defenders on one side, and the victims of such bombings on the other.

The body of the video on terrorism concerns biological weapons, and the "interactive" questions focus on whether biological weapons have been used and how much anthrax can kill how many people. The film literally terrifies viewers with its account of the ease of making and disseminating anthrax and other massively toxic substances. Then, abruptly, the discussion of biological weapons ends (though the terror lingers) and the discussion question is submitted: "Most of the recent acts of terrorism have been committed by Islamic extremists, which raises the issue of racial profiling. Freedom is a precious value in America. Should racial or ethnic profiling be allowed?" No information is offered on the "racial" profile of an Islamic terrorist—that is, on how "race" becomes an index for radical Islamic nationalism or for terrorism. Nor is there any discussion of how racial profiling actually works, who does it and where, who suffers it and how, what kinds of laws it abridges or supplants, or what kind of collateral damage it involves. Racial profiling is simply presented as a tool, with terrorism as the problem for which the tool may be relevant. But because the "Millennium Machine values our opinion," we are given one minute to discuss the acceptability of racial profiling to deter terrorist acts, after which we vote. Reminded again that terrorism has gone from being "a problem over there to one over here," we are offered the two ways we can all help with this problem: (1) "stay informed and tell your political representatives what you think" (racial profiling is good?), and (2) "get involved with organizations like the Wiesenthal Center."[31]

Not only, then, does the Wiesenthal Center hold part of the solution to all the problems presented by the Millennium Machine, but each video ends up positioning the center's political projects as opposing unquestionably terrible things in the world and locates legitimate controversy elsewhere. That is, the Wiesenthal Center is represented as straightforwardly standing for justice against injustice, right against wrong, good against evil, tolerance and civility against terrorism, and not as a partisan player in a range of political conflicts, policy debates, and even wars. Here it becomes clear how the depoliticizing discourse of tolerance is "tacticalized," even weaponized, while the depoliticization itself serves to obscure this move. The advocacy of tolerant views and a tolerant world is the cover under which very specific political positions are advanced, positions that are consecrated by the rubric of tolerance just as their opposites are painted with the brush of intolerance, violence, barbarism, bigotry, or hatred. As we will see, this strategy resurfaces routinely in other Tolerancenter installations.

But before we move on, we need to ask a question that has been developing ever since we entered the Tolerancenter: namely, What is the faux participation about: Why all the voting and button pushing? What is accomplished by the trivial polling, tests for knowledge, and solicitation of opinions? These gimmicks appear aimed, in part, at getting and holding the attention of a generation raised on Nintendo, GameCubes, and touch screens; produced within this technological idiom, otherwise disinterested youth might pay attention to things that are external to them or that potentially challenge their assumptions.[32] Perhaps, too, the interactive moments are meant to be a miniature experience of political participation in a pluralistic world, small steps in learning that one's opinion matters but so also do the viewpoints of others.

Yet there is surely another reason for the frequent but finally irrelevant solicitation of viewer's opinions and choices in the Tolerancenter. At the end of an afternoon spent in the MOT, visitors have been steeped in a sensorily intense, emotional, barely cognitive, and above all fully orchestrated and narrated experience. Not only does the museum deliver experience to its visitors on big screens with wrap-around sound, life-size dioramas, and walk-through facsimiles of concentration camp space, it also delivers the meaning of this experience, from "words kill" to "ordinary people are responsible" to "never again." So while the visitor is subjected to sensory and emotional overload, she or he is simultaneously the recipient of an intense moral-political didacticism. And yet, as already suggested, the museum's overt governing principle is respect for human dignity, individuality, and difference, a doctrine that requires at least a pretense of valuing individual thoughtfulness and reflection. This is the fundamental conundrum of the MOT: How to produce a moral and political consensus—even how to be doctrinaire—when the rubric of the museum is respect for different beliefs and practices, for difference as itself the essence of humanity? That is, how is it possible to get everyone to arrive at the correct moral and political positions while affirming tolerance of difference, plural viewpoints, and individual reflectiveness? How can a universal truth and adherence to particular political positions be generated from a cosmopolitan appreciation of difference and differently situated perspectives?

Organizing the consensus is not the difficult part. Installations, whether on the L.A. riots or the Holocaust, heavily frame and interpret while feigning to only present information. Certain facts are selected and highlighted while other crucial information is omitted; the illusion of a thorough and fair history is produced; moralism is subtly and almost imperceptibly secreted into the narrative; fear is induced and mobilized; metonymic chains of victimization are established; demonization of the enemy is artfully staged. Moreover, the very enterprise of a "museum of tolerance" carries a presumption of innocence and goodness, of openhandedness and evenhandedness, and of a turning aside from power politics to achieve peaceful cohabitation. The mantle of the "museum" is one key to cloaking the politics inside; it exploits the popular conceit that museums do not act or preach but simply harbor and display knowledge and things of value.[33] But the mantle of "tolerance" is equally important to cloaking the political framing of the installations and exhibitions, the dissemination of political positions, and the organization of a political consensus among viewers. Wrapped together, these mantles work as an opaque shroud. If the enterprise were named and framed differently—say, as a Study Center of Political and Social Conflict, or even as a Museum of Current Events—viewers might well be more alert to the political framing of the contents.

Again, however, it is not enough to organize political consensus while pretending not to. Rather, the MOT must make a strong show of valuing individual thoughtfulness and plural viewpoints even as it presses its own political positions and indoctrinates its visitors into them. To this end, the MOT proliferates invitations to deliberation and thoughtfulness, all of which are gestural rather than substantive and none of which subverts its political project. We are asked to vote on myriad minor questions: "Does the media contribute to violence against women?" (What about the contribution of organized patriarchal religions? the sexual division of labor? the feminization of poverty? militaristic nation-states? racism and unemployment? institution-alized male superordination?) It presents controversies and then spins out irrelevant questions to one side of them: "Is a father in the home, or a presentation by an ex-gang member at a school assembly, impor-tant in deterring gang membership?" It poses hard questions, such as those about racial profiling, without providing a hint of the knowl-edge and considerations relevant to forming intelligent opinions about them. It gives us different points of view—public attorneys defending or decrying gang injunctions, or members of different ethnic groups on the L.A. riots—in thirty-second sound bites. It asks us which event, group, or behavior in the L.A. riots makes us angriest—the cops, the looting, or the jury verdict—as if our anger matters or is registered somewhere significant. It invites us to "click to learn more"—about the L.A. riots, a particular hate group, or a viewpoint in a contro-versy—even as the choices are limited and the "more" consists simply of another paragraph or another thirty-second interview.

Above all, the MOT constantly insists that our thinking, our learn-ing, and our participation are crucial. The Millennium Machine videos all conclude by emphasizing the importance of staying informed and letting powerful people know one's opinion; the L.A. riots installation ends with the word "Think" burned across the screen (though it's not clear why, nor what one is supposed to think about); and "In Our Time," a film on contemporary ethnic violence and anti-Semitism, ends with the question "What were we supposed to remember?" These incessant but empty injunctions to think or to offer one's opinion help to obscure the fact that there is very little in the MOT that has not been politically and intellectually premasticated as well as dumbed-down, fictionalized, and fitted into clichés and sound bites. In fact, it is hard not to conclude that in urging its visitors to "think," it is ac-tually urging something closer to the opposite: namely, to accept with-out question the MOT's version of reality and its values, to think ex-actly as one is being taught to think at the MOT. The injunction to think also trades on a set of tropological associations between think-ing and tolerance, on the one hand, and between ignorance, bigotry, and fundamentalism on the other. The tolerant and the civilized think (for themselves); the bigoted and the barbaric merely follow instincts, leaders, crowds, or customs. As chapters 6 and 7 will argue, this set of associations also justifies the *imposition* of a tolerant worldview, and the political-legal apparatus presumed to secure it, on those who do not have it; this is, after all, only forcing them to think and hence to be free.

The staged interest in individual thoughtfulness and viewpoints, and the association of tolerance with thoughtfulness and of bigotry with mindlessness, recurs in the rest of the Tolerancenter. Visitors depart the Millennium Machine to enter a long hall featuring the main exhibits of the Tolerancenter, the place where one could, technically, browse. On one wall is a large installation composed of ten annotated photographs titled "Assuming Responsibility." The collection comprises a "Take Back the Night" march; a group of schoolchildren making a "tolerance banner"; a Montana town unifying in protest after an episode of anti-Semitic violence; a project to help the homeless; a ceremony establishing Cesar Chavez's birthday as a California holiday; "Project Lemonade"—a group that raises funds for tolerance for every minute the Klu Klux Klan marches in the streets of its town; the "Seeds of Peace" youth camp for groups that are warring elsewhere in the world; "Operation Understanding," which connects Jewish and black youth in cities; the signing into law of the Americans with Disabilities Act in 1990; and Long Beach high school students studying Anne Frank and Zlata Filipovic. It is a stirring portrait of local justice efforts, even as it is not clear how all of these scenes connect to one another or fit within the rubric of tolerance. (Was "acceptance of practices and beliefs different from one's own" what Cesar Chavez was trying to gain for farmworkers? Is this bizarre classification of a union struggle itself enabled by a certain racism? That is, is it made possible by the fact that the United Farm Workers organizes mostly *brown* workers, a fact that is more salient in the minds of those producing this installation than its status as a union? Is "tolerance" even an imaginable classification for the goals of the United Auto Workers, and could the UAW appear in this installation? Similarly, are Take Back the Night marches aimed at increasing male tolerance of women in the dark? What makes this a tolerance battle? Do men rape women because they are prejudiced against them or fail to "accept their practices and beliefs"? Or is it a tolerance battle because the marked and subordinate group is subject to violence? That is, could a march for equal pay or reproductive rights qualify as a struggle for tolerance?) In addition to propagating a certain racism and sexism by rendering selected battles for justice and equality as struggles for tolerance, this collection also suggests that tolerance can be invoked whenever two or more of the following are involved in an issue: (1) dark skin, (2) a minority culture or religion, (3) social subordination or marginalization, and (4) violence or extreme deprivation (Palestinians are the notable exception). At the same time, it would seem that the rubric of tolerance, as opposed to the rubric of social justice, eliminates any ambiguity or complexity, as well as any political dimensions, from the issue: there is wrong/violence/intolerance on one side, and right/coexistence/tolerance on the other.

The depoliticization in the MOT's composite portrait of everyday citizens "assuming responsibility" for making the world a more tolerant place makes what is at its center all the more significant: a photograph of American GIs in what is described as the "post-9/11 war against terrorism"—that is, troops in either Iraq or Afghanistan. By virtue of its inclusion in this installation, the wars on Afghanistan and Iraq are linked with the United Farm Workers' struggle for decent wages and working conditions, women's resistence of sexual violence, and citizens' resistence of neo-Nazi and Klan activities in their municipalities. What rhetorically unites these as battles for tolerance? What makes labor exploitation, poverty, terrorism, and sexual, racial, and anti-Semitic violence all part of the same fabric of badness as whatever the United States is fighting in Iraq and Afghanistan? Perhaps they represent the composite evil being battled in Iraq and Afghanistan, even as they are battled singly in the American context. Since, in the Millennium Machine, we learned that terrorism is an attack on civility and civilization and that 9/11 constituted an attack on "our way of life," then those fighting terrorism, as American troops in Iraq and Afghanistan here are said to be doing, are defending a whole way of life against its barbaric enemy. In the context of a portrait of "taking responsibility" for tolerance, this claim effectively

equates tolerance with a civilized way of life and links both to justifications for America's military excursions in the Middle East. Conversely, it equates terrorism, whatever the United States is fighting in
Iraq and Afghanistan, and intolerance. Only through this logic could
the GIs be readily connected to the other images in this installation, a
logic that also forecloses recognition of the imperial aspects of the
American mission in the Middle East and of the Wiesenthal Center's
apparently unqualified support for that mission. Through this logic,
too, the mutual implicatedness of "we are all prejudiced" again gives
way to a Manichean worldview in which there are good and bad people, good and bad regimes, and good and bad causes for which to fight.

The wall across the room from "Taking Responsibility" features the
beginning of the Tolerance Dateline, an extensive listing of events,
laws, and personages in American history, from 1607 through the
present, arrayed under two categories: "Intolerance Persists" or "In
Pursuit of Tolerance." Setbacks for racial and religious minorities,
women, and homosexuals are in the first category; breakthroughs or
achievements are featured in the second. The range in the listing is
enormous; the representation, strikingly random. So, for example,
slave codes, Indian reservations, Dred Scott, the assassination of Robert Kennedy, and Louis Farrakhan's description of Judaism as a "gut-
ter religion" all appear in the "Intolerance Persists" column. Quakers
opposing slavery, the Bill of Rights, Thoreau's tax protests, Harriet
Tubman's underground railroad, an African American army regiment
awarded highest military honors by France in 1918, the defense of
Jews by the Anti-Defamation League, the appointment of Sandra Day
O'Connor to the Supreme Court, the election of a black mayor in Los
Angeles, and Alex Haley's *Roots* are all listed under "In Pursuit of Tolerance." There is no effort to distinguish between advances for "tolerance" and achievements of formal equality, or between episodes of
law-backed discrimination and violence. Moreover, because it actually
requires intensive study, as well as background knowledge about many
of the items listed, and because it is not flashy or interactive yet ex-
tends along the whole length of the hall, the Tolerance Dateline is
probably the least attended exhibit in the museum. One wonders if its
main function is not museum politics—a place to mention groups or

events not featured elsewhere but that certain funders or other guests might care about.

Visitors appear more drawn to the flashier exhibits, starting with a sixteen-screen video on the civil rights movement, "Ain't I Gotta Right." For those who know something about the early 1960s, the video will seem clichéd; for others it may be stirring. But what is notable in the context of the Tolerancenter's promise to focus on "the history of racism and prejudice in the American experience" is that the video starts the story of African Americans with segregation rather than slavery. Is this because slavery could rival the Holocaust as a sustained episode of man's inhumanity to man? (A similar question arises with regard to treatment of Native Americans over three hundred years of American history.) Or does the fact that slavery antedates film and sophisticated photographic technology simply makes the civil rights movement into more conducive material for a high-tech museum? What about lynching, then, that unique form of terror practiced by white men to regulate the behavior of all black people and white women? Certainly the dismantling of Jim Crow and the acquisition of civil rights for African Americans is an important chapter in America's race history, but it hardly captures the severity, longevity, or legacy of this history for the present. In this regard, and because of its strong "we shall overcome" theme—black and white activists are shown working side by side—the video contributes a picture of "the history of racism and prejudice in the American experience" that is strikingly romanticized and contrasts sharply with the narrative of Jewish history contained in the Holocaust section of the museum.

Next is the installation on the 1992 Los Angeles riots, transporting us from tearfulness at the walls of injustice torn down to confusion over images of blacks trashing and looting their own and nearby Korean neighborhoods, beating a white truck driver, and for several days so intimidating the Los Angeles police that officers would not enter the area. The riots, it will be recalled, were precipitated by the chance videotaping of white police officers brutally beating a lone African American, followed by a jury's acquittal of the officers involved. In the main narrative of events in the installation, the beating and the announcement of the verdict are both shown briefly. The focus is the riots themselves, in sensational footage that is neither narrated nor explained. This must leave many visitors perplexed, especially those not old enough to remember the events or those from outside Southern California or the United States. It is also hard to imagine a parallel presentation on Jews or other whites, in which collective rage, but not the overdetermined incitation for the rage (though there is a segment on "conditions in Los Angeles" that one can access), is dominant. As in the Point of View Diner, visitors are given a chance to "vote" on such matters as "Which made you angrier—the verdict or the violence following the verdict?" and "Was the violence justified?" But they are not given much information on which to base their answers; nor, again, is it clear what difference their answers make.

The final installation in the Tolerancenter is a short film titled "In Our Time." Like most of the other video installations, it makes extensive use of split screens and montage, filmic techniques that not only appeal to the MTV generation but displace analytic and other contestable formulations in favor of imagistic and metonymic association. Bosnia, Rwanda, hate groups in Europe and America, terrorism, hate crime, xenophobia, and homophobia are all associated with one another as part of the same phenomenon of evil. Yet the split and multiple screens also convey a certain sense of openness and nondidacticism, appearing merely to expose viewers to contemporary instances of hatred and violence rather than pressing a position.

"In Our Time" does have a narrative, however, and it is a peculiar one. The video begins with this statement: "At the end of World War II, after six years of defending democracy against Nazism, we Americans discovered that we were victors in a great moral crusade against racism, anti-Semitism, and fascism." (Only Hegelian historiography can explain how a nation could make a retrospective discovery of its involvement in a moral crusade, though this same historiography is invoked today to feature wars of empire as wars of civilization against barbarism.) "We Americans learned," the narrator continues, "that hate unchecked becomes mass violence. We also learned that we have to fight racism at home if we are going to fight it abroad." These statements, too, are odd accounts of American postwar ideology and policy, when McCarthyism (never mentioned) seized the nation and the cold war underwrote an unremitting string of incursions and coups in the Third World, of which the Vietnam War was only the longest and most notorious. The video then switches to Bosnia, Kosovo, and Rwanda as episodes of evil in which we (a "we" that is now either the whole world or at least the West) patently failed to remember our World War II lesson. The tragedy of Bosnia is depicted as ethnic groups "picking through old slights and injuries" and "hatred run amok"— a more depoliticized and dehistoricized account would be hard to imagine. No attempt is made to explain the Rwandan genocide; it is simply lamented as the screens fill with scenes of devastation and death. The final collage in the film is of hate rallies, graffiti, and youth groups targeting Jews, homosexuals, and blacks while the narrator lists different kinds of bigotry; she then asks in a haunting tone as the film concludes, "What was it we were supposed to remember?"

Aside from its peculiar historiography and history, this film would seem to root the political violence and political conflict it depicts in an upwelling of hatred itself, that is, in a kind of generic ethnic, cultural, racial, or sexual xenophobia. It does not identify the construction and mobilization of such enmity by political or social power, nor does it distinguish between hate speech, on the one hand, and state policies of ethnic cleansing and genocide, on the other. Rather, the implicit claim is that the former escalates with ease into the latter, that it is made of the same stuff, that xenophobic hatred is the material of mass persecution and violence. Conjoined with the opening claim of the video, that "defenders of democracy" in World War II were (unwittingly) engaged in a great moral crusade against racism, anti-Semitism, and fascism, the film becomes another lesson about civilization versus barbarism, democracy versus its enemies, the free and the tolerant against the bigoted and the fundamentalist. It is a small step from here to George W. Bush's God-inspired mission on behalf of freedom and democracy worldwide.

"In Our Time" is also the last stop before entering the Beit Hashoah, and serves as a segue between the Tolerancenter and the Beit Hashoah, both in its focus on the lessons of World War II and in the claim that various kinds of hate speech (including graffiti), hate crime, and hate groups, along with war, ethnic cleansing, and genocide, are all part of the same fabric. This makes the Holocaust not only something we must never forget but in a certain way always on the horizon, a specter that justifies a great deal of preemptive action and defense, from curtailed civil liberties to war.

Before turning to the Beit Hashoah, let us briefly revisit the question of the place and purpose of the Tolerancenter in the Wiesenthal museum, as well as the question of how it functions in relation to an aim of featuring the Nazi treatment of the Jews as unparalleled in the history of "man's inhumanity to man." As already suggested, the plan for the Tolerancenter clearly assisted in procuring and legitimizing public funding, help evidenced in the state and federal hearings on allocating these monies.[34] But the Tolerancenter also makes racial, religious, and ethnic hatred, as well as misogyny and homophobia, relevant to those visitors, especially young people, who may have strong racial or ethnic identifications but are unworldly and unpolitical, as it links various contemporary targets of hatred or discrimination, and in turn links these contemporary targets with the seemingly more remote problem of anti-Semitism and the Holocaust. Rabbi May, associate dean of the MOT, was explicit about this approach in congressional hearings on federal funding: "in order to best reach children and visitors from all walks of life—non-Jewish children, Jewish children—we have to be able to address the concerns and the threats against them as well. It's not good enough in an educational program only to say we're going to show you what is truly a watershed event—the watershed event—of the 20th century because it doesn't relate to them."[35] More specifically, the Tolerancenter links the contemporary experiences of racial minorities and recent immigrants to those of American Jews; it gathers them all under the rubric of hatred and intolerance and thereby makes the study of the Holocaust more immediate to non-Jews and young secular Jews. It connects anti-Semitism to other kinds of ethnic or racial hatred and helps to close the temporal and spatial gap between contemporary youth and the events of Nazi Germany three-quarters of a century earlier. In this, the Tolerancenter is nothing less than a stroke of genius. It is safe to say that millions of young people would not be learning the story of the Holocaust from the Wiesenthal Center had the Tolerancenter not been built as the front end of the Beit Hashoah.

The Tolerancenter is also important in the way that it prominently features Jews worldwide as victims of hatred and violence, and Israel as the most severe victim of terrorism, without shouting out that it is doing either. When this emphasis is coupled with the general absence of Arabs and Arab Americans in the Tolerancenter, except as haters of Jews, potential candidates for racial profiling, or savage men who gouge out the eyes of their wives or stone them to death for reasons of "honor" (as depicted in the Millennium Machine video on violence against women), the stage is set for unanimous sympathy with Israel, not only as a Jewish homeland after the Shoah but as a beacon of civilization in a barbarous land.[36]

Given the discursive framing of several other conflicts mentioned in the museum, the Israel-Palestine conflict could have been portrayed as driven by ethnic rivalry or hatred (as Hutu against Tutsi in Rwanda) or by religious-ethnic strife (as Serbs against Muslims in Bosnia). But both of these models imply two mutually implicated peoples struggling against one another and thus would cast the Middle East conflict as a tragedy rather than as a moral crusade of civilization against barbarism. They would also frame Israel/Palestine as a site of conflict where hatred and hostility could be replaced by tolerance. But the Israel-Palestine battle is not presented as a candidate for the healing balm of tolerance, because tolerance is not what you extend to the barbarian, by definition an enemy to your way of life—a way of life inclusive of tolerance as exemplified by the very existence of the Simon Wiesenthal Museum of Tolerance.

In the MOT's bare whispers and loud silences about the Middle East, Israel's current woes are also tacitly figured as continuous with the situation of the Jews through history—that is, as besieged by enemies for no reason other than being Jewish. No other context is offered for hostility toward Israel, its policies, or its actions. Jews are depicted as persistently in need of tolerance and, at the same time, as advocates of a tolerant world; indeed, they emerge as the ultimate champions and foot soldiers of tolerance by virtue of their need for it, a championship and soldiering that the Tolerancenter itself exemplifies. If Jews have always been persecuted for their difference, they know better than others why peoples and states that are different must be "tolerated." This conclusion, which precipitates a cosmopolitan and post-universalist worldview out of a parochial status, is one of the most significant achievements of linking the Tolerancenter with the Beit Hashoah. A second significant achievement is using this cosmopolitanism to mask a zealously one-sided perspective on the Israeli-Palestinian conflict.

As their suffering is converted into universal and cosmopolitan wisdom, Jews and Israel take their place at the forefront of the struggle of civilization against barbarism, tolerance against hatred. This is why a project committed to depicting the unique horror of the Holocaust would nevertheless be willing to house it under—or at least alongside, we are never quite sure which—the seemingly mild rubric of "intolerance." Such a rubric enables a defense of Israel that relies less on Jewish exceptionalism vis-à-vis the Holocaust or Jewishness itself than on positioning Jews as defenders of civilization, humanism, civility, and a tolerant order and, conversely, positioning Israel's enemies as enemies to these values. This discourse not only allies Jews and Western Christians but enlists Jews as the beacon of Western values against the barbarous Other, and establishes the West as having more than a guilty or purely strategic investment in the defense of Israel. It replaces an older Jewish nationalism, parochialism, and pariah status with universalism, cosmopolitanism, and centrality in the project of protecting and extending Western civilizational values, and it makes clear that tolerance, though coined to benefit the marginal or the weak, exists only for and among the civilized.

But how does the MOT frame the Holocaust as both connected to and distinct from the episodes and targets of identity-based violence it features in the Tolerancenter? Rhetorically, the Tolerancenter establishes the Holocaust as part of a continuum of intolerance and racialized hatred, its ultimate example, its most horrible instance. And yet, the Beit Hashoah also sets the murder of six million Jews dramatically apart, incomparable and impossible to treat with the same techniques, languages, and rules of interpretation or deliberation as the subjects of the Tolerancenter. The distinction is palpable in the marked shift in representational techniques, staging, and authority between the two sections. The Tolerancenter offers glimpses and fragments of scenes of hatred and violence, largely eschewing histories, contexts, and causes. In it, no one has to gain permission to speak for or about another, and there is no apparent concern with the issue of self-representation. For the most part, the presentations have no authors, claim no viewpoint, and gesture at soliciting diverse responses to the material. There is a casual and overtly popularized quality to some of the installations, and much of the information they offer is accessed at the viewer's discretion. By contrast, the organization and style of the Beit Hashoah makes clear that the Holocaust must have its whole story told, that it must be told authoritatively yet also entirely from the perspective of its Jewish victims. And it must be established as a single narrative, delivered at length without interruption, distraction, or choice on the part of the viewer, and without featuring debate or plural points of view.

Consequently, a dramatic change in museum design, in pedagogy, and in audience positioning takes place between the Tolerancenter and the Beit Hashoah. The entrance to the Beit Hashoah marks the end of interactive media and browsing, of opting in or out of certain exhibits; indeed interactivity is exchanged for the action of the installations *on* the viewer. It also marks the end of fragmentary scenes from a variety of different epochs, geographical locations, and conflicts, the end of indifference to the histories or contexts for the issues raised. And it marks the end of the conceit that any of the material being presented involves difficult interpretive or analytic questions on which there could be several credible views. From the moment the automatic doors sweep open to admit us until we are released through the automatic exit doors sixty-five minutes later, every instant of our experience is narrated and orchestrated and every statement is delivered with certitude. There are no problems or presentations to study at leisure and no documents or annotations to examine at length. With the exception of information to track the fate of the child on one's "passport" (see below), there is almost nothing at all to read, and hence none of the subjective, individual reflection that reading can invite. Instead, the experience inside the Beit Hashoah is continuous and total, surrounding and suffusing. There are no silences, no pauses for questions, no points at which the visitor may seek more or different information, vote her or his viewpoint, or consider a matter from more than one angle. The account is delivered as both impartial and true, lacking even any staged disagreements that might gesture toward interpretive complexity in reporting and receiving meaning.

How are all of these changes accomplished and legitimated? As already noted, *Beit Hashoah*, which is not translated by the docent or in the museum literature, means House of the Holocaust. For those who know Hebrew well, it may metonymically suggest *beit hamidrash* (house of study) and *beit haknesset* (house of assembly or prayer); *beit* connotes gathering and not merely housing.[37] The act of conjuring in Hebrew a gathering place for learning about the Holocaust simultaneously provides scholarly auspices for the enterprise, establishes the Beit Hashoah at a distance from the world of pluralistic opinion constitutive of the Tolerancenter, and distances it from the relativism about belief at the heart of tolerance.[38] The connotation of scholarship from *beit hamidrash* gives the contents of Beit Hashoah truth value; the connotation of religiosity from *beit haknesset* (and simply from using Hebrew) makes those contents sacred and also owned by the Hebrew speakers, the Jews. Together, these associations establish the validity of the Beit Hashoah even as they seal it from external challenges or points of view. We are being invited as guests into a sacred Jewish place to learn the truth about a critical historic episode. This is a radical departure from the profane, relativist, compromised, and finally less profound space of the Tolerancenter, though the likelihood that the casual visitor will not notice the break allows the open and pluralistic discursive practices of the Tolerancenter to extend their legitimating shadow over the Beit Hashoah.

We are also, from the beginning of the Beit Hashoah, interpellated as "witnesses" to the experience of the Holocaust rather than as students of tolerance, individuals implicated in prejudice, participants in debate, or stakeholders in complex social configurations. And yet, we are not witnesses in any ordinary sense: on the one hand, what we are seeing is staged rather than real; on the other hand, the conventional distance between staging and viewer is profoundly reduced by the design and nature of the installations, thereby blinding us to that staging in critical ways.

The Beit Hashoah consists of a series of life-size tableaux and dioramas, featuring talking figures, clips of recordings and film footage
from the Nazi period, and readings from diaries and letters. The story
builds dramatically, from the opening film just outside the entrance,
"The World That Was," a romantic account of the "merriment, sing-
ing, and laughter amid hardship" that constituted the "sweet, charm-
ing, and lovely life" of the shtetl, through Hitler's rise to power to the
stigmatization, ghettoization, deportation, and finally extermination
of the Jews. As the story progresses and we move through the exhibits
and through the years, film gives way to tableaux and then the tableaux move into the space of the audience—brick ruins and abandoned belongings jut out into the rooms in which we are standing—
until, finally, we are fully incorporated into the scene. The installation
culminates with our literal descent into a concentration camp–like
space, replete with barbed wire; entrances that separate the adult and
able-bodied from children, the aged, and the infirm; and uneven rough
cement floors. We issue into the cold, cavernous space of a gas cham-
ber where, for a very long time, we watch images of the camps as actors read the words of inmates and survivors. At this point, we are no
longer mere witnesses to the Holocaust but are *inside* the experience;
and yet, of course, this "experience" is a fascimile. Still, it is not surprising to find scribbled in one of the guest books just beyond the exit
doors of the Beit Hashoah: "I had read some things about the Holocaust, but had never seen it firsthand."

Our receipt, at the entrance to the Beit Hashoah, of a card-sized
"passport" with the picture of a Jewish child on it, whose particular
fate we are to check up on periodically during the course of the war,
also seeks to make us more than mere witnesses, let alone audiences
at a media presentation. The assignment to each visitor of a Jewish
child aims to draw us into identification with the victims, and in particular to feel fear, suffering, and loss through the child or over the
child. Perhaps the child is us, or perhaps, if we are older, the child is
ours. Either way, we are meant not to be disengaged observers but to
merge partially with the action and thus become witnesses to our own
experience. "My [passport] child died," one visitor wrote in the guest
book, "and now I know how it must have felt."

In this way, the conflation of the actual and the virtual, the real and the fictional, that is characteristic of late modernity is simultaneously exploited and condemned (in the name of historical objectivity and accuracy). Moreover, the production of the Holocaust in the Beit Hashoah as an experience that visitors both witness and undergo contains an important truth strategy that settles authority and eliminates the problem of interpretation. As the historian Joan W. Scott argues, in an episteme in which experiencing something is considered to provide authentic and unmediated access to its truth, the fact of witnessing or undergoing something ideologically eliminates the need for interpretation or critical analysis.[39] If a metaphysics of presence equates seeing an event with knowing what really occurred ("I know—I was there"), then actually undergoing something becomes an unimpeachable source of such knowledge ("I know—it happened to me"). By combining both perspectives—witnessing and undergoing—this exhibit seals the authority of its narrative from two directions, even though both what is witnessed and what is undergone are staged.[40]

Still, since the installations in the Beit Hashoah are reproductions of a historical episode, how is their credibility, their faithfulness to the original, initially secured? The first step, just described, is positioning us as witnesses; the second crucial device for eliminating questions about perspective, interpretation, and points of view is a nameless narrator's introduction, in the opening tableau, of three figures identified as the Historian, the Researcher, and the Designer. These life-size, George Segal–esque figures become our virtual docents in the Beit Hashoah, and the division of labor among them is presented at some length in the opening diorama. The crucial rhetorical feature of this belabored account is its seeming openness in explaining how an accurate reconstruction of the Holocaust is undertaken. The crucial content is in the depiction of the Historian as one who "establishes the facts by studying documents, diaries, and letters, checking with other experts, and talking with those who were actually there."[41] In this brief yet comprehensive account of the materials of representing history—primary and secondary sources, consultations, interviews—note what is missing: perspective, interpretation, investments, narrative structure and rendering. Instead, there are only facts to be established and presented.

I will not describe the Beit Hashoah in detail. Like the Tolerancenter, it meets its objectives well in some respects. For those who know little or nothing about the rise of Hitler and the development of Third Reich's policies toward the Jews, it provides a quick primer on these subjects.[42] It offers more than an intimation of the horror and scale of the Holocaust, and it underlines the anti-Semitism that allowed much of the rest of world to turn a blind eye to what was happening to European Jews in the 1930s and early 1940s. An effective diorama devoted to the Warsaw uprising and a lecture by the "historian" debunk the notion that Jews were passive, led "like sheep to the slaughter," in the face of mounting persecution, ghettoization, internment, and extermination. It also elucidates how what begins as relatively mild forms of prejudice can swell into mass persecution and atrocity. Yet this lesson is compromised by the contrapuntal insistence that anti-Semitism and the Shoah stand apart from other forms of ethnic hatred or religious persecution: anti-Semitism because it is singularly historically continuous and geographically ubiquitous, and the Shoah because it represents the collusion between active persecution and this enduring worldwide anti-Semitism. Moreover, it is not clear how tolerance, as "the acceptance of beliefs and practices different from our own," would have prevented the Shoah or prevented the indifference to the plight of the Jews represented here as widespread. As the exhibit itself makes clear, a simple failure to accept the beliefs and practices of Jews does not capture the problems of economic distress, racialized scapegoating, anxiety about racial purity, and imperial ambitions and fascist worldview organizing the basis for the Holocaust. Nor is tolerance itself a sufficiently active posture to combat aggression against an entire people. As defined by the MOT, tolerance is not a doctrine or a mandate but a principle or practice, neither of which produces a basis for the intervention of one sovereign nation into the affairs of another.

In the end, then, the strategic rubric for the House of the Holocaust, however effective in bringing a range of visitors in the door, does not suffice to achieve the goals of "never again." As a consequence, an old and familiar Jewish fatalism courses through this ultracontemporary museum, a fatalism that also explains its central paradox: While visitors are incessantly reminded that every individual has the power and responsibility to shape history, we are directed to confer that power to states and NGOs; there is nothing here that affirms—or trusts—popular power. Similarly, while we are constantly importuned to thoughtfulness, we are not actually trusted to think for themselves. And above all, while tolerance is the ideal or the hope, secure borders and heavily armed checkpoints are the necessary reality, just as freedom may be democracy's *raison d'être* but is ultimately trumped by security.

By now, we rather badly need a bathroom.

TOLERANCE AS DEPOLITICIZATION AND THE DEPOLITICIZATION OF TOLERANCE

The Museum of Tolerance not only promulgates a politics that it dissimulates through the rubric of tolerance, it also promulgates a discourse of depoliticization that is itself a means by which the politics of tolerance—the operations of tolerance as a discourse of normativity and power—are dissimulated. Thus the process is self-reinforcing: tolerance as a moral discourse both works to shroud the specific political investments and positions of the MOT and produces a more generic depoliticization of conflicts and of scenes of inequality and domination.

As chapter 1 argued, there are several strands to the depoliticizing effects achieved by tolerance discourse. First, political conflicts rendered as matters of intolerance reframe inequality or domination as personal prejudice or enmity. The depoliticization occurs both through personalizing a politically produced problem and through attributing cause to attitude. Power disappears as individuals are treated as the agents of the conflict and attitude is treated as its source. The prejudiced individual becomes the cause of and the tolerant one becomes the solution to a variety of social, economic, and political ills.

Second, in this reduction of political conflicts to individuals with attitude, conflict itself is ontologized. History and power analytically vanish as constitutive of the attributes and positioning of those subjects considered to be in need of tolerance. So also do the political and economic orders and the discourses of religion, culture, sex, and gender that generate subordination and marginalization of certain subjects, or that generate antagonism between subjected groups. Thus, for example, the complex social, economic, and political forces securing and reproducing Jim Crow do not appear in the MOT presentation of segregation and the civil rights movement. Rather, segregation appears as attitudinal bigotry backed by law, which is then opposed by a movement of attitudinal equality seeking to become law.

Third, this disappearance of power and history obscures not only the sources of conflict, violence, or subordination but also their subject-making capacity. Tolerance, as the term is used today and circulates in the MOT, casts social differences as natural and humans as naturally responding to difference with diffidence and prejudice. Without a historical, political, and political-economic analysis of how specific identities are produced, and how they become sites of domination and privilege, difference itself appears to engender intolerance, a formulation that also makes difference into something generic. This outcome helps to explain how the MOT can move so promiscuously across fields of identity—gender, sexuality, race, ethnicity, religion, culture—and across fields of conflict—Bosnia, homophobic violence, the Los Angeles riots, domestic violence, Rwanda, Ethiopia. An interlocked series of generalizations—difference as the cause of prejudice, prejudice as the cause of injustice, and tolerance as attenuating the dangers of prejudice—permits the gathering of an extraordinary range of phenomena into the same explanatory rubric and the same justice project, as well as the exile of serious political and historical analysis. The explanations are thin to the point of uselessness and the justice project is more of a moral cry than a coherent political program or undertaking.

Fourth, this amalgamation of differences facilitates slides between them; for example, the United Farm Workers' struggle can be included under tolerance because this economic justice project happens to attach to brown bodies. The amalgamation makes possible an especially pernicious interchangeability between religion, culture, ethnicity, and race, an interchangeability that isn't entirely reducible to analytic sloppiness or to the effect of extending the model of Judaism to everything else. Rather, these categories become fungible when identity is ontologized such that belief and practice are derived from blood or phenotype. This ontologization is what makes perversely intelligible the inclusion of racial difference as a candidate for tolerance within a definition of tolerance as "the acceptance of beliefs and practices that differ from one's own." It also permits the slip from religion to race when the Millennium Machine video on terrorism asks viewers whether racial profiling is an acceptable security measure in the aftermath of an attack by Islamic terrorists. The implication is that people of a certain phenotype or appearance inherently hew to a particular set of beliefs and that those beliefs, in turn, can produce a certain set of diabolical practices. Once culture, ethnicity, race, and religion are all part of the generic problem of difference, and once identity itself is ontologized, this chain of logic becomes possible.

Yet this derivation of belief and practices from race is what the MOT elsewhere defines as stereotyping and condemns as an enemy of tolerance. Moreover, the naturalization and amalgamation of difference inscribes the very racism, sexism, and homophobia it purports to redress. It makes identity ontological rather than an effect of the powers that produce it—indeed, that produce every Us and Them, whether women and men, Korean and black, homosexual and heterosexual, or Jew and Christian. In casting difference as an inherent ground of hostility, this logic affirms the tribalism it claims to deplore. But this is also the logic that permits a definition of tolerance as "the acceptance of beliefs and practices that differ from one's own" to be sustained when dealing with categories such as race and gender that would seemingly undermine it. If difference is natural and deep, then it contours belief and practice even where these do not take expressly religious or cultural shape. So race and gender, as sites of deep difference, constitute the basis for disparate beliefs and practices; in the process, sexism and racism are reduced to the failure to treat "difference" with respect, to accord it human dignity despite its strangeness. In this radically depoliticized account of subordination and domination, hegemony and marginalization, the natural diffidence of difference becomes the engine of human history.

On the one hand, this kind of depoliticization is so American, and so late modern, that the Simon Wiesenthal Center cannot be blamed: it is simply fashioning its installations from the basic cloth of contemporary American (un)political culture. On the other hand, this chapter has argued that the MOT employs this cloth to cloak its own political agenda, suggesting a paradoxical political mindfulness about the uses of a certain discourse of depoliticization, a cynically strategic rather than unwitting or naive deployment of it. I want to argue for this purposefulness in a qualified way, suggesting that there is both wiliness and clumsiness, unconscious adaptation and intentionality in the MOT's mobilization of the depoliticizing rubric of tolerance for its political project. That is, insofar as the MOT requires a discourse of depoliticization for its political task, it is not itself fully produced from within this discourse but, rather, wields it purposefully and navigates it carefully. While the museum may be maddeningly incoherent in certain places, none of the installations are intellectually or politically careless or self-contradictory. They do not slip up in their politics or make self-undermining or self-revealing mistakes. Nor, despite the depoliticization that they traffic in and the weak notion of political participation that they promote, are they themselves created from innocence about where power resides or about how to present history to make certain points. The MOT represents an admirable craftiness about power and politics, and even about the politics of history.

Yet it is also the case that tolerance discourse produces occasional problems for the MOT and must be navigated accordingly. For example, the very conflation of ethnicity, race, and culture that tolerance discourse permits, and the "culturalization of conflict" that it promotes, must be resisted to contest the racialization of the Jews adapted and exploited by the Nazis. In fact, the Historian explains early on in the Beit Hashoah that racialization sealed the fate of the Jews under Hitler: "Cultures could be absorbed, the religious could convert, but races could only be eliminated."[43] The narrator also insists that Hitler's demonization and persecution of the Jews was enabled by a racialization that was not simply anti-Semitic but forthrightly wrong in rendering Jews as a race.[44] This careful attunement to distinctions between race, religion, culture, and ethnicity, and to the significance of

conflating them when dealing with Jews, makes all the more disturbing the discussion of racial profiling to deter "Islamacist" terrorist attacks. The Beit Hashoah explicitly rebuts the racialization of Jews and
is highly sensitive to the implications of this racialization in Nazi discourse and practices; at the same time, however, the MOT casually
racializes Muslims when talking about terrorism.

In the Millennium Machine film on violence against women, similarly careful parsing occurs at a crucial moment. The narrator specifies at one point that female circumcision is a "social, not a religious
practice." This striking claim would seem to serve several purposes.
One is to establish that opposing female circumcision is not an act of
religious intolerance. A second is to prevent concern over female circumcision from redounding on the Jewish practice of male circumcision or even the requirement of head shaving for Orthodox women.
Such religious practices are protected by the mantle of tolerance.
Third, the social is distinguished not only from the religious but the
cultural, since culture, too, has acquired standing in tolerance discourse and is covered by the MOT's definition of tolerance. Thus the
"social" appears to have been quite carefully selected as that which
has no hallowed status, belongs to no one in particular, and hence does
not harbor beliefs or practices in need of protection by tolerance. Cod-
ing a practice as social rather than as religious, ethnic, or cultural suggests that it does not issue from deep difference, and is therefore contestable by outsiders and available to being judged by considerations
that could include safety, pain, social utility, social damage, or a
generic and vague notion of human dignity.

In short, within contemporary tolerance discourse, practices one
wants to contest, outlaw, or banish must be categorized as social or
political, while practices one wishes to protect must be classified as
cultural or, better still, religious. Of course, these categories have none
of the fixity implied by the MOT. What is social to one person may be
cultural or religious to another: for example, corporal punishment for
children, wife beating, and taboos on abortion, cremation, sex outside
of marriage, eating certain animals, the abomination of homosexuality. Indeed, male circumcision, performed in the United States for reasons that may be religious, hygienic, "cultural," or aesthetic, is a good

example of the capacity of practices to migrate across the categories the MOT attempts to fix in the statement that female circumcision is a social rather than religious custom.

There are other moments in the MOT that reveal how much political awareness goes into its installations so as to simultaneously make use of the depoliticizing discourse of tolerance and carefully navigate its terms. For example, while the Tolerancenter puts the question of truth in the background and respect for belief or diverse viewpoints in the foreground, we saw that the Beit Hashoah requires a settled, uncontestable truth that is at once objective and concordant with the experience of the victims. This requirement is met via incisive and deliberate recourse to a number of devices, from the construction of the "Historian" and the "Researcher" to the abandonment of interactive media to the featuring of live Holocaust survivors as repositories of truth beyond hermeneutics. Similarly, even as continuity is established between the Tolerancenter and the Beit Hashoah for purposes of gaining our investment in the story of the Holocaust, that continuity also must be disrupted—not only at the level of epistemology and viewpoint but also at the level of what constitutes acceptable levels of complicity. While the Tolerancenter prevails on us to become less bigoted and more responsible in the struggle against bigotry, from the beginning it also confers acceptance on our parochial and prejudiced nature, and thus accepts, and to a degree depends on, the permanence of the problem it is devoted to exposing. The vision in the Tolerancenter is not one of a world in which prejudice has been rooted out and differences no longer explode into conflict; rather, it is one of coping with difficult differences and points of view, and trying to keep things from getting out of hand. The Beit Hashoah, by contrast, works to establish all anti-Semitism as having dire if not holocaustal consequences and thus as requiring a zero-tolerance policy. A narrative structured by the idea that what starts as words, naming practices, and prejudice can escalate into a genocidal project makes ominous any *and every* expression of anti-Semitism. This is the narrative that makes the Holocaust relevant as a defense of contemporary Israel, one that is different from casting the Holocaust as the history out of which the seeming necessity of a Jewish state emerged. For all manifestations of anti-

Semitism to be an immediate and live danger to the existence of all Jews, the specter of the Holocaust must lurk in every anti-Semitic slogan or icon, every terrorist act within Israel, indeed, every challenge to the legitimacy of the Israeli state. By this logic, anti-Semitism and challenges to Israel become one and the same, just as tolerance of Jews and tolerance of Israel become one and the same.

In sum, in the very dissimulation on which it relies—cloaking its politics by recourse to a culturally familiar discourse that eschews a political vocabulary and an analysis of inequality, domination, and colonialism in favor of an emphasis on personal attitude, prejudice, difference, hatred, and acceptance—the MOT has produced a masterful political achievement. The Wiesenthal Center is expert in making use of the quintessentially American as well as classically liberal diffusion of politics and institutional power to stage a political position while appearing to promulgate only unimpeachably good values. And if it succeeds in conveying its didactic message that intolerance does not merely hurt feelings or injure self-esteem but literally kills, it does so by renewing the memory of the Holocaust for the present, a renewal that also ensures that "never again" continues to have a singular meaning, single referent, and single contemporary relevance. As the Museum of Tolerance founder Rabbi Hier said to Pope John Paul II in 1983: "Never again will the Jewish People be victims of another 'Final Solution.' For G-d has bestowed upon us the gift of the State of Israel."[45]

■ ■ ■ ■

SIX

SUBJECTS OF TOLERANCE: WHY WE ARE CIVILIZED AND THEY ARE THE BARBARIANS

Primitive men . . . are uninhibited: thought passes directly into action.
> —Sigmund Freud, *Totem and Taboo*

If intolerance and narcissism are connected, one immediate and practical conclusion might seem to be: we are only likely to love others more if we also learn to love ourselves a little less.
> —Michael Ignatieff, "Nationalism and Toleration"

Since a group is in no doubt as to what constitutes truth or error, and is conscious, moreover, of its own great strength, it is as intolerant as it is obedient to authority. It respects force and can only be slightly influenced by kindness, which it regards merely as a form of weakness. What it demands of its heroes is strength, or even violence. It wants to be ruled and oppressed and to fear its masters. Fundamentally, it is entirely conservative, and it has a deep aversion to all innovations and advances and an unbounded respect for tradition.
> —Freud, *Group Psychology and the Analysis of the Ego* citing (Gustave) Le Bon

The murder of [a U.S. civilian working in Saudi Arabia] shows the evil nature of the enemy we face—these are barbaric people.
> —President George W. Bush, 18 June 2004

In recent years, culture has become a cardinal object of tolerance and intolerance. In part, this development reflects changes in liberal democratic societies, which have become increasingly multicultural as a consequence of late modern population flows and of the affirmation of cultural difference over assimilation. But it is also tied to what Mahmood Mamdani calls the "culturalization" of political conflict: "It is no longer the market (capitalism), nor the state (democracy), but culture (modernity) that is said to be the dividing line between those in favor of a peaceful, civic existence and those inclined to terror."[1] Mamdani credits Samuel Huntington and Bernard Lewis with catapulting the notion of culture to the status of a political dividing line between good and evil, progress and reaction, peaceability and violence. In a 1990 article, "The Roots of Muslim Rage," Bernard Lewis put forward the "clash of civilizations" thesis to describe relations between what he termed the Judeo-Christian and Islamic civilizations; a few years later, Huntington generalized the thesis to argue that "the velvet curtain of culture" had replaced the cold war's "iron curtain of ideology."[2]

When political or civil conflict is explained as a cultural clash, whether in international or domestic politics, tolerance emerges as a key term for two reasons. The first is that some cultures are depicted as tolerant while others are not: that is, tolerance itself is culturalized insofar as it is understood to be available only to certain cultures. The second is that the culturalization of conflict makes cultural difference itself into a (if not *the*) salient site for the practice of tolerance or intolerance. The border between cultures is taken to be inherently volatile *if* those cultures are not subdued by liberalism. So tolerance, rather than, say, equality, emancipation, or power sharing, becomes a basic term in the vocabulary describing and prescribing for conflicts rendered as cultural.

As chapter 1 argued, the culturalization of conflict and of difference discursively depoliticizes both, while also organizing the players in a particular fashion, one that makes possible that odd but familiar move within liberalism: though "culture" is what nonliberal peoples are imagined to be ruled and ordered by, liberal peoples are considered to *have* culture or cultures. In other words, what Mamdani terms the ideological culturalization of politics does not uniformly reduce all conflict or difference to culture. Rather, "we" have culture while culture has "them," or we *have* culture while they *are* a culture. Or, we are a democracy while they are a culture. This asymmetry turns on an imagined opposition between culture and individual moral autonomy, in which the former vanquishes the latter unless culture is itself subordinated by liberalism. The logic derived from this opposition between nonliberalized culture and moral autonomy then articulates a further set of oppositions between nonliberalized culture and freedom and between nonliberalized culture and equality. This chapter maps that logic in order to reveal how and why liberalism conceives of itself as unique in its capacity to be culturally neutral and culturally tolerant, and conceives of nonliberal "cultures" as disposed toward barbarism.

The overt premise of liberal tolerance, when applied to group practices (as opposed to idiosyncratic individual beliefs or behaviors), is that religious, cultural, or ethnic differences are sites of natural or native hostility. Tolerance is conceived as a tool for managing or lessening this hostility to achieve peaceful coexistence. Yet within a liberal paradigm, this premise already begs a number of questions: What makes groups cohere in the first place, that is, what binds them within and makes them hostile without; and what makes group identity based on culture, religion, or ethnicity, as opposed to other kinds of differences, an inherent site of intolerance? Within liberal society, what are culture, religion, or ethnicity imagined to contain within and repel without that makes their borders so significant? What do we imagine to be deposited in these sites such that they feature a relatively solidaristic inside and inherently hostile outside? Given a liberal account of human beings as relatively atomized, competitive, acquisitive, and insecure, what makes common beliefs or practices a site for overcoming this prickliness? What kinds of beliefs are thought to bind us, and is the binding achieved through something in the nature of the beliefs themselves or in an order of *affect* attached to belief? Put differently, what is the relation between the binding force of the social contract and the binding force of culture or religion? Why doesn't the social contract suffice to reduce the significance of subnational group hostilities?[3]

In short, what, according to liberal theory, makes multiculturalism a political problem that tolerance is summoned to solve? And from what noncultural, nonethnic, or secular place is tolerance imagined to emanate for this work? These are not easy questions to ask, or even to formulate properly, from within a liberal, modernist, or rationalist paradigm. The difficulty arises in part because the methodological individualism of liberal theory produces the figure of an individuated subject by abstracting and isolating deliberative rationality from embodied locations or constitutive practices. The formulation of rationality that has nonreason as its opposite presumes a Cartesian splitting of mind from embodied, historicized, cultured being. Across Lockean, Kantian, Millian, Rawlsian, and Habermasian perspectives, rationality transcends—or better, exceeds—embodiment and cultural location to permit a separation between rational thought on one side and the constitutive embodiment of certain beliefs and practices on the other. For deliberative rationality to be meaningful apart from "culture" or "subjectivity," the conceit must be in play that the individual *chooses* what he or she thinks. This same choosing articulates the possibility of an optional relationship with culture, religion, and even ethnic belonging; it sustains as well the conceit that the rationality of the subject is independent of these things, which are named as contextual rather than constitutive elements. But if the deliberative rationality that generates choice entails the capacity of the subject to abstract from its own context, then individuation itself posits a will (to reason, as well as to do other things) that enables such independence. The idea of individuation is thus enabled on the one side by rationality and on the other by a notion of will; together they produce the possibility of the autonomous liberal subject.

The quintessential theorist of this formulation, of course, is Kant, for whom intellectual and moral maturity consists in using "one's own understanding without the guidance of another."[4] Rational argument and criticism, indeed the rationality of criticism, are not simply the sign but also the basis of the moral autonomy of persons, an autonomy that presupposes independence from others, independence from authority in general, *and* the independence of reason itself. From this perspective, a less individuated person, one who has what social theorists term an organicist identity, appears as neither fully rational nor fully in command of a will. That is, the liberal formulation of the individuated subject as constituted by rationality and will figures a non-individuated opposite who is so *because* of the underdevelopment of both rationality and will. For the organicist creature, considered to lack rationality and will, culture and religion (culture *as* religion, and religion *as* culture—equations that work only for this creature) are saturating and authoritative; for the liberal one, in contrast, culture and religion become "background," can be "entered" and "exited," and are thus rendered extrinsic to rather than constitutive of the subject.

Through individuation, so this story goes, culture and religion as forms of rule are dethroned, replaced by the self-rule of men. But this very dethroning changes the meaning of culture and religion within liberal and organicist orders. In liberal societies, culture is positioned as "background" of the subject, as something one may opt in or out of and also deliberate about. (This is what makes rational choice theory intellectually coherent as a form of social theory for liberal societies, but only for liberal societies.) Put the other way around, if not only rule but subject constitution by culture and religion are equated with organicist orders, then this rule and this constitution are imagined to disappear with the emergence of the autonomous individual; indeed, their vanquishing is the very meaning of such autonomy. For liberal subjects, culture becomes food, dress, music, lifestyle, and contingent values. Culture *as* power and especially as rule is replaced by culture as mere way of life; culture that preempts individuality transmogrifies into culture as a source of comfort or pleasure for the individual, akin to the liberal idealization of the domestic sphere as "a haven in a heartless world." Similarly, religion as domination, tyranny, or source of irrationality and violence is presumed to transform, where the individual reigns, into religion as a choice and as a source of comfort, nourishment, moral guidance, and moral credibility. This is the schema that allows President Bush's prayers about political matters, routine consultations with radical Christian groups on foreign policy, and even his personal conviction that his military mission in the Middle East is divinely blessed to be sharply differentiated from the (dangerous) devotion to Allah of a Muslim fundamentalist. Bush's religi-

osity is figured as a source of strength and moral guidance for his delib-
erations and decisions, while the devotee of Allah is assumed to be without the individual will and conscience necessary to such ratiocination.[5]

Moral autonomy, the name liberalism gives to this individuated figure, is widely understood by theorists of tolerance to constitute *the* un-
derlying value of the principle of liberal tolerance.[6] As Susan Mendus
writes, "The autonomy argument is sometimes referred to as the char-
acteristically liberal argument for toleration." For Will Kymlicka,
"Liberals are often defined as those who support toleration because
it is necessary for the promotion of autonomy." And for Bernard
Williams, "If toleration as a practice is to be defended in terms of its
being a value, then it will have to appeal to substantive opinions about
the good, in particular the good of individual autonomy."[7] But while
autonomy is the liberal good that tolerance aims to promote, tolerance
is also understood as that which can be generated only by autonomous
individuals—that, in part, is the significance of its status as a civic offering rather than a legal mandate. Tolerance thus requires in advance
what it also promotes. Conversely, tolerance as the abiding of behaviors or convictions other than those to which one subscribes is conceived within liberalism as unavailable to the unindividuated or nonliberal subject. The making of a tolerant world, then, literally requires
the liberalization of the world, a formulation endorsed by liberal democratic theorists, pundits, and political actors ranging from Will Kymlicka to Thomas Friedman. As Michael Ignatieff argues, "the culture
of individualism is the only reliable solvent of the hold of group identities and the racisms that go with them." The "essential task in teaching 'toleration,'" he adds, "is to help people see themselves as individuals, and then to see others as such."[8]

While Kant functions as the foundation stone for contemporary liberal theorists subscribing to this formulation, the contribution of
Freud to the ideology of the tolerant liberal self and its intolerant organicist Other is an interesting one. Many liberals concerned with tolerance implicitly or explicitly place Freudian assumptions at the heart
of their work or have tucked him into their arguments as a kind of au-
thorizing signature. What Freud offers, among other things, is an ac-

count of why liberal orders, in their affirmation of the individual, represent themselves as the only possible regime type for cultivating and practicing tolerance, while simultaneously promoting the pluralistic belief structure understood to necessitate tolerance. Though Freud ratifies the "mature" (or "advanced") status of the individuated Westerner in this regard, he does not make an ontological or permanent distinction between the individual and group. On Freud's view, individuated subjects can regress into organicist formations at any moment, forfeiting the definitive elements of proper individuation when they do so. Strong group identity thus constitutes not an opposition to but a regression from the mature individuated psyche. Even as Freud pathologizes the group (as irrational and dangerous), he does not reify the rational individual as a permanent cultural achievement radically differentiated from organicist subjects.

In what follows, then, Freud's thinking will be both criticized and appropriated for a critique of liberal thinking about tolerance. On the one hand, Freud's progressive historical-anthropological narrative in which tolerant liberal orders represent the highest stage of "maturity" for man and are equated with civilization will be read critically, especially insofar as these themes are manifest in contemporary theorists of tolerance.[9] That is, Freud's equation of individuation with both ontogenic and phylogenic maturity, and of solidarity or organicism with primitivism or regression, will offer a basis for grasping the civilizational discourse that frames contemporary tolerance talk and converts it to the purposes of liberal imperialism. On the other hand, Freud's appreciation of the contingency of groups, their basis in affect rather than essential traits, is valuable in deconstructing the ontologization of "blood and belonging" at play in the modern liberal theory and practice of cultural tolerance.[10]

FREUD

In *Civilization and Its Discontents* and *Totem and Taboo*,[11] Freud is conventionally read as explaining how men overcome what he posits as a natural asociality rooted in sexual rivalry and primary aggression.

As accounts of how men come to live together without perpetual strife, these stories have been read as Freud's version of the emergence of humans from a state of nature into a social contract and from primary satisfaction of the instincts to the instinctual repression productive (via sublimation) of civilization. But there is another cross current in Freud's depiction of our struggle for sociality, one that concerns how subjects progress not just from primary hostility to relative peaceability but from organicist identities—groups—to being civilized individuals. These two tales are neither identical nor fully reconcilable—in fact, they represent two different tropes of "the primitive": the lone savage and the submissive tribal follower. The second figure is the problematic of *Group Psychology and the Analysis of the Ego*;[12] it makes a shadowy appearance in *Civilization and Its Discontents* as well. And it is the narrative of this figure, with its "ontogeny recapitulates phylogeny" trajectory from childlike primitivism to mature liberal cosmopolitanism, that is detectable at the foundations of most liberal tolerance talk. Where this talk does not actually reference Freud, it remains convergent with Freud's accounts of what binds groups, what signals primitivism and civilization, what the tensions are between the individual and the group, and what is so dangerous—internally oppressive, externally threatening—about organicist societies. Together these accounts coin tolerance as something available only to liberal subjects and liberal orders and fashion the supremacy of both over the dangerous alternatives. They also establish organicist orders as a natural limit of liberal tolerance, as intolerable in consequence of their assumed intolerance.

Freud's challenge to himself in *Group Psychology and the Analysis of the Ego* is to explain *Massenpsychologie*—variously translated as "mass," "mob," or "crowd psychology" but inherently pejorative across all translations—as consonant with, rather than a departure from, the individual psychology he devoted his life to mapping. Unlike others working on the problem (whom he considers at length in the book's first chapter), Freud does not treat group behavior or feeling as issuing from a different structure of desire from that of individual affect. His concern here, in addition to ratifying the basic architecture of the psyche he spent years theorizing, is to affirm the individual as a primordial unit of analysis and action *and thereby* pathologize the group as a dangerous condition of de-individuation and psychological regression. Freud's beginning point thus works normatively to align maturity, individuation, conscience, repression, and civilization and to oppose these to childishness, primitivism, unchecked impulse, instinct, and barbarism. This is the alignment and opposition that make their way into contemporary tolerance discourse.

Yet Freud's contrast between primitive groups and civilized individuals is not a straightforward story of emergence from an undifferentiated mass to self-reflective individuality. As is well known, it is the repression of *individual instinct*, and not the disaggregation of a group, that animates the drama of *Civilization and Its Discontents* as human happiness, satisfaction, and self-love are all sacrificed at the altar of civilization. It could even be said that for Freud there is only ever the individual, that is, the individual is both the ontological a priori and the telos of civilization; groups are not primary or natural, nor are they stable. To the contrary, Freud's insistence on our "primary mutual hostility" and natural "sexual rivalry"[13] makes associations of any sort an achievement, whether they are relatively permanent and organized structures arrived at through the complex covenant of the totemic system depicted in *Totem and Taboo*, or more contingent and unstructured, as with those diagnosed in *Group Psychology*. Man is not a "herd animal" but a "horde animal," Freud writes at the conclusion of his lengthy critical discussion of other theorists of group psychology (*Group Psychology*, 68). A herd animal has an instinctual affinity for closeness, a primary gregariousness, while the horde animal is constituted by an external organizing principle that brokers a complex need for, rivalry with, endangerment by, and aggression toward others.

Still, Freud, like other nineteenth-century European thinkers, conceives "primitive" peoples as organized by principles of tribalism rather than individualism. Individuation is both the agent and sign of civilization for Freud, while groups signify a condition—whether temporary or enduring—of barbarism. Organicist orders, in other words, denote not simply pre-civilized social relations and subject formations but *de-civilized* ones in which the demands of civilization have been loosened or shed. This is why, despite his quarrel with their analyses of the source of *Massenpsychologie*, Freud allows fellow psychologists Gustave Le Bon and William McDougall to characterize the problem he joins them in wishing to understand, namely that the mental life of "unorganized" groups is comparable to that of "primitive people *and* of children" (13). For Le Bon, "by the mere fact that he forms part of an organized group, a man descends several rungs in the ladder of civilization. Isolated, he may be a cultivated individual; in a crowd, he is a barbarian—that is, a creature acting by instinct. He possesses the spontaneity, the violence, the ferocity, and also the enthusiasm and heroism of primitive beings" (12). McDougall says the behavior of the group "is like that of an unruly child or an untutored passionate savage in a strange situation, rather than like that of its average member; and in the worst cases it is like that of a wild beast, rather than like that of human beings" (24).

So we have in Freud the paradox of an analytical a priori individualism (the lone savage) and a colonial historiography of the emergence of modern individualized man out of organicism (the primitive tribalist). Savage man is nonhuman animal, lacking instinctual repression, while primitive man is human infant, lacking individuation and rationality. This paradox, which is distributed across the several Freudian texts mentioned thus far, also appears in many contemporary liberal discussions of culture and tolerance. To the degree that there is a reconciliation of the paradox in Freud, it is hinged on the a priori status of the individual: regressed man, unindividuated man, isn't regressed *to* the group but *by* the group to a more instinctual psychic state. And his de-individuation derives from his relation not to others but to his own instincts. He is without the independence of will and deliberation yielded by a developed superego. Man in a group does not simply merge—Freud quarrels overtly with "contagion theory"—but bears both a shared attachment to something external to the group and a shared lack, a lowered or absent superego. Man in a group ceases to be directed by his own deliberation and conscience. He ceases to be organized by free will and rationality, those two crucial features of the individuated liberal subject.

Through this lens, the brutal murders and public torching of four American civilians by a Fallujan mob in March 2004 converge with the torture scenes orchestrated by American troops in Abu Ghraib revealed a month later. Both could be read as a decline of individual deliberation, conscience, and restraint in the context of morally depraved group enthusiasms.[14] Yet this convergence still permits a divergent assessment of the two peoples from which the acts emerged— such that President Bush could declare that the Fallujan incident or Nicholas Berg's decapitation confirmed the "true nature of the enemy" while insisting that the torture at Abu Ghraib did not express the "the nature of the men and women who serve our country."[15] We will return to this matter after we examine the basis for the liberal conviction that group ties cancel rational deliberation and moral conscience.

For this purpose, we need to enter the story Freud tells in *Group Psychology and the Analysis of the Ego*. Freud's commitment to a methodological and social individualism requires that his analysis of group psychology commence with the question of how a group is possible at all before considering why certain group formations induce or produce animal-like, passionate, and mentally defective behavior among its members. That is, primary rivalry and atomization have to be overcome, an overcoming that can issue only from the drive that binds humans—namely, Eros. Love for another is all that can challenge the primary narcissism generative of social hostility and rivalry. Immediately, however, Freud cautions against imagining that the bonds of a group consist in a simple love of group members for one another—to do so would be to eschew both our primary self-regard and what Freud, borrowing from Schopenhauer, identifies as the "porcupine problem," which goes as follows: A number of porcupines, feeling cold, huddle together in order to benefit from each other's warmth. But in drawing close, they feel one another's quills and sense danger, leading them to draw apart again, a separation that returns them to suffering from the cold. The repetition of this movement, in which "they were driven backwards and forwards from one trouble to the other," produces for Freud a metaphor of human desire and explains an oscillation he associates with inherent ambivalence in love (41)

while Eros impels us toward closeness with another, this very closeness makes us terribly vulnerable to injury and suffering. So we pull
away, only to feel endangered by loneliness and fearful isolation.[16]

Explaining the phenomenon of the human group, then, necessitates
explaining how this oscillation between two unacceptable dangers—
closeness that produces vulnerability to another and isolation that
produces a sense of unprotectedness—is overcome in favor of pro-
longed closeness. How do we become continuously huddling porcupines? The answer lies not in the dynamics of Eros within the group
but rather in the group's constitution by something external to which
we are each libidinally bound—a leader or an ideal. A group is formed
out of mutual identification in love or idealization (they turn out to be
the same) of something outside the group. But what is the nature of
this identification such that it actually binds those who share it? In
Group Psychology, Freud specifies three types of identification in love:
"First, identification is the original form of emotional ties with an object; secondly, in a regressive way it becomes a substitute for a libidinal object-tie, as it were by means of introjection of the object into the
ego; and thirdly, it may arise with any new perception of a common
quality shared with some other person who is not the object of the sexual instinct. The more important this common quality is, the more successful may this partial identification become, and it may thus represent the beginning of a new tie." Freud hypothesizes that "the mutual
tie between members of a group is in the nature of this [third] kind"
(50); thus, we are bound to members of a group by virtue of a perceived shared quality, in this case love for the leader or external ideal.
But his hypothesis in turn requires that we understand the psychical
phenomenon of "being in love" to appreciate why identification with
others in this state would produce a strong bond.

So what is it to be in love? In the beginning, goes Freud's oft-
rehearsed tale, there is only sexual desire. What we call *love* precipitates out of the inhibition of this desire. Love—whether that of a
child for its parents or that of an adult for a lover or friend—is aim-
inhibited Eros. Aim inhibition entails a displacement or rerouting of
libidinal energy; in the case of love, this energy goes into idealization
of the object. But idealization itself, Freud explains, is more than rev-

erence for the object. Rather, it is a way of satisfying one's own need to be loved by projecting one's ideals of goodness onto another. Idealization thus involves a circuitry of projection from the ego ideal of the lover onto the love object, a projection that produces a feeling (being in love) that in turn gratifies the ego's own desire for love or self-idealization.[17]

In short, the idealization of a loved one, in which the object is inevitably "sexually overvalued" (only the lover sees the beloved's bottomless charms) and rendered relatively free from criticism, involves a great deal of our own narcissistic libido spilling onto the object. Here is Freud's account of how these two sources of the affect of love—the inhibition of Eros and the gratification of the lover's own ego—combine:

> If the sensual implications are more or less effectively repressed or set aside, the illusion is produced that the object has come to be sensually loved on account of its spiritual merits, whereas on the contrary these merits may really only have been lent to it by its sensual charm.
>
> The tendency which falsifies judgement in this respect is that of *idealization*. . . . We see that the object is being treated in the same way as our own ego, so that when we are in love a considerable amount of narcissistic libido overflows on to the object. . . . [I]n many forms of love choice . . . the object serves as a substitute for some unattained ego ideal of our own. We love it on account of the perfections which we have striven to reach for our own ego, and which we should now like to procure in this roundabout way as a means of satisfying our narcissism. (56)

Idealization is narcissistic projection necessitated by aim inhibition. But precisely because this experience of narcissism is so heady for the ego—headier, indeed, than any mere sexual satisfaction, which, Freud notes, "always involves a reduction in sexual overvaluation"—idealization can grow quite extreme. And as the idealization intensifies, so also does the narcissistic gratification it produces, until the latter eventually overtakes the ego ideal of the lover altogether: "the ego [of the lover] becomes more and more unassuming and modest, and the object more and more sublime and precious, until at last it gets possession of the entire self-love of the ego, whose self-sacrifice thus follows as a natural consequence" (56).

Here lies the secret of the love of individual group members for a leader or ideal. Originally driven by Eros, the (sexless) love for the leader or ideal develops into an ardent idealization of the loved object; what starts as a gratification of the ego's own narcissism ends with the idealized object taking the place of the ego ideal itself and consuming the ego as well. This last move explains the familiar phenomenon in group psychology of a severe deterioration in individual judgment and conscience:

> Contemporaneously with this "devotion" of the ego to the object, which is no longer to be distinguished from a sublimated devotion to an abstract idea, the functions allotted to the ego ideal entirely cease to operate. The criticism exercised by that agency is silent; everything that the object does and asks for is right and blameless. Conscience has no application to anything that is done for the sake of the object; in the blindness of love remorselessness is carried to the pitch of crime. The whole situation can be completely summarized in a formula: *The object has been put in the place of the ego ideal.* (57)

So this is the nature of the love that individual group members bear toward the leader or idea. But what binds group members to one another? How is it possible for these individual lovers of a distant figure or ideal to become attached to one another, especially given Freud's hypothesis of primary rivalry in love? Here Freud returns to identification: *a group is a number of individuals who have put one and the same object in the place of their ego ideal, and in so doing, identify with one another in their ego.* The group coheres to the extent that individual ego ideals have been replaced or absorbed by a common object. In such coherence the group not only shares a love object and ego ideal but also becomes something of a common ego, a "common me" to a degree that no mere social contract could produce.[18]

The group's foundation on the collective experience of being in love with something external to it is what engenders mutual identification rather than mutual rivalry among the lovers. The distant (or abstract) character of the love object secures the impossibility of any group member actually, and hence exclusively, possessing the object. The nonsexual nature of the love both perpetrates the idealization and ensures this impossibility.[19] Nonsexual love also allows for a persistent oscillation between love of a leader and love of an ideal—the group is bound by idealization that is at once detachable from a particular person and sustained through a particular person. The person remains abstract and idealized because the sexual consummation that would reduce the idealization does not occur.

In this rendering of love and identification as the basis of groups, Freud believes he has explained two crucial things: (1) how groups can exist at all when we are naturally rivalrous and antisocial, that is, when we are porcupines; and (2) why groups represent a regressed state of the psyche, that is, why group behavior episodically becomes mob behavior, even among the highly educated or civilized. With regard to the first, our natural rivalry is resolved through collective identification, the mechanism of which is love for an external object or ideal. We do not actually love each other but are bound together through an identification that is experienced as love even as it is a way of living our love for the unattainable object. With regard to the second, for Freud, being in love inherently entails a certain regression, a withdrawal from the world and a loss of boundaries—a state of abandon as well as slavishness. Moreover, being in love entails a loss of the individual ego ideal and of the conscience and inhibition it sustains. Not the group as a group but rather each of its individuals is in this condition vis-à-vis something external to the group. Collective identification of group members with one another's love heightens this state and also forms the basis for the group tie.

Freud's theory of group formation is quite suggestive for thinking about nationalism, not to mention fascism. However, we have rehearsed this story not for its explanatory value but in order to explore its assumptions and explanations as they operate in liberal figurations of the inherent intolerance and dangerousness of organicist societies. In *Group Psychology*, Freud masterfully articulates an ideology of the civilized, individuated subject and pathologizes groups and group identities. Basing the group tie on the dynamics of love and identification produces group enthrallment as a regression from rationality, conscience, and impulse control. The group is dangerous because it has these qualities, and it also signifies a literal undoing of the individuated subject who must be, in Freud's words, "conquered" by the requirements of civilization.[20]

While Freud elsewhere links civilization, instinctual repression, and maturity at both the ontogenic and phylogenic levels, only in *Group Psychology* does he elaborate the political-theoretical implications of these relatively conventional metonymies: organicist societies are inherently less civilized than liberal individualistic ones because non-individuation signals a libidinally charged psychic economy that constrains rational deliberation and impulse control. This formulation renders individuation both an effect and sign of instinctual repression, conscience, and the capacity for self-regulation. It renders groups inherently dangerous because of the de-repressed human condition they represent—the psychic state of urgency, unbridled passion, credulousness, impulsiveness, irritability, impulsiveness, extremism, and submissiveness to authority that Freud, drawing on Le Bon and MacDougall, takes to be characteristic of the group (*Group Psychology*, 13–15).

Freud also figures organicist societies as problematic because in them love operates in the public or social realms, instead of being (properly) confined to the private and the familial ones. Such societies represent the dangerousness of public ardor and signify the importance of containing love in the domestic domain so that civilization can produce the rationality and individuation that is its mark.[21] If love civilized is love domesticated, then ardent attachments of any sort— to a god, a belief system, a people, or a culture—must remain private and depoliticized or take the abstract form of patriotism lest they endanger civilization and the autonomous individual who signifies a civilized state. Culture is thus dangerous if it is public rather than private, a key formulation in distinguishing liberal from nonliberal states and, even more significantly, "free" societies from "fundamentalist" ones. What is achieved by starting with the egoistic individual who then sacrifices his individuality as a member of the group is the valorization of the liberal individual as a rational, self-regulating subject, and hence as a modestly free subject. This trajectory becomes especially clear if we remember that Freud's pathologization of the group pertains not just to its crude and dangerous behavior but also to its enthrallment, its constitution through domination: "It wants to be ruled and oppressed and to fear its masters" (15). If what holds a group together is slavish devotion to something external to it, and if such devotion entails the naturally egoistic subject giving up a significant part of its individuality, then Freud has succeeded in defining group membership as the inherent sacrifice of individual freedom (rooted in deliberation, self-direction, and conscience) on the alter of love for that which dominates it. Strong social bonds arise only and always as an effect of domination and as a sign of dangerous regression to a de-individuated and hence de-repressed state.

Above all, Freud has made organicist societies signify a condition in which subjects are less conscience-bound and civilized than the mature individual and less individualized *because* they are less conscience-bound—that is, because their ego ideals are conferred to the external ideal or leader. If the fall into primitivism is seen as a fall away from superegoic self-regulation, then "civilization" becomes coterminous with self-regulating individuals and the diminution of groups inherently dominated by a leader or ideal, on the one hand, and unrepressed instincts on the other. Individuation (vis-à-vis one another and authority) represents ontogenic and phylogenic "childhood" thrown off and instinctual repression, deliberation, conscience, and freedom acquired.[22] In this light, the gleeful mob violence against the American security workers in Fallujah appears iconographic of an absent liberalism—such violence appears as the rule rather than the exception for an order construed as desperately in need of the very liberal democratic transformation that it is resisting. Indeed, such violence becomes a vindication of George W. Bush's newfound liberation theology, his mission to free the unfree world both in the name of what is good for others and in the name of what makes the world a safer place.[23] For by this account, to be without liberalism is to be not simply oppressed but exceptionally dangerous.[24] Conversely, American torture and humiliation of Iraqis at Abu Ghraib was rendered as sheer aberration: "not the America I know," as Bush put it. Or, in the words of British Prime Minister Tony Blair, "what we came to put an end to, not to perpetrate," a formulation that deftly reverses the source of violence, attributing it to Iraqi political culture while ruling it out of character for the Western occupiers.[25]

This argument implies that the individual must be cultivated and protected and that group identities of all kinds must be contained insofar as they represent both the absence of individual autonomy and the social danger of a de-civilized formation. Organicist orders are not only radically Other to liberalism but betoken the "enemy within" civilization and the enemy to civilization. Most dangerous of all would be transnational formations that link the two—Judaism in the nineteenth century, communism in the twentieth, and today, of course, Islam.[26]

LIBERALISM AND ITS OTHER: WHO HAS
CULTURE AND WHOM CULTURE HAS

The governmentality of tolerance as it circulates through civilizational discourse has, as part of its work, the containment of the (organicist, non-Western, nonliberal) Other.[27] As pointed out earlier, within contemporary civilizational discourse, the liberal individual is uniquely identified with the capacity for tolerance and tolerance itself is identified with civilization. Nonliberal societies and practices, especially those designated as fundamentalist, are depicted not only as relentlessly and inherently intolerant but as potentially intolerable for their putative rule by culture or religion and their concomitant devaluation of the autonomous individual—in short, their thwarting of individual autonomy with religious or cultural commandments. Out of this equation, liberalism emerges as the only political rationality that can produce the individual, societal, and governmental practice of tolerance, and, at the same time, liberal societies become the broker of what is tolerable and intolerable. Liberalism's promotion of tolerance is equated with the valorization of individual autonomy; the intolerance associated with fundamentalism is equated with the valorization of culture and religion at the expense of the individual, an expense that makes such orders intolerable from a liberal vantage point.

These logics, more fully adumbrated in the next chapter, share the assumptions about individuals and groups appearing both in Kant's grammar of moral autonomy and Freud's pathologization of groups. They entail two particular conceits about autonomy in liberal orders:

the autonomy of the subject from culture—the idea that the subject is prior to culture and free to choose culture; and the autonomy of politics from culture—the idea that politics is above culture and free of culture. Each of these will be outlined here; their operation and their implications will be examined in chapter 7.

"Culture is one of the two or three most complicated words in the English language," Raymond Williams begins the entry on "culture" in *Keywords*. The term emerges as a noun, he tells us, only in the eighteenth century, not coming into common use until the middle of the nineteenth century.[28] Originally deployed mainly as a synonym for civilization, the noun described the secular process of human development.[29] But in our time, Williams writes, culture has acquired four broad categories of meaning: (1) a physicalist usage that reaches back to the old synonymic relationship that the verb *culture* had with husbandry; (2) a usage that approximates "civilization" and that refers to a general process of intellectual, spiritual, and aesthetic development; (3) an anthropological usage that indicates a particular way of life of a people, period, or group or of humanity in general; and (4) a usage that refers to a body of artistic and intellectual heritage or activity.[30]

Williams mentions briefly that these meanings do not remain distinct today, but we must scrutinize their admixture more closely to appreciate the problematic of culture within contemporary liberal democratic discourse. If culture signifies a material process, a common way of life, a process of development of the distinctly human faculties of intellect and spirit, and a valuation of selected products of these faculties, then this very complex of meanings actually represents a certain vexation within liberalism. On the one hand, liberal societies generally regard themselves as representing the world-historical apex of culture and cultural productions. On the other hand, liberalism conceives of itself as freeing individuals from the mandate of culture in any of its senses, that is, as producing the moral and intellectual autonomy of the individual to self-determine the extent of his or her participation in culture(s) in every sense of the word. Whether construed as high art, the acquisition of knowledge, or as an ethnically inflected "way of life," culture in liberal societies is largely deemed an objectifiable good that is optional and privately enjoyed—hence the common reference in multicultural schools today to "sharing one's culture" (by which is usually meant sharing food, holiday rituals, or performing arts) or "respecting another's culture" (by which is usually meant respecting another's dietary practices, holidays, or ways of dress). But on this account, liberalism cannot feature culture as a public good or even a public bond. The closest liberals generally come to the notion of a publicly shared culture is "national culture," which conveys a loose link between particular national histories, social mores, and habits of thought, or "market culture," which, ironically, redounds to the physicalist meaning of culture as a form of husbandry or cultivation that exceeds individual choice and that produces conditions of subsistence and existence. Some liberal theorists also speak of "Western culture," a term by which they are mostly alluding to the habits of life and thought organized by liberalism, Christianity, and the market.

The conceptual positioning of culture as extrinsic to the liberal subject (and to the liberal state, about which more shortly) is exemplified by the normative conditions that the political philosopher Seyla Benhabib sets out for the resolution of multicultural dilemmas, each of which presumes the capacity to grasp and negotiate culture from the outside: universal respect, egalitarian reciprocity, voluntary self-ascription, and freedom of exit and association.[31] Benhabib is attempting to establish limits on the claims of culture that would respect individual autonomy without violating the fabric of culture, certainly an admirable endeavor. But in order for us to assess and limit the claims of culture according to such criteria, culture must be graspable as knowable and as containable from some noncultural place. Similarly, Benhabib speaks about limiting minority cultural claims in terms of the "rights" they have over their members: "nomoi communities do *not* have the right to deprive their children of humankind's accumulated knowledge and civilizational achievement; . . . they *do* have a right to transmit to their children the fundamentals of their own ways of life *alongside* other forms of knowledge shared with humankind."[32] Again, the very language of rights implies an ability to isolate various parties—the culture and the individual, respective forms of cultural knowledge—that rests on an autonomous, precultural, Kantian subject to whom such judgment and assertion is available.[33]

From such ground, it is not surprising that a range of contemporary theorists of tolerance—Bernard Williams, Joseph Raz, Michael Ignatieff, and Will Kymlicka, along with the Rawlsians and the Habermasians—tacitly or expressly argue that a tolerant worldview is available only to peoples or societies with a deep value and practice of individualization, an investment in individual rather than group identity. But while collective identity, today linguistically denoted as "culture," is affirmed as important to human beings by these thinkers, it is also problematic for liberalism's attachment to the secularism that guarantees both individual autonomy and deliberative rationality. Beyond representing a local claim on the individual, and in this regard an attenuation of individuality and autonomy, culture undermines the aspiration to a public rationality that overcomes cultural particularism in favor of putatively a-cultural concerns with justice as fairness. Thus even as a deliberative democratic theorist such as Benhabib struggles to recognize cultural belonging and identity in excess of what is offered by the nation-state, and dismisses as "institutionally unstable and analytically untenable" efforts to separate "background culture" from "public political culture," she also insists on a set of norms, metanorms, and principles to produce "free and reasoned deliberation among individuals considered as moral and political equals" as the basis of democracy.[34]

Most importantly, if, for liberals, collective identities represent the dangerousness of the group, then liberalism stands for that which has found a solution to this dangerousness without abolishing collective identity altogether. Liberalism prides itself on having discovered how to reduce the hungers and aggressive tendencies of collective identity while permitting individuals private enjoyment of such identity. This solution involves a set of interrelated juridical and ideological moves in which religion and culture are privatized and the cultural and religious dimensions of liberalism itself are disavowed. Culture and religion are private and privately enjoyed, ideologically depoliticized, much as the family is; and, like the family, they are situated as "background" to *homo politicus* and *homo oeconomicus*. Culture, family, and religion are all formulated as "havens in a heartless world" rather than as sites of power, politics, subject production, and norms. In this way, far from being conceived as that which constitutes the subject, culture becomes something that, in Avishai Margalit and Moshe Halbertal's phrase, one may "have a right to."[35]

These analytic moves to situate culture as extrinsic to the individual, as forming the background of the individual, as that which the individual "chooses" or has a right to, do not merely confirm the autonomy of the individual but also figure culture as inherently oppressive when it saturates or governs law and politics. In liberalism, the individual is understood to have, or have access to, culture or religious belief; culture or religious belief does not have him or her. The difference turns on which entity is imagined as governing in each case: sovereign individuals in liberal regimes, culture and religion in fundamentalist ones. At the same time, liberal legalism and the liberal state are identified as fully autonomous of culture and religion. These two forms of autonomy, that of the individual and that of the state, are importantly connected: liberalism is conceived as juridically securing the autonomy of the individual from others *and* from state power through its articulation of the autonomy of the state from cultural and religious authority. Liberal politics and law are self-represented as secular not only with regard to religion but also with regard to culture, and above and apart from both. This makes liberal legalism at once cultureless and culturally neutral (even as legal decisions will sometimes allude to standards of "national culture" or "prevailing cultural norms"). Put the other way around, liberalism figures culture as separable from political power and political power as capable of being cultureless. These same moves render liberal legal principles as universal and culture as inherently particular, a rendering that itself legitimates the subordination of culture to politics as the subordination of the particular to the universal. They are also what permit principles of liberal democracy to be *universalizable* without being culturally imperialist; as universals, these principles are capable of "respecting" particular cultures. Conversely, nonliberal orders themselves represent the crimes of par-

ticularism, fundamentalism, and intolerance, as well as the dangerousness of unindividuated humanity.

Maintaining a distinction and presumed separation between politics and culture within liberalism is crucial to sustaining the fiction of
the autonomous individual and the fiction of its imagined opposite—
the radically de-individuated, culturally or religiously bound creature
of a fundamentalist order. Seen from the other direction and in a more
deconstructive grammar, the liberal construction of its fundamentalist
Other as one ruled by culture and religion enables liberal legalism's
discursive construction of culture as a form of power only when it is
formally imbricated with governance, which is how this discourse represents most nonliberal regimes. The autonomy of the state from culture is therefore just as important as the autonomy of the individual
from culture in distinguishing liberal orders from their Other. Nonliberal polities are depicted as "ruled" by culture or religion; liberalism is depicted as ruled by law, with culture dispensed to another domain—a depoliticized and voluntary one. In this way, individual
autonomy is counterposed to rule by culture, and subjects are seen to
gain their autonomy not through culture but against it. Culture is individual autonomy's antimony and hence what the liberal state presumes to subdue, depower, and privatize, as well as detach itself
from.[36]

The twin conceits of the autonomy of liberal legalism from culture
and the autonomy of the self-willing and sovereign subject from culture enable liberal legalism's unique positioning as fostering tolerance
and liberal polities' unique position as capable of brokering the tolerable. As chapter 7 will argue more extensively, tolerance is extended
to almost all cultural and religious practices seen to be "chosen" by
liberal individuals, but it may be withheld from those practices seen
to be imposed by culture inscribed as law, as it may be withheld from
whole regimes considered to be ruled by culture or religion. This logic
effectively insulates all legal practices in liberal orders from the tag of
barbarism while legitimating liberal aggression toward non-Western
practices or regimes deemed intolerable. And this logic allows for the
disavowal of the cultural imperialism that such aggression entails be-

cause the aggression is legitimated by the rule of law and the inviolability of rights and choice, each of which is designated in liberal discourse as universal and noncultural. Ubiquitous in all liberal theoretical discussions of tolerance and the intolerable, this logic was succinctly expressed by George W. Bush during the initiation of the U.S. war on Afghanistan in 2002: "We have a great opportunity during this time of war to lead the world toward the values that will bring lasting peace. . . . We have no intention of imposing our culture. But America will always stand firm for the non-negotiable demands of human dignity: the rule of law, limits on the power of the state, respect for women; private property; free speech, equal justice; and religious tolerance."[37] None of these "non-negotiable demands"—which hail not from the United States but from a paradoxically transcendent or sacred place called human dignity, where the individual is a priori—is portrayed as cultural, nor as conditioned by the sovereignty of states or nations.[38] Rather, each is set out as a universal political principle both independent of culture and capable of being neutral with regard to culture, as well as innocent of the particulars of political regimes. Each, importantly, presumes the autonomy of the subject and the state from culture. And each so-called demand also figures a dark Other against which it obtains its own identity. The "rule of law" is opposed to rule by the sword, religious leaders, or cultural custom; "limits on the power of the state" are opposed to absolutism or state power imbricated with other powers, such as culture or religion; "respect for women" is opposed to the degradation of women (by culture or religion) but also, interestingly, to the equality of women; "private property" is opposed to collective ownership, national or state ownership, or public property; "free speech" is opposed to controlled, bought, muffled, or conditioned speech; "equal justice" is opposed to differentiated justice; and "religious tolerance" is opposed to religious fundamentalism. These dark others, metonymically associated with each other, together signal the presence of barbarism, liberalism's putative opposite. This construction also implies that liberalism itself is inherently clear of all of these dark others, that each belongs exclusively to nonliberal regimes and cultures, and, further, that where liberalism does not prevail, neither does civilization.

This chapter began with a consideration of the anxiety about organicist orders evident in liberal thought, and it explored Freud's theory of group identity to plumb liberal assumptions about the civilizational supremacy of orders featuring high levels of individuation. Freud's story revealed the ways in which liberal thought equates organicism with primitivism, and especially with subjects who lack the capacity for self-regulation, conscience, instinctual repression, and rational deliberation. Such organicism, I have been suggesting, is equated with rule by "culture," "religion," and "ethnic identity"; liberal legalism is the sign that these things do not rule, the sign that a secular state and an autonomous individual have usurped their power and put them in their appropriate place.

Liberal tolerance, which simultaneously affirms the value of autonomy and consecrates state secularism, is understood as a virtue available only to the self-regulating individual, as a political principle available only to secular states, and as a good appropriately extended only to individuated subjects and regimes that promote such individuation. Conversely, those captive to organicism and organicist practices are presumed neither to value tolerance, to be capable of tolerance, nor to be entitled to tolerance. The governmentality of tolerance deploys the formal legal autonomy of the subject and the formal secularism of the state as a threshold of the tolerable, marking as intolerable whatever is regarded as a threat to such autonomy and secularism.

Yet even as tolerance is mobilized to manage the challenges to this logic posed by the eruptions of subnational identities in liberal polities occasioned by late modern transnational population flows, its invocation also functions as a sign of the breakdown of this logic of liberal universalism. Tolerance arises as a way of negotiating "cultural," "ethnic," and "religious" differences that clash with the hegemonic "societal culture" within which they exist. The conflict that emerges when those differences emerge or erupt into public life poses more than a policy problem—for example, whether Muslim girls in France can wear the *hijab* to public schools, or whether female circumcision or bigamy can be practiced in North America. Rather, the conflict itself exposes the nonuniversal character of liberal legalism and public life: it exposes its cultural dimensions.

This exposé is managed by tolerance discourse in one of two ways. Either the difference is designated as dangerous in its nonliberalism (hence not tolerable) or as merely religious, ethnic, or cultural (hence not a candidate for a political claim). If it is a nonliberal political difference, it is intolerable; and if it is tolerated, it must be privatized, converted into an individually chosen belief or practice with no political bearing. Tolerance thus functions as the supplement to a liberal secularism that cannot sustain itself at this moment. Still, the very fact of the eruption that challenges liberalism's putative a-culturalism, and the mobilization of tolerance to respond to it, suggests alternative political possibilities that might affirm and productively exploit rather than disavow liberalism's culturalism.

In a passing remark about the contemporary language of "cultural or ethnic minority," Talal Asad identifies another a site of contemporary leakage in the purity aspirations of liberal legalism. Within liberalism, Asad notes, *majority* and *minority* are political terms with political relevance. As such, they "presuppose a constitutional device for *resolving* differences"—which is not, of course, how the language of tolerance approaches difference. "To speak of cultural majorities and minorities is therefore to posit ideological hybrids," Asad continues. "It is also to make the implicit claim that members of some cultures truly belong to a particular politically defined place, but those of others (minority cultures) do not."[39] Without acknowledging or thematizing this slippage between the cultural and the political within liberalism, tolerance is adduced to handle it, indeed, to re-depoliticize what erupts into the political as a cultural, religious, or ethnic claim. Again tolerance appears as a supplement for liberalism at the point of a potential crisis in its universalist self-representation. And again, the alternative is not abandoning or rejecting liberalism but rather using the occasion to open liberal regimes to reflection on the false conceits of their cultural and religious secularism, and to the possibility of being transformed by their encounter with what liberalism has conventionally taken to be its constitutive outside and its hostile Other. Such openings would involve deconstructing the opposition between moral autonomy and organicism, and between secularism and fundamentalism, both for the polyglot West and for the polyglot Islamic world.[40]

These deconstructive moves bear the possibility of conceiving and nourishing a liberalism more self-conscious of and receptive to its own always already present hybridity, its potentially rich failure to hive off organicism from individuality and culture from political principles, law, or policy. This would be a liberalism potentially more modest, more restrained in its imperial and colonial impulses, but also one more capable of the multicultural justice to which it aspires. Above all, it would be a liberalism less invested in the absolute and dangerous opposition between us and them, thereby losing one of its crucial justifications for empire under the flag of liberal democracy.[41]

■ ■ ■ ■

TOLERANCE AS/IN
CIVILIZATIONAL DISCOURSE

Alongside an infinite diversity of cultures, there does exist
one, global civilization in which humanity's ideas and beliefs meet and develop peacefully and productively. It is a
civilization that must be defined by its tolerance of dissent, its celebration of cultural diversity, its insistence on
fundamental, universal human rights and its belief in the
right of people everywhere to have a say in how they are
governed.
>   —UN Secretary Kofi Annan, 5 September 2000

We meet here during a crucial period in the history of our
nation, and of the civilized world. Part of that history was
written by others; the rest will be written by us. . . . And
by acting, we will signal to outlaw regimes that in this
new century, the boundaries of civilized behavior will be
respected.
>   —President George W. Bush, 26 February 2003

America and the West have potential partners in these [Is-
lamic] countries who are eager for us to help move the
struggle to where it belongs: to a war within Islam over its
spiritual message and identity, not a war with Islam . . . a
war between the future and the past, between development and underdevelopment, between authors of crazy
conspiracy theories versus those espousing rationality. . . .
Only Arabs and Muslims can win this war within, but we
can openly encourage the progressives.
  The only Western leader who vigorously took up
this challenge was actually the Dutch politician Pim
Fortuyn. . . . Fortuyn questioned Muslim immigration to
the Netherlands . . . not because he was against Muslims

but because he felt that Islam had not gone through the
Enlightenment or the Reformation, which separated
church from state in the West and prepared it to embrace
modernity, democracy and tolerance.

As a gay man, Fortuyn was very much in need of tolerance, and his challenge to Muslim immigrants was this: I
want to be tolerant, but do you? Or do you have an authoritarian culture that will not be assimilated, and that
threatens my country's liberal, multicultural ethos?
— *New York Times* editorialist Thomas Friedman,
2 June 2002

The War on Terrorism is a war for human rights.
—Secretary of Defense Donald Rumsfeld, 12 June 2002

Every terrorist is at war with civilization. . . . And so,
America is standing for the expansion of human liberty.
—President Bush, 18 May 2004

In the modern West, a liberal discourse of tolerance distinguishes "free" societies from from "fundamentalist" ones, the "civilized" from the "barbaric," and the individualized from the organicist
or collectivized. These pairs are not synonymous, are not governed
precisely the same way by tolerance discourse, and do not call up precisely the same response from that discourse. Yet, as the previous chapter argued, they do assist in each other's constitution and in the constitution of the West and its Other. Whenever one pair of terms is
present, it works metonymically to imply the others, in part because
these pairs are popularly considered to have an organic association
with one another in the world. Thus the production and valorization
of the sovereign individual are understood as critical in keeping barbarism at bay, just as fundamentalism is understood as a breeding
ground of barbarism, and individuality is what fundamentalism is presumed to attenuate if not deny. But there is a consequential ruse in the
association of liberal autonomy, tolerance, secularism, and civilization
on the one hand, and the association of group identity, fundamentalism, and barbarism on the other. This chapter seeks to track the operations of that ruse.

CIVILIZATIONAL DISCOURSE

Tolerance as a political practice is always conferred by the dominant, it is always a certain expression of domination even as it offers protection or incorporation to the less powerful, and tolerance as an individual virtue has a similar asymmetrical structure. The ethical bearing of tolerance is high-minded, while the object of such high-mindedness is inevitably figured as something more lowly. Even as the outlandish, wrongheaded, or literal outlaw is licensed or suffered through tolerance, the voice in which tolerance is proffered contrasts starkly with the qualities attributed to its object. The pronouncement "I am a tolerant man" conjures seemliness, propriety, forbearance, magnanimity, cosmopolitanism, universality, and the large view, while those for whom tolerance is required take their shape as improper, indecorous, urgent, narrow, particular, and often ungenerous or at least lacking in perspective.[1] Liberals who philosophize about tolerance almost always write about coping with what they cannot imagine themselves to be: they identify with the aristocrat holding his nose in the agora, not with the stench.

Historically and philosophically, tolerance is rarely argued for as an entitlement, a right, or a naturally egalitarian good in the ways that liberty generally is. Rather, one pleads for tolerance as an incorporative practice that promises to keep the peace through such incorporation. And so the subterranean yearning of tolerance—for a universally practiced moderation that does not exist, a humanity so civilized that it would not require the virtue of tolerance—sits uneasily with the normative aspect of tolerance that reaffirms the characterological superiority of the tolerant over the tolerated.

Attention to these rhetorical aspects of tolerance suggests that it is not simply asymmetrical across lines of power but carries caste, class, and civilizational airs with it in its work. This chapter scrutinizes that conveyance by considering the logic of tolerance as a civilizational discourse. The dual function of civilizational discourse, marking in general what counts as "civilized" and conferring superiority on the West, produces tolerance itself in two distinct, if intersecting, power functions: as part of what defines the superiority of Western civilization, and as that which marks certain non-Western practices or regimes as intolerable. Together, these operations of tolerance discourse in a civilizational frame legitimize liberal polities' illiberal treatment of selected practices, peoples, and states. They sanction illiberal aggression toward what is marked as intolerable without tarring the "civilized" status of the aggressor.

Shortly after September 11th, George W. Bush asserted: "Those who hate all civilization and culture and progress . . . cannot be ignored, cannot be appeased. They must be fought."[2] Tolerance, a beacon of civilization, is inappropriately extended to those outside civilization *and* opposed to civilization; violence, which tolerance represses, is the only means of dealing with this threat and is thereby self-justifying. When this statement is paired with remarks in February 2002, in which Bush declared the United States to have a "historic opportunity to fight a war that will not only liberate people from the clutches of barbaric behavior but a war that can leave the world more peaceful in the years to come,"[3] it is not difficult to see how an opposition between civilization and barbarism, in which the cherished tolerance of the former meets its limits in the latter (limits that also give the latter its identity), provides the mantle of civilization, progress, and peace as cover for imperial militaristic adventures.

But civilization is a complex term with an even more complex genealogy. According to the *Oxford English Dictionary*, since the eighteenth century it has referred to "the action or process of civilizing or of being civilized" and also denoted "a developed or advanced state of human society."[4] In *Keywords*, Raymond Williams notes that while "civilization is now generally used to describe an achieved state or condition of organized social life," it pertained originally to a process, a meaning that persists into the present.[5] The static and dynamic meanings of civilization are easily reconciled in the context of a progressivist Western historiography of modernity in which individuals and societies are configured as steadily developing a more democratic, reasoned, and cosmopolitan bearing. In this way civilization simultaneously frames the achievement of European modernity, the promised fruit of modernization as an experience, and, crucially, the effects of exporting European modernity to "uncivilized" parts of the globe. European colonial expansion from the mid–nineteenth through the mid–twentieth century was explicitly justified as a project of civilization, conjuring the gifts of social order, legality, reason, and religion as well as regulating manners and mores.[6]

However, civilization did not remain a simple term of colonial domination that led all the subjects it touched to aspire to European standards. Not only did non-European elites and various anticolonial struggles reshape the concept to contest and sometimes forthrightly oppose European hegemony, but the idea of civilization was also pluralized in both scholarly and popular discourses during the past century. From Arnold Toynbee to Fernand Braudel to Samuel Huntington, there has been a concerted if variously motivated effort to pry civilization apart from Europe and even from modernity to make it more widely define structured "ways of life" comprising values, literatures, legal systems, and social organization.

Plural accounts *of* civilization, however, do not equate to a pluralist sensibility *about* civilization. Samuel Huntington's thesis (best known as an argument about the mutual flashpoints among what he designates as the world's distinct and incommensurate civilizations) makes abundantly clear that such pluralization can cloak rather than negate the Western superiority charging the term. Although Huntington insists that Western civilization "is valuable not because it is universal but because it *is* unique" (in its cultivation of the values of individual liberty, political democracy, human rights, and cultural freedom),[7] this apparent gesture toward cultural relativism does not materialize as a principle of mutual valuation. For one thing, Huntington's argument about Western civilization's uniqueness forms the basis for intolerance of multiculturalism *within* the West (famously, Huntington argues that "a multicultural America is impossible because a non-Western America is not American. . . . [M]ulticulturalism at home threatens the United States and the West").[8] Equally important, *The Clash of Civilizations and the Remaking of World Order* concludes with a warning about the current vulnerability of what Huntington calls "civilization in the singular": "on a worldwide basis Civilization seems to be in many respects yielding to barbarism, generating the image of an unprecedented phenomenon, a global Dark Ages, possibly descending on humanity." This danger is evident, Huntington continues, in a worldwide breakdown of law and order, a global crime wave, increasing drug addiction, a general weakening of the family, a decline in trust and social solidarity, and a rise in ethnic, religious, and civilizational violence. And what is occasioning this dark specter of what Huntington terms "a global moral reversion?" Nothing less than the decline of Western power, that which established the rule of law as a civilizational norm and decreased the acceptability of "slavery, torture and vicious abuse of individuals."[9] So even as Huntington argues for all civilizations to bond together in fighting barbarism—the intolerable—only the values of the West can lead this fight: what will hold barbarism at bay is precisely what recenters the West as the defining essence of civilization and what legitimates its efforts at controlling the globe.

When these two arguments of Huntington's are combined—the argument for mutual accord among civilizations governed by what he sets out as the distinctly Western value of tolerance, together with the argument that the barbarism into which the world now threatens to slide is attributable to the decline of the West—there appears an unmistakable chain of identifications of the West with civilization ("in the singular"), of civilization with tolerance, and of the intolerant and the intolerable with the uncivilized. That these identifications occur despite Huntington's sincere effort to disrupt them is only a sign of how powerful civilizational discourse is in liberal theories of tolerance, even (and perhaps especially) when that discourse is most thoroughly inflected by political realism.

Huntington's work also makes clear that even when civilization is rendered in the plural, its signifying opposite remains barbarism. *Barbarian*, it will be remembered, derives from the ancient Greek term denoting all non-Greeks. With the rise of Rome, its meaning shifted to refer to those outside the Empire; in the Italian Renaissance, barbarian defined all those imagined unreached by the Renaissance, that is, non-Italians. A barbarian is thus technically "a foreigner, one whose language and customs differ from the speaker's"; but crucially, this foreignness has been continually established vis-à-vis empire and imperial definitions of civilization. And so the *OED* provides the second meaning: a condition of being "outside the pale of . . . civilization." Outside the pale (a term defining the limits of England's colonial jurisdiction in Ireland in the sixteenth century)—not merely beyond geographical bounds but unreached by civilization, beyond its canopy. It is not difficult, then, to see the path from the ancient meaning of barbarian as foreigner to its contemporary signification, the third and fourth listings in the *OED*: "a rude, wild, uncivilized person; . . . an uncultured person, or one who has no sympathy with literary culture."[10] As we will see shortly, Susan Okin's designation of selected nonliberal cultural practices as barbaric, and her inability to see "barbaric" practices anywhere within liberal orders, perfectly mimics the etymological slide of barbarian from *foreigner* to *uncivilized* to *wild brute*, inhabiting as well the blindness to colonial or imperial domination that this slide entails. Again, this slide also underwrites George W. Bush's routine accounts of his military engagements in the Middle East as a struggle of the civilized world against barbarism: "Now is the time, and Iraq is the place, in which the enemies of the civilized world are testing the will of the civilized world."[11]

If being beyond the pale of civilization is also to be what civilization cannot tolerate, then tolerance and civilization not only entail one another but mutually define what is outside of both and together constitute a strand in an emerging transnational governmentality. To be uncivilized is to be intolerable is to be a barbarian, just as to declare a particular practice intolerable is to stigmatize it as uncivilized. That which is inside civilization is tolerable *and* tolerant; that which is outside is neither. This is how, even amid plural definitions of civilization, the discourse of tolerance recenters the West as the standard for civilization, and how tolerance operates simultaneously as a token of Western supremacy and a legitimating cloak for Western domination. This is also why Kofi Annan, in one of the epigraphs for this chapter, had to bring all the world's cultures into a discursive meeting place governed by a liberal political idiom named "global civilization." In no other way could these diverse cultures attain or keep their status as civilized.

TEACHING TOLERANCE

According to Huntington, the West will save itself by valuing itself and will save the world by developing global practices of civilizational tolerance, but the latter requires enlightening others about the value of tolerating difference and eschewing fundamentalism. This formulation renders tolerance as pedagogically achieved, a rendering inscribed in the very name of the "Teaching Tolerance" project of the Southern Poverty Law Center.[12] Or, in the words of K. Peter Fritzsche of the International Tolerance Network, "Tolerance has to be learned. One has to be made capable of tolerance, and it is one of the utmost tasks of tolerance education to promote the elements of this capability."[13] And Jay Newman, a contemporary philosopher of tolerance, introduces his volume on religious tolerance with a similar declaration: "Intolerance is the most persistent and the most insidious of all sources of hatred. It is perhaps foremost among the obstacles to civilization, the instruments of barbarism." Newman's cure for intolerance? Education, which he equates with "a process of civilizing."[14] So strongly does the binary of the ignorant and parochial hater and the cosmopolitan sophisticate govern Newman's argument that he does not even feel compelled to specify what *kind* of education is needed; knowledge and thinking are themselves the engine that dispel tribal enthusiasms and replace them with reflective individuals.[15]

The notion that tolerance must be taught articulates intolerance as the "native" or "primitive" response to difference, an articulation consonant with the equation of tolerance and individuation considered in chapter 6. The rhetoric of "teaching tolerance" relegates enmity or intolerance to the construed narrow-mindedness of those who are more childlike, less formally educated, and, above all, less individuated than enlightened moderns. Hence the equation of the "bigot" with "ignorance," and also the popular journalistic use of tropes such as "primitive blood feuds" or "archaic enmity" to frame contemporary ethnic conflict in eastern Europe, Rwanda, or Ethiopia (which, it will be recalled from chapter 5, appear together in the video "In Our Time" at the Museum of Tolerance). Hence, too, another popular journalistic trope figuring Islamacist violence as the consequence of a premodern sensibility. At work here is a familiar Orientalist narrative of the cosmopolitan Westerner as more rational and peaceful because more enlightened than the native, with a rationality and peacability understood to derive from and generate tolerance. This is a narrative in which, as Barry Hindess argues, difference itself is temporalized, and in which progressivism tied to Western notions of the individual, as well as of knowledge and freedom, is fundamentalized.[16]

The native, the fanatic, the fundamentalist, and the bigot are what must be overcome by the society committed to tolerance; from the perspective of the tolerant, these figures are premodern or at least have not been thoroughly bathed in modernity, a formulation endlessly rehearsed by Thomas Friedman in his *New York Times* editorials on Islam.[17] This reminds us that it is not really Western civilization *tout court* but the identification of modernity and, in particular, liberalism with the West—indeed, the identification of liberalism as the telos of the West—that provides the basis for Western civilizational supremacy.

What wraps in a common leaf the native, the fanatic, the fundamentalist, and the bigot—despite the fact that some may be religiously orthodox or members of an organicist society while others may be radical libertarians—is a presumed existence in a narrow, homogeneous, unquestioning, and unenlightened universe, an existence that inherently generates hostility toward outsiders, toward questioning, toward difference. "Learning tolerance" thus involves divesting oneself of relentless partiality, absolutist identity, and parochial attachments, a process understood as the effect of a larger, more cosmopolitan worldview and not as the privilege of hegemony. It is noteworthy, too, that within this discourse the aim of learning tolerance is not to arrive at equality or solidarity with others but, rather, to learn how to put up with others by weakening one's own connections to community and claims of identity—that is, by becoming a liberal pluralist and thereby joining those who, according to Michael Ignatieff, can "live and let live" or "love others more by loving ourselves a little less."[18] Tolerance as the overcoming of the putative natural enmity among essentialized differences issues from education and repression, which themselves presume the social contract and the weakening of nationalist or other communal identifications. Formulated this way, the valuation and practice of tolerance simultaneously confirm the superiority of the West; depoliticize (by recasting as nativist enmity) the effects of domination, colonialism, and cold war deformations of the Second and Third Worlds; and portray those living these effects as in need of the civilizing project of the West.

Undergirding this conceptualization of enmity toward difference as natural and primitive is the conceit, explored in chapter 6, that the rational individual is inherently more peaceable, civil, farseeing, and hence tolerant than are members of "organicist societies." Thomas Friedman is one of the most widely read and unabashed promulgators of this view; Michael Ignatieff is one of its more subtle exponents. For Ignatieff, racism and ethnically based nationalism are the effects of being "trapped in collective identities," the cure for which is "the means to pursue individual lives" and especially individual routes to success and achievement.[19] Thus, it will be recalled, Ignatieff argues that "the culture of individualism is the only reliable solvent of the hold of group identities and the racisms that go with them" and that the "essential task in teaching 'toleration' is to help people see themselves as individuals, and then to see others as such." Ignatieff also understands this way of seeing as bringing us closer to the truth of "actual, real individuals in all their specificity" as opposed to the "procedures of abstraction" constitutive of group interpellation[20]; it brings us closer, in other words, to the truth of what human beings really are. This makes the individual a distinctly Hegelian a priori in Ignatieff's analysis—ontologically true yet historically achieved. And the more developed and rewarded this individual is *as* an individual, the more that collective identity is eroded or undercut by individualism and especially individual ego strength, and the greater the prospects for a tolerant world. This equation not only posits liberalism as superior because true and posits tolerance as the sign of a fully and rightly individualized society (one that has arrived at the core truth of human beings); it also invokes liberalism's self-representation, considered in chapter 6, as both a-cultural and anti-cultural, beyond culture and opposed to culture.

CONFERRING AND WITHHOLDING TOLERANCE

Tolerance is generally conferred by those who do not require it on those who do; it arises within and codifies a normative order in which those who deviate from rather than conform to the norms are eligible for tolerance. The heterosexual proffers tolerance to the homosexual, the Christian tolerates the Muslim or Jew, the dominant race tolerates minority races . . . each of these only up to a point. However, the matter is rarely phrased this way. Rather, power discursively disappears when a hegemonic population tolerates a marked or minoritized one. The scene materializes instead as one in which the universal tolerates the particular in its particularity, in which the putative universal therefore always appears superior to that unassimilated particular—a superiority itself premised upon the nonreciprocity of tolerance (the particular does not tolerate the universal). It is the disappearance of power in the action of tolerance that convenes the hegemonic as the universal and the subordinate or minoritized as the particular. The mechanics of this evocation are familiar: homosexuals discursively appear as more thoroughly defined by their sexuality and hence less capable of participation in the universal than are heterosexuals, just as Jews, Catholics, Mormons, and Muslims appear more relentlessly saturated by their religious/ethnic identity than are other Americans. (Thus, vice presidential candidate Joseph Lieberman's Orthodox Judaism became a significant campaign issue, as did John F. Kennedy's Catholicism, while the strongly avowed Christianity of Jimmy Carter, Ronald Reagan, and both Bushes did not.) This quality of saturation results from the normative regime and not from some quality inherent in the identities or practices. However, in aligning itself with universality and relative neutrality, the unmarked-because-hegemonic identity also associates tolerance with this standing and, conversely, associates objects of tolerance with particularity and partiality.

When the heterosexual tolerates the homosexual, when Christians tolerate Muslims in the West, not only do the first terms *not* require tolerance but their standing as that which confers tolerance establishes their superiority over that which is said to require tolerance; the tolerating and tolerated are simultaneously radically distinguished from each other and hierarchically ordered according to a table of virtue. That which tolerates is not eligible for tolerance; that which is tolerated is often presumed incapable of tolerance. This aspect of the binary structure of tolerance discourse circulates not just power but superordination and subordination with the term. Through the alignment of the object of tolerance with *difference*, its inferiority to that which is aligned with sameness or universality is secured. Its association with difference places the object of tolerance outside the universal, positioning it as needing tolerance and hence as a lower form of life.[21] But this positioning is a discursive trick, one that disguises the extent to which it is power, and not inherent qualities of openness or rigidity, moral relativism or orthodoxy, that produces the universal and the particular, the tolerant and the tolerated, the West and the East, the pluralist and the fundamentalist, the civilized and the barbaric, the same and the other. This discursive trick also purifies the first term, the tolerant entity, of all intolerance; and it saturates the second term, the tolerated, with difference nearly to (and sometimes arriving at) the point of intolerability.

In liberal theories of tolerance concerned with liberalism's orientation toward putatively nonliberal cultures, or practices, liberalism acquires moral superiority through its ability to tolerate in its midst those thought not to be able to tolerate liberalism in their midst. This superiority is sustained by the conceit that liberalism can tolerate religions without being conquered by them, or tolerate certain fundamentalisms without becoming fundamentalist. In contrast, fundamentalism cannot tolerate or incorporate liberalism; the superior entity is the more capacious one, the one that can harbor difference and not be felled by it. In this regard, tolerance valorizes both size and strength; its virtue rests in a presumption about the value of being large, and that which cannot be large is its inferior. Thus tolerance discourse rewards power's potential for capaciousness with the status of virtue.[22]

Politically, then, the capacity for tolerance is itself an expression of power and of a certain security in that power. At the collective and individual levels, the strong and secure can afford to be tolerant; the marginal and insecure cannot. A polity or culture certain of itself and its hegemony, one that does not feel vulnerable, can relax its borders and absorb otherness without fear. Thus the Ottoman Empire could be modestly tolerant and so could Euro-Atlantic liberalism, though the latter has reified tolerance as a continuous principle even as the actual practice of tolerance in liberal societies varies dramatically according to perceived threats and dangers. Indeed, liberal commitments to tolerance are always modified by anxieties and perceived dangers—from the effect of racial integration on neighborhood property values to the effect on schoolchildren when avowed homosexuals are teachers. While tolerance is an index of power, it is also a practice of vulnerability within this power, an instrument of governance that regulates vulnerability according to a variety of governmental aims.

This suggests that tolerance is also crucial to the shell game that liberal political thought plays with Christianity and with liberal capitalist culture more generally, the ways it denies its involvement with both while promulgating and protecting them.[23] A trivial example: the University of California academic instructional calendar, like that of most state schools, is prepared without deference to major religious holidays for Jews, Muslims, or Eastern Orthodoxy believers. One year, a faculty member complains that the first day of fall instruction, when students risk losing their place in oversubscribed courses if they are not present, falls on Yom Kippur. The registrar responds that the academic calendar honors no religious holidays but that faculty are urged to tolerate all recognized religions by offering makeup exams and other nonpunitive accommodations for students whose religious commitments require them to miss selected classes. The faculty member notes that classes are never held on Christmas, Easter, or, for that matter, the Christian Sabbath. The registrar replies that this is a coincidence of the timing of "winter break" and of Easter and Sundays always falling on a weekend.

Liberal tolerance discourse not only hides its own imbrication with Christianity and bourgeois culture, it sheaths the cultural chauvinism that liberalism carries to its encounters with nonliberal cultures. For example, when Western liberals express dismay at (what is perceived as mandatory) veiling in fundamentalist Islamic contexts, this dismay is justified through the idiom of women's choice. But the contrast between the nearly compulsory baring of skin by American teenage girls and compulsory veiling in a few Islamic societies is drawn routinely as absolute lack of choice, indeed tyranny, "over there" and absolute freedom of choice (representatively redoubled by near-nakedness) "over here." This is not to deny differences between the two dress codes and the costs of defying them, but rather to note the means and effects of converting these differences into hierarchicalized opposites. If successful American women are not free to veil, are not free to dress like men or boys, are not free to wear whatever they choose on any occasion without severe economic or social consequences, then what sleight of hand recasts their condition as freedom and individuality contrasted with hypostasized tyranny and lack of agency? What makes choices "freer" when they are constrained by secular and market organizations of femininity and fashion rather than by state or religious law? Do we imagine the former to be less coercive than the latter because we cling to the belief that power is only and always a matter of law and sovereignty, or, as Foucault put it, because we have yet to "cut off the king's head in political theory"? A less politically innocent account of this analytic failure would draw on the postcolonial feminist insight that the West encodes its own superiority through what Chandra Mohanty identifies as the fantasy of Western women as "secular, liberated, and having control over their own lives," an identity derived in part from the very figure of an oppressed Third World opposite.[24] To acknowledge that we have our own form of compulsory feminine dress would undercut this identity of superiority: we *need* fundamentalism, indeed, we project and produce it elsewhere, to represent ourselves as free.[25]

One of the most crucial mechanisms of this projection is the reification and totalization of "intolerant societies," the representation of such societies as saturated by intolerance and organized by the very principle of intolerance. Conversely, the political principle of tolerance is almost always imagined to exhaustively define the polity that harbors it, even as the question of the limits of tolerance may be hotly debated within that polity.[26] This division of the world into the tolerant and the intolerant, the fundamentalist and the pluralist, the parochial and the cosmopolitan, allows the political theoretical and philosophical literature on tolerance to repeatedly pose the question "What should be the attitude of the tolerant toward the intolerant?" as if these dire opposites truly existed, embodied in radically different entities. The point, again, is not that there are no differences between regimes that expressly advocate tolerance and those that do not, but that civilizational discourse converts these differences into opposites and attributes a distorting essence to each—"fundamentalist/intolerant/unfree" on one side and "pluralist/tolerant/free" on the other—as it aligns liberalism with civilization.

It is not only liberal advocates of tolerance who participate in this Manichean rhetorical scheme. Liberal anti-relativists, on the right and the left, who seek to limit tolerance, indeed who regard current deployments of cultural tolerance as abetting a loathsome relativism, also depict the world as divided between the tolerant and free (West) and the fundamentalist and oppressive (non-West). In a special issue of *Daedelus* titled "The End of Tolerance: Engaging Cultural Difference" and in Susan Okin's *Is Multiculturalism Bad for Women?* a concerted argument emerges for articulating standards of the humane and acceptable and limiting tolerance to those cultural practices or even to those cultures that meet such standards.[27] Western refusals to condemn and legally ban practices such as genital mutilation, widow suttee, or polygamy are treated as relativism run amok (tacitly if not expressly attributed to something called "postmodernism"), which thoroughly compromises liberal values of autonomy and freedom. Tolerance is not here repudiated as a value but rather becomes a practice of demarcation, drawing the line at the "barbaric" or the coerced.

Intrinsically unobjectionable as this argument may sound, the problem is that all instances of the barbaric and the coerced are found on the non-Western side of the line—that is, where culture or religion are taken to reign and hence where individual autonomy is unsecured. No legal Western practice is marked as *barbaric* (which is only to say that Western culture, like all cultures, affirms itself), including feasting on a variety of animals except those fetishized as pets; polluting the planet and plundering its resources; living and dying alone; devoting life to the pursuit of money; making available human eggs, sperm, and infants for purchase by anonymous strangers; performing abortions;

stockpiling nuclear weapons; tolerating sex clubs, indigency, and home-lessness; enjoying flagrant luxury in the presence of the poor; consuming junk food; or undertaking imperialist wars. Any of these might be considered violent, dehumanizing, or degrading from another cultural perspective. But what Okin and others consider beyond the pale of tolerance are selected non-Western practices, each of which is taken to be promulgated by culture, religion, or tradition, three forces that, in Okin's view, cannot infect liberal legalism. The effect is to tar the non-West with the brush of the intolerable for harboring certain practices that are not only named barbaric, that is, uncivilized in contrast to our practices, but coerced, that is, unfree compared to our practices. The limits of tolerance are thus equated with the limits of civilization or with threats to civilization. Indeed, insofar as both invoke a civilizational discourse to broker the tolerable, those who worry about tolerating what portends the unraveling or decline of Western civilization (Samuel Huntington, the neoconservatives, right-wing Christians) converge ideologically with those who worry about tolerating non-Western practices that are outside civilization's pale (Susan Okin, liberals, human rights activists). Conservatives and liberals alike deploy this colonially inflected discourse to establish a civilizational norm by which the tolerable is measured, a norm that tolerance itself also secures.

Moreover, for purposes of distinguishing the civilized from the un-civilized, the discourse of tolerance at its limits is as effective as the discourse of tolerance in a more capacious mode, where it demeans what it abides by making it an object of tolerance. The former marks the barbaric, the latter the abject or deviant. Together, they figure the West *as* civilization and produce liberalism itself as uniquely generative of rationality, freedom, and tolerance; at the same time, they designate only certain subjects as rational and free, and only certain practices as normative. A closer examination of Susan Okin's argument in *Is Multiculturalism Bad for Women?* will help us to grasp this logic.[28]

Okin's basic claim is that multiculturalism—which she takes to be a relatively unqualified respect for various cultures and which may assume the juridical form of group rights or cultural defenses of particular practices—is in high tension with feminism, the opportunity for women to "live as fulfilling and as freely chosen lives as men can" (10). Reduced further, Okin's argument is that respect for culture collides with respect for gender equality, even that culture *tout court* is in tension with feminism. If culture and sex difference are something that all peoples everywhere have, there is, of course, no logical reason for culture and gender equality to be antagonists, especially when one considers that the gender equality valued by Okin itself emerges from within some culture.[29] Or does it? What Okin mostly means by culture is not the conventions, ideas, practices, productions, and self-understandings that bind and organize the lives of a particular people. Rather, for Okin, culture comprises ways of life that are not markedly liberal, Enlightenment-bound, rational-legal, and, above all, secular. Culture is implicitly premodern or at least incompletely modern, in her account. For Okin, nonliberal societies *are* cultures; liberal societies are . . . states, civil societies, and individuals. Culture appears when a collectivity is not organized by individual autonomy, rights, or liberty. Culture is nonliberal; liberalism is *kulturlos*.

Okin does not explicitly argue this view of culture; to the contrary, she manages to utter the phrase "liberal culture" when acknowledging and lamenting that Western democracies harbor some sexist practices. In other words, culture makes an appearance in the West whenever Okin has to explain how sexist practices have persisted into a time and place formally governed by individual rights. But this usage only confirms the pejorative standing of "culture" in her analysis—culture is what a complete realization of liberal principles will eradicate or at least radically subdue. Moreover, the gesture of recognizing liberalism as bearing culture seems disingenuous when one notices the incessant slide from culture to religion in Okin's argument. Not only does she repeatedly pair "culture and religion," but she begins a paragraph with a claim about the drive of most *cultures* to control women and ends the same paragraph with a series of examples from Judaism, Islam, and Christianity (13–14). And that paragraph is followed by one that treats together the shared patriarchal tendencies of orthodox monotheism and "Third World cultures." For Okin, the link between what she calls culture and religion is their common focus on domestic life, which she takes to be a crucial site for women's oppression and the transmission of gender ideology: "obviously culture is not only about domestic arrangements, but they do provide a major focus of most contemporary cultures. Home is, after all, where much of culture is practiced, preserved, and transmitted to the young" (13). So culture and religion both organize domestic life patriarchically and are transmitted through domestic life. What is the standing of liberalism in this regard? Its sharp ideological and political-economic divide between public and private (which other feminists have spent the past thirty years subjecting to critique for its role both in structurally producing women's economic dependence and in depoliticizing women's subordination) is here affirmed by Okin because of the barrier it ostensibly erects between gendered family values and gender-neutral civic and public law. Though the private realm in liberal societies harbors gender inequality, Okin tacitly suggests, though this is where sexist culture lingers and is reproduced, the harm is potentially redressed by the public, juridical principles of abstract personhood and autonomy. In liberal democracies, the formal commitment to secularism and to individual autonomy can be mobilized to erode sexist culture, and this possibility is what Okin wants for the rest of the world.

"Most cultures," Okin writes, "have as one of their principal aims the control of women by men" (13). But "Western liberal culture" (her phrase) is a little different: "While virtually all of the world's cultures have distinctly patriarchal pasts, some—mostly, though by no means exclusively, Western liberal cultures—have departed far further from them than others" (16). What distinguishes Western cultures, which "still practice many forms of sex discrimination," from others is that in them women are "legally guaranteed many of the same freedoms and opportunities as men" (16–17). In other words, it is not the law or the doctrine of liberalism that is sexually discriminatory but some cultural remainder that the law has not yet managed to reform or extinguish. Whatever the remains of culture in Western liberal orders, and whatever the remains of sexism within those cultures, liberalism as a political-juridical order is, or has the capacity to be, gender-clean. This account, of course, is warmed-over John Stuart Mill: in a progress narrative led by liberalism (indeed, by the bourgeoisie), male dominance is the barbaric stuff of the old regime; of a time when might, custom, and religion rather than the law of equality and reason ruled the world; and of a time before the individual reigned supreme. Thus, if liberal regimes continue to house deposits of misogyny and female subordination, this residue must be the result of something other than liberalism, which, with its legal principles of autonomy, liberty, and equality, constitutes the remedy to such ills within the societies it orders.

But what if liberalism itself harbors male dominance, what if male superordination is inscribed in liberalism's core values of liberty—rooted in autonomy and centered on self-interest—and equality—defined as sameness and confined to the public sphere?[30] Many feminists have argued that liberal categories, relations, and processes are inseparable from a relentlessly gendered division of labor and a far-reaching public/private distinction by which everything associated with the family—need, dependence, inequality, the body, relationality—is identified with the feminine and constitutes both the predicate and the opposite of a masculinist public sphere of rights, autonomy, formal equality, rationality, and individuality. In this critique, masculinist social norms are part of the very architecture of liberalism; they structure its division and population of the social space and govern its production and regulation of subjects. These are norms that produce and privilege masculine public beings—free, autonomous, and equal—while producing a feminine Other as a familial being—encumbered, dependent, and different.[31]

Okin does not simply elide such feminist critiques of liberalism.[32] The presumption of ungendered liberal principles counterposed to gendered cultural ones is fundamental to the argument that liberalism is the best cure for the patriarchal ills of culture. Okin perfectly expresses the ideology, critically assessed in chapter 6, of the autonomy of the liberal state and individual from (what is named) culture, an autonomy that positions the liberal state as singularly freeing and the liberal individual as singularly free. Culture is not only historically sexist in her account, it is corrosive of autonomy and corrupting of juridical universalism. For Okin, individual autonomy prevails only when culture recedes (a view that makes clear why *multi*culturalism is so bad for women: it multiplies enemies to autonomy). Where there is autonomy, there is choice; and where there is choice, there is freedom, especially women's freedom. In this way, Okin positions both culture and patriarchy (as opposed to mere "sexist attitudes or practices") as always elsewhere from liberalism. Culture and religion perpetuate inequality by formally limiting women's autonomy, while the constraints on choice in a liberal capitalist order—say, those experienced by a single mother with few job skills—are either not cultural or not significant. The formal existence of choice is the incontestable (hence noncultural?) good, regardless of its actualizability. Thus Okin concludes:

> In the case of a more patriarchal minority culture in the context of a less patriarchal majority culture, no argument can be made on the basis of self-respect or freedom that the female members of the culture have a clear interest in its preservation. Indeed, they *might* be much better off if the culture into which they were born were either to become extinct (so that its members would become integrated into the less sexist surrounding culture) or, preferably, to be encouraged to alter itself so as to reinforce the equality of women—at least to the degree to which this value is upheld in the majority culture. (23)

This passage involves several remarkable claims. First, in arguing that women who have self-respect and want freedom will necessarily oppose (not simply be ambivalent about) their culture, Okin rehearses a false consciousness argument always reserved today for the practices of women: a woman who defends cultural or religious practices that others may designate as patriarchal cannot be thinking for herself, and so cannot be trusted to think clearly about her attachments and investments. Consequently, self-respecting liberals like Susan Okin must think for her. Second, the passage implies that female subordination is sufficient grounds for wanting one's culture dead, an extraordinary claim on its own but made more so by its issuance from one as wedded to Western culture as Okin is. Third, it argues that minority cultures are to be measured not against an abstract standard of freedom, equality, and self-respect for women but rather against that superior *degree* of these things found in the majority culture as determined by the values of the majority culture. In this strict quantification of sexism—more there, less here—and inattention to the *varieties* of male superordination, it is hard to imagine a more naked version of Enlightenment progressivism and the brief for liberal imperalism it entails.

Where does tolerance fit into this picture? In Okin's view, liberal orders and liberal legalism should *not* stretch to accommodate the overtly misogynist or sexist practices of minority cultures—for example, child brideship, polygamy, clitoridectomy—and should not permit cultural defenses any standing in criminal trial cases concerned with rape, wife-murder, or infanticide (18). Okin draws the line for tolerance at the point of what she calls not simply "sex inequality" but the "barbaric" treatment of women. Tolerance is for civilized practices; barbarism is on the other side of the line, beyond the pale.

But consider: American women spend upward of nine billion dollars annually on plastic surgery, cosmetic implants, injections, and facial laser treatments, and untold more on over-the-counter products advertised to restore youthful looks. In the past half decade, tens of thousands of women have opted to smooth their forehead lines with regular injections of Botox, a diluted version of what the American Medical Association has identified as "the most poisonous substance known," far more deadly than anthrax: "a single gram, evenly dispersed, could kill more than one million people, causing 'symmetric, descending, flaccid paralysis' and eventually cutting off its victims' power to breathe, swallow, communicate, or see." [33] How many noses have been cut, flattened, or otherwise rearranged to fit an Aryan ideal of feminine beauty? How many breasts reduced, and how many enlarged? How many women have submitted to painful electrolysis and other means of removing body hair? What of the rising trend among well-off American women to have their feet surgically reconfigured to fit high-fashioned shoes or their labia surgically "corrected" to be symmetrical? Or what of the popularity of plastic surgery—for noses, lips, breasts, and hips—among high school girls? [34] Are these procedures less culturally organized than the procedures Okin condemns in other "cultures"? Is their "voluntariness" what spares them from being candidates for her attention? Does a liberal frame mistake elective surgery for freedom from coercive power, as it tends to mistake elections for political freedom? What is voluntary about treatments designed to produce conventional ideals of youthful beauty for an aspiring

Hollywood actress, a trophy wife on the verge of being traded in for a younger model, or an ordinary middle-aged, middle-class woman in Southern California?

Similarly, why is Okin more outraged by clitordectemy than by the routine surgical "correction" of intersexed babies in the United States —babies whose genitals are sexually ambiguous and who have no say whatsoever in these surgeries but are condemned to live the rest of their lives with the (often botched) outcome?[35] Is Western anxiety about sexual dimorphism, and in particular about female availability for penile penetration, any less cultural than the anxieties about female sexual pleasure that she condemns in parts of Africa and the Middle East? Why isn't Okin alarmed by the epidemic of eating disorders among American teenage girls or by the epidemic of American women being pharmaceutically treated for depression? Why doesn't Okin find drugging such women rather than transforming their life conditions barbaric and intolerable? In sum, why is Okin more horrified by the *legal* control of women by men than by the controlling cultural norms and market productions of gender and sexuality, including norms and productions of beauty, sexual desire and behavior, weight and physique, soul and psyche, that course through modern Western societies?

When individual rights and liberties are posited as the solution to coercion, and liberalism as the antidote to culture, women's social oppression or subordination (as opposed to their contingent or domestic violation or maltreatment) appears only where law openly avows its religious or cultural character—that is, where it has not taken the vow of Western secularism. But as the examples above suggest, by formulating freedom as choice and reducing the political to policy and law, liberalism sets loose, in a depoliticized underworld, a sea of social powers nearly as coercive as law, and certainly as effective in producing subjectivated subjects. Indeed, as a combination of Marcusian and Foucaultian perspectives remind us, choice can become a critical instrument of domination in liberal capitalist societies; insofar as the fiction of the sovereign subject blinds us to powers producing that subject, choice both cloaks and potentially eroticizes the powers it engages.[36] Moreover, Okin's inability to grasp liberalism's own cultural norms—in which, for example, autonomy is valued over connection or the responsibility for dependent others (with which women are typically associated), liberty is conceived as freedom to do what one wants (for which women are often faulted), and equality is premised on sameness (while women are always conceived as different)—blinds her to the deep and abiding male superordination within liberalism: not just in "liberal cultures" or in the sphere of the family but in liberal legalism and political principles.

In sum, the putative legal autonomy of the subject combines with the putative autonomy of the law from gendered norms and from culture more generally to position women in the West as free, choosing beings who stand in stark contrast to their sisters subjected to legally sanctioned cultural barbarism. From this perspective, liberal imperialism is not only legitimate but morally mandated. "Culture" must be brought to heel by liberalism so that women are free to choose their antiwrinkle creams.

There is a final irony in Okin's formulation of "culture" as the enemy of women. This focus sustains an elision of the conditions imposed on Third World women by global capitalism, conditions to which Western critics could be responsive without engaging in cultural imperialism or endorsing political and military imperialism. These hardships range from the hyperexploitation of labor in export platforms and free trade zones to global capitalism's often violent disruptions and dislocations of family and community. If the aim is to secure possibilities for modest self-determination for Third World women, what could be more important than addressing and redressing these circumstances? Instead, in her obsession with culture over capitalism, indeed in her apparent indifference to the mechanics of poverty, exploitation, and deracination, Okin repeats a disturbing colonial gesture in which the alleged barbarism of the native culture, rather than imperial conquest, colonial political and economic deformation, and contemporary economic exploitation, is made the target of progressive reform. As the final turn of this chapter suggests, such a gesture is characteristic of tolerance discourse in its civilizational mode.

There is a second colonial gesture in a Western feminism that targets "culture" as the problem. The liberal construction of tolerance as respect for individual autonomy secured by a secular state, a construction shared by liberal theorists on both sides of the "group rights" debates, means that the practice of tolerance is inconceivable where such autonomy is not a core political principle and juridical norm. Such an account of tolerance not only consecrates liberalism's superiority but reiterates liberalism's obliviousness to social powers other than law, thereby sustaining the conceit of the thoroughgoing autonomy of the liberal subject. At the same time, in its dependence on legally encoded autonomy—rights—this definition rules out the possibility of nonliberal political forms of tolerance. But what if tolerance of differing beliefs and practices could (and does) attach to values other than autonomy—for example, to formulations of plurality, difference, or cultural preservation that do not devolve on individual liberty?[37] Conversely, what if individual liberty were decentered (without being rejected) as the sign of civilization, grasped as but one way of gratifying the richness and possibilities in being human and also as fictional in its absolutism? That is, what if autonomy were recognized as relative, ambiguous, ambivalent, partial, and also advanced by means other than law?[38] Such recognition would not only make nonliberal tolerance practices conceivable, it would serve as a starting point for a more critical understanding of liberal practices than is permitted by liberalism's self-affirming vocabulary and dubious syllogisms.

TOLERANCE, CAPITAL, AND LIBERAL IMPERIALISM

In considering how the entwining of liberal and postcolonial discourse positions tolerance in a contemporary civilizational discourse, I have dwelt on Okin at length. This is not because she is the most sophisticated exponent of this use of tolerance but because she is among the most forthright. But other liberal theorists make similar moves. Recall Michael Ignatieff's argument that tolerance is the fruit of individuation and hence the achievement of societies governed by individualism. Recall, too, that Ignatieff portrays such individualism as the primordial truth of human beings—who we really are—as opposed to the abstract human being entailed in collective conceptions of identity. This positing of the individual as a priori not only renders collective

identity as ideological, deformative, and dangerous, it also tacitly as-
signs culture and all other forms of collective identification uncon-
quered by liberalism to a premodern past and nonhuman elsewhere.
Paralleling the political implications of Freud's thought discussed in
chapter 6, this argument depicts liberal democracy as representing the
truth of human beings and depicts those mired in collective identity—
or, as Francis Fukuyama would have it, "mired in history"—as at once
misguided, irrational, and dangerous.

On a closer reading of Ignatieff, however, tolerance appears as the
fruit not simply of individualism but of prosperity—it is not the individual as such but individual success that breeds a tolerant moral psychology. On the one hand, "the German man who can show you his
house, his car, and a family as measures of his own pride rather than
just his white skin may be less likely to wish to torch an immigrant
hostel." On the other hand, "if the market fails, as it is failing upwards
of twenty million unemployed young people in Europe alone, then it
does create the conditions in which individuals must turn to group hatreds in order to assert and defend their identities."[39] Here tolerance
appears less a moral or political achievement of liberal autonomy than
a *bourgeois* capitalist virtue, the fruit of power and success . . . even
domination.

As the passage above suggests, while affirming the value of economic prosperity in generating a tolerant outlook, Ignatieff is fully
confident that globalization brings with it a more tolerant world. He
worries that its economic depression of certain populations may incite
racial or ethnic nationalisms in a kind of last-gasp attempt to maintain supremacy or privilege.[40] However, the moral philosophers
Bernard Williams and Joseph Raz have no such anxieties; for them,
the market inherently waters down fundamentalism, puts the brakes
on fanaticism, and "encourages scepticism about religious and other
claims to exclusivity." In short, it erodes cultural, nationalistic, and religious forms of local solidarity or belonging.[41] Williams and Raz differ in their accounts of how neoliberal globalization enriches the
ground from which tolerance grows. For Raz, market homogenization
counters the fragmenting effects of multiculturalism in the era of
global capitalism. That is, the market helps to dampen the "culture"

in the multicultural civic and national populations produced by globalization *because* it tends to brings liberal democratic politics along with it, thereby producing a common (cultureless) political and economic life to attenuate the substance and contentiousness of (culturally based) claims of difference. For Williams, the globalized market does not need to import liberal democracy as a political form in order to effect an increase in religious and ethnic tolerance. For him, the market itself loosens the grip (by greasing the palm?) of the fundamentalist, thereby reducing intolerance by recourse to the principle of utility rather than by any other moral or "civilizing" principle. In Williams's words, "when such scepticism [induced by international commercial society] is set against the manifest and immediate human harms generated by intolerance, there is a basis for the practice of toleration—a basis that is indeed allied to liberalism, but is less ambitious than the pure principle of pluralism, which rests on autonomy. It is closer to the tradition that may be traced to Montesquieu and to Constant, which the late Judith Shklar called 'the Liberalism of Fear.'"[42] Indeed, not only the politics of fear configured by the rightest liberal tradition of Hobbes, Montesqueiu, and Constant but a forthright neoliberal political rationality appears on Williams's pages, as unfettered capitalism is imagined to produce a normative social order and calculating subject, neither of which need be codified in liberal law or letters. For attentive students of the history of capitalism, of course, the erosion of nonmarket practices and customs by capital is old news. What is striking is the enthusiasm with which political liberals such as Williams and Raz applaud this phenomenon, cheering raw Western liberal imperialism and neoliberal globalization for their combined effectiveness in destroying local culture.

Other political liberals are less confident about the ease with which tolerance can be exported to nonliberal sites. Examining multiculturalism within liberal democratic societies, Will Kymlicka concludes that there is no way to impose the value of tolerance on minority cultures for which individual autonomy is not a primary value other than to make it part of the deal of being tolerated by the majority or hegemonic culture. For a culture to be tolerated by liberalism, in Kymlicka's view, it must itself become tolerant, even if doing so compromises crucial principles of the culture.[43] Thus Kymlicka effectively advocates exploiting the power position of the tolerating culture, which means deploying Kantian liberalism in a distinctly non-Kantian way: that is, treating tolerance as a means for transforming others rather than as an end in itself, and treating individual autonomy as a bargaining chip rather than as an intrinsic value. The demand for cultural transformation, of course, also compromises the gesture of tolerance at the moment it is extended. Kymlicka's proposal to extend tolerance to nonliberal cultures tacitly exposes the antiliberal aspects of this aim, along with the absence of cultural and political neutrality in tolerance itself. It reminds us that tolerance in its liberal mode is more than a means of achieving civil peace of freedom: it is an exercise of hegemony that requires extensive political transformation of the cultures and subjects it would govern.

There are important analytic and prescriptive differences between Okin and Ignatieff, Huntington and Raz, Williams and Kymlicka. But together, they paint a picture of tolerance as a civilizational discourse that draws from and entwines postcolonial, liberal, and neoliberal reasoning. This discourse encodes the superiority of the West and of liberalism by valorizing (and even ontologizing) individual autonomy, by positioning culture and religion as extrinsic to this autonomy, and by casting governance by culture and religion as individual autonomy's opposite. The cultural norms carried by the market and organizing liberal democracy are not made visible within the discourse.

That tolerance is preferable to violent civil conflict is inarguable. What this truism elides, however, is the discursive function of tolerance in legitimating the often violent imperialism of international liberal governmentality conjoined with neoliberal global political economy.[44] The practice of tolerance does not simply anoint the superior or advanced status of the tolerant. Withholding tolerance for designated practices, cultures and regimes does not simply mark them as beyond the pale of civilization. The economy of this offering and this refusal also masks the cultural norms of liberal democratic regimes and of the West by denying their status *as* cultural norms. What becomes clear when we consider together the above-named thinkers is that the discourse of tolerance substantively brokers cultural value—

valorizing the West, othering the rest—while feigning to do no more than distinguish civilization from barbarism, protect the former from the latter, and extend the benefits of liberal thought and practices. Insofar as tolerance in its civilizational mode draws on a political-juridical discourse of cultural neutrality, in which what is at stake is said to be rationality, individual autonomy, and the rule of law rather than the (despotic) rule of culture or religion, tolerance is crucial to liberalism's denial of its imbrication with culture and the colonial projection of culture onto the native. It is crucial to liberalism's conceit of independence from culture, of neutrality with regard to culture . . . a conceit that in turn shields liberal polities from charges of cultural supremacy and cultural imperialism. This was precisely the conceit that allowed George W. Bush to declare, without recourse to the infelicitous language of "crusade," that "we have no intention of imposing our culture" on others while insisting on a set of liberal principles that others cannot brook without risking being bombed (see chapter 6).

Tolerance *conferred* as well as tolerance *withheld* serves this function; both are essential in the circuitry that tolerance travels as a civilizational discourse. *Tolerance conferred* on "foreign" practices shores up the normative standing of the tolerant and the liminal standing of the tolerated—a standing somewhere between civilization and barbarism. It reconfirms, without reference to the orders of power that enable it, the higher civilizational standing of those who tolerate what they do not condone or share—their cosmopolitanism, forbearance, expansiveness, catholicity, remoteness from fundamentalism. It is only against this backdrop that *tolerance withheld* succeeds in marking the other as barbaric without implicating the cultural norms of the tolerant by this marking. When a tolerant civilization meets its limits, it says not that it is encountering political or cultural difference but that it is encountering the limits of civilization itself. At that point, the tolerant civilization is justified not only in refusing to extend tolerance to its Other but in treating it as hostile, both internally oppressive *and* externally dangerous, and, as chapter 6 made clear, externally dangerous *because* internally oppressive. This hostile status in turn legitimates the tolerant entity's suspension of its own civilizational principles in dealing with this Other, principles that range from political

self-determination and nation-state sovereignty to rational deliberation, legal and international accountability, and reasoned justification.
Such legitimate abrogation of civilizational principles can be carried
quite far, up to the point of making preemptive war on the Other.

The circuitry of tolerance in civilizational discourse also abets the
slide from terrorism to fundamentalism to anti-Americanism that legitimates the rhetorical Manicheanism often wielded by the Bush
regime: "You're either with the civilized world, or you're with the terrorists." It facilitates the slide from Osama bin Laden to Saddam Hussein as the enemy to civilization, and from a war *on* terrorism to wars
for regime change in Afghanistan and Iraq. And likewise it indulges a
slide from a war justified by Iraq's *danger* to the "civilized world" to
one justified by the Iraqi people's *need* for liberation (by the West). Tolerance in a liberal idiom, both conferred and withheld, does not merely
serve as the *sign* of the civilized and the free: it configures the *right* of
the civilized against a barbaric opposite that is both internally oppressive and externally dangerous, neither tolerant nor tolerable.

In these operations, tolerance has a slim resemblance to its founding
impetus as a response to the fracturing of church authority, an instrument for consolidating emerging nation-state power and dominion,
even as a modus vivendi among cohabiting belief communities. That
tolerance has acquired such a troubling relationship to Western empire today does not add up to an argument to scrap the term or jetti-
son its representation of a practice for living with what is undesirable,
offensive, or repugnant. Rather, it calls for becoming savvy about the
ways of tolerance today and contesting the anti-political language of
ontology, affect, and ethos that tolerance circulates with a language of
power, social forces, and justice. This means becoming shrewd about
the ways that tolerance operates as a coin of liberal imperialism, intersects with racialized tropes of barbarism or of the decline of the
West, and at times abets in legitimizing the very violence it claims to
abhor or deter. It means apprehending how tolerance discourse articulates normal and deviant subjects, cultures, religions, and regimes,
and hence how it produces and regulates identity. It means tracking
the work of tolerance in iterating subordination and marginalization,

in part by functioning as a supplement to other elements of liberal discourse, such as universalism and egalitarianism, that are associated with remedying subordination and marginalization. It means grasping tolerance as discursively depoliticizing the conflicts whose effects it manages by analytically occluding the histories and powers constitutive of these conflicts, and by casting "difference" as ontological and as an inherent site of hostility. It means attending to the ways that tolerance draws on its reputation as a civilizing moment in the early modern West—reducing persecution in the field of religion—for the legitimation of its current work as a civilizational discourse that masks the violence in its dealings with the non-West. It means, in sum, grasping tolerance as a mode of national and transnational governmentality today.

The development of this kind of political intelligence does not entail rejecting tolerance outright, declaring it a necessarily insidious value, or replacing tolerance with some other term or practice. Rather, becoming perspicacious about the contemporary operations and circuitries of tolerance suggests a positive political strategy of nourishing counterdiscourses that would feature power and justice where antipolitical tolerance talk has displaced them. We can attempt to strengthen articulations of inequality, abjection, subordination, and colonial and postcolonial violence that are suppressed by tolerance discourse. We can configure conflicts through grammars of power rather than ontologized ethnic or religious feuds. And we can labor to expose the cultural and religious norms organizing liberalism along with the ethnic, racial, sexual, and gendered norms it harbors. In short, without foolishly positioning ourselves "against tolerance" or advocating "intolerance," we can contest the depoliticizing, regulatory, and imperial aims of contemporary deployments of tolerance with alternative political speech and practices. Such work constitutes a modest contribution to the larger project of alleviating human suffering, reducing violence, and fostering the political justice for which the twenty-first century howls.

NOTES

CHAPTER ONE. TOLERANCE AS A DISCOURSE OF DEPOLITICIZATION

1. Critics of tolerance also cross party lines: where the cultural right sometimes finds it a code word for approval of homosexuality, the cultural Left sometimes declaims tolerance as an impoverished substitute for equal rights for homosexuals. (See, for instance, the recent controversy generated by James Dobson's denunciation of the SpongeBob SquarePants "We Are Family" music video; "US Right Attacks Spongebob Video," bbc.co.uk, 20 January 2005 ⟨http://news.bbc.co.uk/1/hi/world/americas/4190699.stm⟩, accessed 20 July 2005.) Similarly, while the Christian Right may decry the erosion of morality produced by "excesses of tolerance," there are also progressives who assail a tolerant multiculturalism for its hesitation to condemn cultural practices such as female genital circumcision or, as in France, the wearing of a *hijab* by Muslim girls.

2. As chapter 4 argues in detail, the circuitry of tolerance—not only its extension from the state through the fibers of the social and the local but the intermittent nature of its invocation in various sites—both organizes and dissimulates its workings as a form of governmentality. For example, the challenge to Protestant, white, heterosexual superordination posed by the legal equality of those of other races, religions, and sexualities is a threat that is contained by tolerance discourse through its propagation of hegemonic social norms. When those identified with minority religions, ethnicities, and sexualities are simultaneously rendered as objects of *social* tolerance yet formally enfranchised, their marginal status in the nation is continuously inscribed by the former while their political inclusion is established by the latter. Tolerance

discourse in the social thus restores the hegemony that state-sponsored egalitarianism threatens to undermine. Far from de-implicating the state in tolerance, this partnership reveals the importance of a state that stands for tolerance without expressly administering it.

This is but one instance of the governmentality of tolerance disseminated across state and civil society and across a range of public, semi-public, and private sites and subjects. Such dissemination, as opposed to consolidation in a sovereign or juridical site, is not only a signature of governmentality but also a sign of power in postsovereign political organization. Thus the very resistance of tolerance to codification, combined with its lack of instantiation in any institution and its peculiar hybridity of cultural, political, and social regulation, suggests its potency in the production of marked subjects, social stratification, and global ordering.

3. I am grateful to Stuart Hall, Mahmood Mamdani, and an anonymous reviewer for pushing me toward this recognition. Useful works on the subject include Paul Gilroy, *The Black Atlantic: Modernity and Double Consciousness* (Cambridge, MA: Harvard University Press, 1993); Uday Mehta, *Liberalism and Empire: A Study in Nineteenth-Century British Liberal Thought* (Chicago: University of Chicago Press, 1999); and Sankar Muthu, *Enlightenment against Empire* (Princeton: Princeton University Press, 2003).

4. There is a vast philosophical literature on tolerance. A sampling includes David Heyd, ed., *Toleration: An Elusive Virtue* (Princeton: Princeton University Press, 1996); Preston King, *Toleration* (London: Allen and Unwin, 1976); Susan Mendus, ed., *Justifying Toleration: Conceptual and Historical Perspectives* (Cambridge: Cambridge University Press, 1988); John Horton, "Three (Apparent) Paradoxes of Toleration," *Synthesis Philosophica* 9 (1994): 7–20; John Horton and Susan Mendus, eds., *Aspects of Toleration: Philosophical Studies* (London: Methuen, 1985); Susan Mendus and David Edwards, eds., *On Toleration* (Oxford: Oxford University Press, 1987); Bernard Williams, *Ethics and the Limits of Philosophy* (London: Fontana, 1985); Glen Newey, *Virtue, Reason and Toleration* (Edinburgh: Edinburgh University Press, 1999); and Mehdi Amin Razavi and David Ambuel, eds., *Philosophy, Religion, and the Question of Intolerance* (Albany: State University of New York Press, 1997).

5. Again, while the literature is enormous, one might profitably begin with John Rawls, *A Theory of Justice* (Cambridge, MA: Harvard University Press, 1971) and *Political Liberalism* (New York: Columbia University Press, 1995);

John Horton, ed., *Liberalism, Multiculturalism and Toleration* (London: Macmillan, 1993); Thomas Nagel, *Equality and Partiality* (Oxford: Oxford University Press, 1991); Joseph Raz, *The Morality of Freedom* (Oxford: Oxford University Press, 1986); Will Kymlicka, *Liberalism, Community and Culture* (Oxford: Oxford University Press, 1989) and *Multicultural Citizenship: A Liberal Theory of Minority Rights* (Oxford: Oxford University Press, 1996); Michael Walzer, *On Toleration* (New Haven: Yale University Press, 1999); Susan Okin, *Is Multiculturalism Bad for Women?* (Princeton: Princeton University Press, 1999); Susan Mendus, ed., *The Politics of Toleration in Modern Life* (Durham: Duke University Press, 1999); Mendus and Edwards, eds., *On Toleration*; Susan Mendus, *Toleration and the Limits of Liberalism* (London: Macmillan, 1989); J. Budziszewski, *True Tolerance: Liberalism and the Necessity of Judgment* (New Brunswick, NJ: Transaction, 1992); Andrew R. Murphy, *Conscience and Community: Revisiting Toleration and Religious Dissent in Early Modern England and America* (University Park: Pennsylvania State University Press, 2003); William Connolly, *The Ethos of Pluralization* (Minneapolis: University of Minnesota Press, 1995); Bhikhu Parekh, *Rethinking Multiculturalism: Cultural Diversity and Political Theory* (Basingstoke: Macmillan, 2000); and Chandran Kukathas, *The Liberal Archipelago: A Theory of Diversity and Freedom* (Oxford: Oxford University Press, 2003). The classical modern theorists include Pierre Bayle, John Locke, John Stuart Mill, and Voltaire; the early moderns include, among others, Marsiglio of Padua, John of Salisbury, Nicolas of Cusa, Gottfried Leibniz, Samuel Pufendorf, Jean LeClerc, Thomas More, Erasmus, and Daniel Defoe.

6. See Ingrid Creppell, *Toleration and Identity: Foundations in Early Modern Thought* (New York: Routledge, 2003); Perez Zagorin, *How the Idea of Religious Toleration Came to the West* (Princeton: Princeton University Press, 2003); John Boswell, *Christianity, Social Tolerance, and Homosexuality* (Chicago: University of Chicago Press, 1980); John Christian Laursen, ed., *Religious Toleration: "The Variety of Rites" from Cyrus to Defoe* (New York: St. Martin's Press, 1999); Herbert Butterfield, "Toleration in Early Modern Times," *Journal of the History of Ideas* 38.4 (October 1977): 573–84; Ole Peter Grell et al., eds., *From Persecution to Toleration: The Glorious Revolution and Religion in England* (Oxford: Clarendon Press, 1991); Ole Peter Grell and Bob Scribner, eds., *Tolerance and Intolerance in the European Reformation* (Cambridge: Cambridge University Press, 1996); John Christian

Laursen and Cary J. Nederman, eds., *Beyond the Persecuting Society: Religious Toleration before the Enlightenment* (Philadelphia: University of Pennsylvania Press, 1998); Cary J. Nederman, *Worlds of Difference: European Discourses of Toleration, c. 1100–c. 1550* (University Park: Pennsylvania State University Press, 2000); and Gary Remer, *Humanism and the Rhetoric of Toleration* (University Park: Pennsylvania State University Press, 1996).

7. See David A. J. Richards, *Toleration and the Constitution* (New York: Oxford University Press, 1986); James Tully, *Strange Multiplicity: Constitutionalism in an Age of Diversity* (Cambridge: Cambridge University Press, 1995); and Lee Bollinger, *The Tolerant Society* (Oxford: Oxford University Press, 1988).

8. Certainly I am not the first to do make such an effort, and, within the literatures cited above, there are a handful of important exceptions to the general characterization I have offered of each disciplinary approach. Most well-known is Herbert Marcuse's essay "Repressive Tolerance," itself published alongside Robert Paul Wolff's "Beyond Tolerance" and Barrington Moore, Jr.'s "Tolerance and the Scientific Outlook" in a volume titled *A Critique of Pure Tolerance* (Boston: Beacon, 1965). But there are others: Katherine Holland, "Giving Reasons: Rethinking Toleration for a Plural World," *Theory and Event* 4.4 (2000); Anne Phillips, "The Politicisation of Difference: Does This Make for a More Intolerant Society?" in *Toleration, Identity, and Difference*, ed. John Horton and Susan Mendus (New York: St. Martin's Press, 1999); and Jeremy Stolow, "Transnational Religious Social Movements and the Limits of Liberal Tolerance," unpublished MS, Departments of Sociology and Communication Studies, McMaster University, Ontario, 1998.

9. This view of tolerance varies sharply from its seventeenth- and eighteenth-century deployments, which often took shape as formal "declarations," "edicts," and "indulgences" that at once incorporated, protected, and regulated practitioners of minority religions—Protestant sectarians in Anglican England and Holland, Jews in various Christian European states, Protestants in Catholic France. See Zagorin, *How the Idea of Religious Toleration Came to the West*; Joseph Lecler, *Toleration and the Reformation*, trans. T. L. Westow (New York: Association Press, 1960); and Henry Kamen, *The Rise of Toleration* (New York: McGraw-Hill, 1967).

10. For example, the proposed Constitution of the European Union (18 June 2004) includes tolerance in Article I-2, titled "The Union's Values": "The

Union is founded on the values of respect for human dignity, freedom, democracy, liberty, equality, the rule of law and respect or human rights, including the rights of persons belonging to minorities. These values are common to the Member States in a society in which pluralism, non-discrimination, tolerance, justice, solidarity, and equality between women and men prevail" (⟨http://europa.eu.int/constitution/en/ptoc2_en.htm⟩, accessed 28 November 2005).

Even the United Nations Declaration on the Elimination of All Forms of Intolerance and of Discrimination Based on Religion or Belief (proclaimed by General Assembly resolution 36/55 of 25 November 1981), which sounds like it might attempt a doctrinal codification of tolerance and intolerance, ends up referring intolerance to discrimination and then codifying the unacceptability of discrimination. This move is performed in Article 2: "1. No one shall be subject to discrimination by any State, institution, group of persons, or person on the grounds of religion or other belief. 2. For the purposes of the present Declaration, the expression 'intolerance and discrimination based on religion or belief' means any distinction, exclusion, restriction or preference based on religion or belief and having as its purpose or as its effect nullification or impairment of the recognition, enjoyment or exercise of human rights and fundamental freedoms on an equal basis." The rest of the declaration then proceeds to work with the term *discrimination*, while tolerance and intolerance vanish from the text (⟨http://www.unhchr.ch/html/menu3/b/d_intole.htm⟩, accessed 4 October 2005).

11. Occasionally, tolerance is invoked to indicate a willingness to abide certain kinds of "victimless crimes" or to indicate a lack of accord between the law and prevailing social norms. But we are more likely to use *lenience* than *tolerance* here, a word that suggests lassitude or indifference toward the issue or the subject by the authorities in charge rather than their coping with or managing a threat or challenge.

12. See, for example, Walzer, *On Toleration*, xi.

13. There are two theoretical difficulties in this claim, neither of which can be fully explored here:

(1) First is the question of intention. Is depoliticization the result of a scheme to enact it? Is it traceable to the interests of a dominant political group? While depoliticization may not be an explicit aim of the powerful, it does conserve the status quo and dissimulates the powers that organize it. The depoliticization entailed in liberalism, American political culture, and neolib-

eral rationality discussed in this study involves casting the existing order of things as inevitable, natural, or accidental rather than as the issue of orders or networks of power that privilege some at the expense of others. Thus depoliticization serves the powerful, but that service does not mean that the powerful intentionally and consciously develop and deploy this strategy to shore up their position. To the contrary, depoliticization may well issue from a certain blindness about power and dominance that is the privilege of the powerful. Certainly this would seem to be the case with tolerance and with liberal discourse more generally. This notion of a profound power effect absent a master choreographer but correspondent to the standpoint of the dominant is consonant not just with Marx's argument about the emergence of political ideology in the *German Ideology* but also with Foucault's account of the emergence of certain discourses of power in *The Order of Things, Discipline and Punish*, and *The History of Sexuality*, vol. 1.

(2) The notion of depoliticization also attributes an a priori political nature to certain relations, phenomena, or events, a nature that is then said to be mystified or veiled by depoliticizing narratives. The tricky epistemological and ontological issue here is not so much whether certain things can be classified as a priori political as how to insist on this classification without claiming that there is a single narrative through which political phenomena can be grasped or explained.

14. See Sarah Bullard, *Teaching Tolerance: Raising Open-minded, Empathetic Children* (New York: Doubleday, 1996).

15. Richard Rorty, *Achieving Our Country: Leftist Thought in Twentieth-Century America* (Cambridge, MA: Harvard University Press, 1998).

16. Kukathas, *The Liberal Archipelago*, 119.

17. Mahmood Mamdani, *Good Muslim, Bad Muslim: America, the Cold War, and the Roots of Terror* (New York: Pantheon, 2004).

18. The alternative to this relentlessly self-made and agentic individual is equally depoliticized: this is the disease model of behavior (from alcoholism to serial rape) or the related culturalist model, which Bonnie Honig indicts as a "my culture made me do it" approach to action and subjectivity. Both the disease model and the culturalist model are suffused with a determinism and a behaviorism that are the simply the other side of the individualist coin. Both are radically ahistorical and acontexual; both ignore the varieties of social, economic, and political powers producing subjects and conditioning their

thinking and actions. See Honig, "My Culture Made Me Do It," in Okin, *Is Multiculturalism Bad for Women?*

19. The "Finding Our Families, Finding Ourselves" exhibit in the Los Angeles Museum of Tolerance is an extreme example of this depoliticization. The main installation of the exhibit features biographical portraits of Joe Torres, Carlos Santana, Billy Crystal, and Maya Angelou. Each figure, the docent explains before one enters the installation, faced "a hurdle that had to be overcome and a role model to help him or her." Each embodies the story of an immigrant or American minority who rose to fame or success despite obstacles. Yet the obstacles featured are contingently personal—an abusive father, abandonment by a mother—rather than the racism, anti-Semitism, or poverty one expects these "heroes" to encounter. See chapter 5 for a detailed discussion of the Museum of Tolerance.

20. See Wendy Brown, "Neo-liberalism and the End of Liberal Democracy," *Theory and Event* 7.1 (2003), republished as chapter 3 in *Edgework: Essays on Knowledge and Politics* (Princeton: Princeton University Press, 2005).

21. See the Museum of Tolerance online teachers' guide, "Definitions," under "Define: Vocabulary and Concepts" (⟨http://teachers.museumoftolerance .com/mainjs.htm?s=4&p=1⟩, accessed 4 October 2005).

22. Okin, *Is Multiculturalism Bad for Women?*, 13–14.

23. Mamdani, *Good Muslim, Bad Muslim*, 17.

24. Two examples of such rhetoric are "We saw the nature of this enemy again . . . when terrorists in Iraq beheaded an American citizen, Nicholas Berg" ("President Speaks to the American Israel Public Affairs Committee," Washington, DC, Office of the Press Secretary, 18 May 2004 ⟨http://www .whitehouse.gov/news/releases/2004/05/20040518=1.html⟩, accessed 3 October 2005) and "We see the nature of the enemy in terrorists who exploded car bombs along a busy shopping street in Baghdad, including one outside a mosque. We see the nature of the enemy in terrorists who sent a suicide bomber to a teaching hospital in Mosul. We see the nature of the enemy in terrorists who behead civilian hostages and broadcast their atrocities for the world to see" ("Remarks by the President on the War on Terror," Fort Bragg, NC, 28 June 2005 (⟨http://www.globalsecurity.org/wmd/library/news/iraq/ 2005/iraq=050628=whitehouse01.htm⟩ accessed 3 October 2005).

25. Samuel Huntington, *The Clash of Civilizations*; quoted in Mamdani, *Good Muslim, Bad Muslim*, 21.

26. Mamdani, *Good Muslim, Bad Muslim*, 18.

27. This opposition between culture and universality is notably contemporary. In eighteenth- and nineteenth-century usage, culture, like civilization, could be identified with the (universal) common historical project of humankind, with Europeans in the vanguard. And Lévi-Strauss posited the rules of culture, centered on kinship regulation, as universal (see *The Elementary Structures of Kinship*, trans. James Harle Bell, John Richard von Sturmer, and Rodney Needham, editor, rev. ed. [Boston: Beacon, 1969]). For especially useful discussions of the complex lineages behind and contradictions within contemporary deployments of culture, see Amelie Rorty, "The Hidden Politics of Cultural Identification," *Political Theory* 22.1 (February 1994): 152–66; Tully, *Strange Multiplicity*; Seyla Benhabib, *The Claims of Culture: Equality and Diversity in the Global Era* (Princeton: Princeton University Press, 2002), esp. chap. 1; and Joshua Parens, "Multiculturalism and the Problem of Particularism," *American Political Science Review* 88.1 (March 1994): 169–81. Others who wrestle with the concept of culture as they explore the politics and possibilities of multiculturalism include Joseph H. Carens, *Culture, Citizenship and Community: A Contextual Exploration of Justice as Evenhandedness* (Oxford: Oxford University Press, 2000); Kymlicka, *Liberalism, Community and Culture* and *Multicultural Citizenship*; and Amy Gutmann, *Identity in Democracy* (Princeton: Princeton University Press, 2003).

28. For a more extended version of this argument, which focuses on Michael Ignatieff's brief for the moral discourse of human rights, see my "'The Most We Can Hope For . . .': Human Rights and the Politics of Fatalism," in "And Justice for All? The Claims of Human Rights," ed. Ian Balfour and Eduardo Cadava, special issue, *South Atlantic Quarterly* 103.2/3 (Spring/Summer 2004): 451–63.

CHAPTER TWO. TOLERANCE AS A
DISCOURSE OF POWER

1. *Oxford English Dictionary*, compact ed. (1971), s.v. "tolerance"; my emphasis. The entry for *toleration* lists two additional definitions worth noting: "the action or practice of tolerating or allowing what is not actually approved" and "allowance (with or without limitations), by the ruling power,

of the exercise of religion otherwise than in the form officially established or recognized."

2. But what of the tolerance exercised by those enduring sustained oppression or violence, e.g., those who stoically "tolerate" slavery, colonial rule, male dominance, or apartheid? How is this kind of tolerance accounted for by the argument that tolerance is always extended from the hegemonic to the liminal, from the powerful to the weak, from the insiders to the outsiders? As suggested in chapter 1, tolerance as an orientation or capacity, which is what the dominated or suffering subject exhibits, is different from a *regime* of tolerance and especially from the positive political valuation of tolerance as a feature of pluralist or secular societies. Indeed, the forbearance of oppression by the oppressed is rarely cast as a positive *political* value by democrats, though it may be covertly preferred to the moment at which such tolerance gives way to rebellion or subversion.

3. It is noteworthy that the *Oxford English Dictionary* definitions feature power much more centrally than does the definition from the (less historically minded) *American Heritage Dictionary*, a definition that also serves as an epigraph for the magazine *Teaching Tolerance*, a publication of the Southern Poverty Law Center: "the capacity for or the practice of recognizing and respecting the beliefs or practices of others."

4. Michel Foucault, *History of Sexuality, Vol. 1, An Introduction*, trans. Robert Hurley (New York: Random House, 1978), 139–41.

5. Here one can see the blurring between the Other within and the Other outside the body that was identified in chapter 1 as linking tolerance as a practice of domestic governmentality to tolerance as a dimension of civilizational discourse shaping international relations.

6. See "'. . . That Dangerous Supplement . . .'" in Jacques Derrida, *Of Grammatology*, trans. Gayatri Spivak, corrected ed. (Baltimore: Johns Hopkins University Press, 1997). That which represents itself as whole, continuous, or autarkic actually requires what is cast as "mere supplement," a requirement that belies the wholeness, continuity, or autarky of the primary term. "The supplement adds itself, it is a surplus, a plenitude enriching another plenitude. . . . But the supplement . . . adds only to replace. It intervenes or insinuates itself *in-the-place-of*; if it fills, it is as if one fills a void . . . its place is assigned in the structure by the mark of an emptiness" (145). For Derrida, the very appearance of the supplement is also a sign of crisis in coher-

ence or narrative continuity. The operation of tolerance as supplement to liberal equality and to Western secularism is elaborated in detail in chapters 3 and 7, respectively.

7. In zero-sum accounts of power, it is difficult to stage the possibility of mutual and discordant benefits for diverse parties. Thus, even Foucaultians tend to equate "regulatory power" with oppression, though regulation may closely protect and even empower what it also subordinates.

8. For example, a skin graft that takes is no longer "tolerated," and we do not speak of a community extending tolerance to those who have come to belong to it unproblematically. Thus it is possible for tolerance to give way to acceptance. But we cannot conclude that political tolerance is the *cause* of eventual and inevitable political acceptance, a commonly held teleological view of democratic inclusion that positions tolerance as a midway point between a naturalistic hostile exclusion of designated others and an achieved cosmopolitan acceptance of them. This view animates one of the most common dismissals of the critique of tolerance developed in this book. Here is how it goes: "Once upon a time, there was a homogeneous people, (e.g., Anglo-Saxons) or a widely accepted norm (e.g., heterosexuality). Then other kinds of people began to present themselves for membership or other practices emerged to contest the norm. Initially, the nation met this presentation or contestation with hostile rejection, then with tolerance, and finally with respect, equality, and full inclusion. Therefore, one should not fret too much over the politics of tolerance, because it is an imperfect but necessary stage on the way toward membership and equality." Not only does this narrative depend on a starkly progressivist historiography whose telos is universal equality; it also is unable to account for the simultaneous operation of tolerance and egalitarian inclusion—that is, for the fact that peoples who have full civil and political rights in a liberal democracy may remain subjects of tolerance or may be episodically returned to the status of being tolerated (e.g., Jews, Muslims, homosexuals, and particular racial or ethnic groups).

9. Similarly, George W. Bush's apparent willingness, in spring of 2003, to tolerate North Korea's development of weapons of mass destruction but not those fantasized in Iraq demonstrated both a significant designation of unilateral purview and a capacity to decide what was and was not tolerable.

10. Gary Remer, *Humanism and the Rhetoric of Toleration* (University Park: Pennsylvania State University Press, 1996), 5–7.

11. There are several fine intellectual histories of early modern toleration, among them Zagorin's *How the Idea of Religious Toleration Came to the West* (Princeton: Princeton University Press, 2003) and W. K. Jordan's *The Development of Religious Toleration in England*, 4 vols. (Cambridge, MA: Harvard University Press, 1932–40). Carey J. Nederman offers an excellent synthesis of premodern European advocates of toleration in *Worlds of Difference: European Discourses of Toleration, c. 1100–c. 1550* (University Park: Pennsylvania State University Press, 2000). *Religious Toleration: "The Variety of Rites" from Cyrus to Defoe*, ed. John Christian Laursen (New York: St. Martin's Press, 1999), contains a useful annotated bibliography of early modern tolerance thought.

12. John Locke, "A Letter Concerning Toleration," in *Political Writings*, ed. David Wootton (London: Mentor, Penguin, 1993); this edition is hereafter cited parenthetically in the text. See Ingrid Creppell, *Toleration and Identity: Foundations in Early Modern Thought* (New York: Routledge: 2003), for an argument that Bodin and Montaigne may be considered as important as Locke in setting out early modern theories of toleration.

13. Sheldon S. Wolin draws this subjectivism of belief toward the concept of interest that would come to dominate the characterization of the liberal individual in the next century: "what was controlling in Locke's argument was that conscience stood for a form of conviction rather than a way of knowing. Thus conscience meant the subjective *beliefs* held by an individual, and from this definition flowed the same characteristics which were later attached to interest. . . . That interest and conscience had coalesced was not lost upon the men of the eighteenth century; freedom to pursue one's interests was interchangeable with the freedom to worship as one saw fit" (*Politics and Vision: Continuity and Innovation in Western Political Thought* [Boston: Little, Brown, 1960], 339–40).

14. Locke's brief for religious freedom, like most others of the period, did not encompass intellectual freedom. His argument for tolerating religious choice was based on the individual nature of conscience and faith, the individual matter of caring for one's own soul, such that, as Voltaire phrased it impishly a century later, "an Englishman goes to heaven by whatever route he likes" (*Letters on England*, trans. Leonard Tancock [Harmondsworth: Penguin, 1980], letter 5). The arguments for religious and intellectual freedom would not be conjoined until the eighteenth century, under the sway of

the Enlightenment, at which point liberty rather than tolerance becomes the governing rubric of the argument. Although this shift can be understood in terms of an increasing valuation of individual liberty in all things as a good both in itself and in the development of reason, it also highlights an interesting feature of tolerance; it is addressed to humans not as bearers of reason or truth, but as bearers of belief and faith, as bearers of subrational convictions and attachments, or, later, as bearers of culture or desire. As a civic practice, tolerance is never adduced to handle Truth; it is always about features of us that escape or exceed the domain of Truth or even reason.

15. Persecuted as they were, Puritans in England were notably intolerant, hating Catholicism and opposed to separatist sects. See Zagorin, *How the Idea of Religious Toleration Came to the West*, 190.

16. A point made by Robert Paul Wolfe, "Beyond Tolerance," in *A Critique of Pure Tolerance* (Boston: Beacon, 1965), 12.

17. Will Kymlicka, "Two Models of Pluralism and Tolerance," in *Toleration: An Elusive Virtue*, ed. David Heyd (Princeton: Princeton University Press, 1996), 96.

18. The transformations in the governance aim, subject production, and other political effects consequent to these changes in the object of tolerance are explored in chapters 3 and 4.

19. Again, as discussed at the beginning of this chapter, I am using supplement here in Derrida's sense, as that which completes a putatively self-sufficient or coherent whole yet is simultaneously disavowed as it does so.

20. This point about tolerance's associations is made somewhat differently by Herbert Marcuse in "Repressive Tolerance," in *A Critique of Pure Tolerance*.

21. Gordon Graham and Jay Newman, among others, have attempted to refute toleration's entailment of a metaethic of relativism, to my mind unconvincingly. See Graham, "Tolerance, Pluralism, and Relativism," in Heyd, ed., *Toleration*, and Newman, *Foundations of Religious Tolerance* (Toronto: University of Toronto Press, 1982).

22. Both quotations appear in Kevin Boyle and Juliet Sheen, eds., *Freedom of Religion and Belief: A World Report* (New York: Routledge, 1997). The first is from the 'United Nations Declaration on the Elimination of all Forms of Intolerance and of Discrimination Based on Religion or Belief (1981) proclaimed by the General Assembly of the United Nations on 25 November

1981 (Resolution 36/55)' (xvii), and the second is from their 'Introduction' (11).

23. Foucault, *History of Sexuality*, 43.

24. Michel Foucault, *Discipline and Punish: The Birth of the Prison*, trans. Alan Sheridan (New York: Vintage, 1979).

25. Ibid., 192.

26. Ibid., 193.

27. Docent lecture, Simon Wiesenthal Center Museum of Tolerance, Los Angeles, 28 January 1999.

CHAPTER THREE. TOLERANCE AS SUPPLEMENT: THE "JEWISH QUESTION" AND THE "WOMAN QUESTION"

1. It is also insufficient to argue, as one well-regarded political theorist did in response to a presentation of this chapter, that women are not subjects for tolerance because "everyone has a mother." Not only could mothers be prime subjects for tolerance in a book (not this one) on psychoanalysis and tolerance, but I think everyone also has a Jew.

2. In *Out of the Ghetto: The Social Background of Jewish Emancipation, 1770–1870* (Cambridge, MA: Harvard University Press, 1973), Jacob Katz argues that however different the national stories of Jewish emancipation across western and central Europe—Germany, Hungary, Austria, France, Holland, and England—"Jewish emancipation, in its wider sense, occurred more or less simultaneously. It can also be said to have followed a similar, if not identical course" (3). He argues further that "the story of Jewish emancipation in any of the Western European countries could be told separately but not for each country in isolation. For there is a reciprocal influence here that cannot be ignored. The example and teaching of German reformers like Moses Mendelssohn had their effect on French Jews; and the political advances gained by French Jews through the French Revolution had their impact on German Jewry" (3–4).

3. David Vital, *A People Apart: A Political History of the Jews in Europe, 1789–1939* (Oxford: Oxford University Press, 1999), 42.

4. Ibid., 44.

5. Clermont-Tonnerre, quoted in ibid., 44.

6. Vital, *A People Apart*, 48.

7. Salo Baron, "Newer Approaches to Jewish Emancipation," *Diogenes*, no. 29 (Spring 1960): 57.

8. Vital, *A People Apart*, 50.

9. One clear instance of this change in political orientation toward the Jews is the difference in both tenor and aim between two Viennese policies separated by less than twenty years. Empress Maria Theresa's *Judenordnung* of 1764 was hostile and punitive, while Emperor Joseph II's *Toleranzpatent* of 1782 was rational, benevolent, and administrative. Neither policy made the Jews citizens, and both aimed to reform Jewish practice and behavior in order that Jews could be tolerated; but the *Toleranzpatent* took up this task of reform in the style of an administrative and regulatory state rather than an antagonistic one.

10. Michael R. Marrus, *The Politics of Assimilation: The French Jewish Community at the Time of the Dreyfus Affair* (Oxford: Clarendon Press, 1971), 91–92.

11. Here is the French historian Théodore Reinach's formulation of the historico-ontological effect of Jewish emancipation: "the Jews, since they have ceased to be treated as pariahs, must identify themselves, in heart and in fact, with the nations which have accepted them, renounce the practices, the aspirations, the peculiarities of costume or language which tended to isolate them from their fellow citizens, in a word cease to be a dispersed nation, and henceforth be considered only a religious denomination" (*Histoire des Israélites: depuis la ruine de leur indépendance nationale jusqu'à nos jours*, 5th ed. [Paris; Hachette, 1914]; quoted in Marrus, *Politics of Assimilation*, 94).

12. As already suggested, the Protestant character of religious tolerance in the West, in which religion is cast as a private matter of individual conscience and belief, is a poor fit for Jews as members of a *Volk* or nation. Patchen Markell underscores this misfit in his reading of the Prussian Emancipation Edict of 1812. The edict, Markell notes, refers to Jews as "persons of the Jewish faith," a gesture that discursively severs them from the Jewish nation and portrays them instead as "individual subscribers to a religious creed, akin to Lutheranism or Catholicism" (*Bound by Recognition* [Princeton: Princeton University Press, 2003], 135–36).

13. Tourasse, quoted in Marrus, *Politics of Assimilation*, 15.

14. Sander Gilman, *The Jew's Body* (New York: Routledge, 1991), 175–80.

15. In a passage quoted at length in chapter 2, above, Foucault makes a convincing case that in parallel fashion, nineteenth-century discourses of sexuality produced a subject exhaustively defined by desires marked as perverse, the homosexual (*History of Sexuality, vol. 1, An Introduction*, trans. Robert Hurley [New York: Random House, 1978], 43). Though it is beyond the purview of this study to explore the issue, significant intercourse and even interconstitutiveness existed between the emerging discourses of racialization and sexualization; the racialization of the Jew had a substantial sexual component.

16. As Sander Gilman notes, much of the racial theory marking Jews as "black" in nineteenth-century Germany and Austria was rooted in speculations about Jewish interbreeding with Africans during the period of the Alexandrian exile, thus constituting Jews as a mongrel rather than pure race and producing mongrelization as an explanation for Jewish inferiority. Gilman adds that Jews were regarded as having inherently endogamous kinship practices that resulted in impurity from the beginning. The mongrelization (as opposed to healthy mixing) of Jewishness did not make it any less categorizable (or reviled) as a race (*The Jew's Body*, 174).

17. Marrus, *Politics of Assimilation*, 111–12.

18. One can only wonder how much guilt associated with assimilation was relieved by an embrace of the racialization thesis.

19. Marrus, *Politics of Assimilation*, 114, 120.

20. Ibid., 158–62.

21. Thomas Laqueur, *Making Sex: Body and Gender from the Greeks to Freud* (Cambridge, MA: Harvard University Press, 1990).

22. Needless to say, these emerging discourses of racialization and gender were not entirely distinct, though they tend to be treated as such in the literature. Laqueur, for example, discusses the sexualization of gender largely without reference to race, while Gilman tends to treat even the sexualized racialization of the Jew without reference to the discourses of gender upon which Laqueur draws. This is a sad irony of compartmentalized scholarship, for as even the popular imagination knows, the nineteenth-century racialization of Jews and Africans, and that of "Orientals" too, was markedly sexual, achieving its subordinating effects through feminization (in the case of the

Jew) or through animalization (in the case of the African) of both the sex drive and sexual morphology of male members of the "race."

23. Laqueur, *Making Sex*, 5; see Jacques-Louis Moreau, *Histoire naturelle de la femme*, vol. 1 (Paris, 1803).

24. J. L. Brachet, *Traité de l'hystérie* (Paris, 1847); quoted in Laqueur, *Making Sex*, 5 (his ellipsis).

25. Laqueur, *Making Sex*, 152.

26. Karl Marx and Friedrich Engels, "Manifesto of the Communist Party," in *The Marx-Engels Reader*, ed. Robert C. Tucker (New York: Norton, 1978), 477.

27. Mary Wollstonecraft, *A Vindication of the Rights of Woman*, ed. Carol H. Poston, 2nd ed. (New York: Norton, 1988), 42, 51; Poullain de la Barre, quoted in Londa Schiebinger, *The Mind Has No Sex: Women in the Origins of Modern Science* (Cambridge, MA: Harvard University Press, 1989), 1.

28. Wollstonecraft, *Vindication*, 33, 34, 39. If what currently ruins women is an education that neglects or deforms their rational capacities, what is it that ruins men in the existing sexual order of things? Here, Wollstonecraft draws on the Enlightenment conviction that illegitimate rank corrupts; that men born to high station rather than earning it is the toxic stuff of the ancien régime. Thus, privilege by birth, which is what men in male-dominant regimes everywhere possess, must be eliminated not just for the sake of an egalitarian ideal but to promote social virtues ranging from authenticity to industriousness. For Wollstonecraft, this is particularly important in the family, where virtue is nourished in the young (see 44–45, 146–50).

29. Ibid., 39, 51.

30. John Stuart Mill, *The Subjection of Women*, in *On Liberty; with The Subjection of Women; and Chapters on Socialism*, ed. Stefan Collini (Cambridge: Cambridge University Press, 1989), 148: "However brutal a tyrant she may unfortunately be chained to—though she may know that he hates her, though it may be his daily pleasure to torture her, and though she may feel it impossible not to loathe him—he can claim from her and enforce the lowest degradation of a human being, that of being made the instrument of an animal function contrary to her own inclinations."

31. Ibid., 134, 136–37.

32. To an even greater degree than Wollstonecraft, Mill flirts with the notion that women may be inferior as a group in certain areas, and he even entertains the possibility of a mental difference related to their sex; but these dif-

ferences are never expressly tied to the sexual or reproductive dimensions of the female body (see *Subjection of Women*, 175–88).

33. See chapter 5 of *Émile*. Rousseau's position is echoed a century later in British moral psychology. In his manifesto against educating women in the same way as men, Herbert Cowell declares: "Physiologists are . . . agreed that there is sex in mind as well as in body, and that the mental qualities of the sexes correlate their physical differences" ("Sex in Mind and Education: A Commentary," in *Gender and Science: Late Nineteenth-Century Debates on the Female Mind and Body*, ed. Katharina Rowold [Bristol: Thoemmes Press, 1996], 82; originally published in *Blackwood's Edinburgh Magazine* 115 [1874]).

34. G.W.F. Hegel, *Elements of the Philosophy of Right*, ed. Allen W. Wood, trans. H. B. Wisbet (Cambridge: Cambridge University Press, 1991), § 166 and addition, 206–7.

35. Other strategies for legitimating women's foreclosure from political, intellectual, or economic life rely less directly on the sexual or reproductive body and more on another kind of heterosexual functionalism, one that harks back to the status-based arguments for gender subordination preceding what Laqueur describes as the sexualization of the gendered body commencing in the late eighteenth century.

36. Joan W. Scott, *Only Paradoxes to Offer: French Feminists and the Rights of Man* (Cambridge, MA: Harvard University Press, 1996), x.

37. This formulation of public equality on the back of privatized difference, of course, would give rise to many of feminism's internal tensions and stumbling blocks over the next two centuries.

38. Indeed, this was precisely the worry voiced initially about vice presidential candidate Lieberman's fitness for the job: Could he come to work, could he wage a war, on the Jewish Sabbath or holy days? Was he too much of a Jew to be a universal representative of the people?

39. Michel Foucault, *The Order of Things: An Archaeology of the Human Sciences* (New York: Random House, 1973), chap. 7.

40. Le Bon, quoted in Marris, *Politics of Assimilation*, 14.

41. See Michel Foucault, "Omnes et Singulatim: Towards a Criticism of Political Reason," in *The Tanner Lectures on Human Values*, vol. 2, ed. Sterling McMurrin (Salt Lake City: University of Utah Press, 1981), 225–28, and *Discipline and Punish: The Birth of the Prison*, trans. Alan Sheridan (New York: Vintage, 1979), 231–56.

42. Markell, *Bound by Recognition*, 146; his emphasis.

43. Immanuel Kant, *The Metaphysics of Morals*, excerpted in *Kant's Political Writings*, ed. Hans Reiss, trans. H. B. Nisbet (Cambridge: Cambridge University Press, 1970), 139; Sir William Blackstone, *Blackstone's Commentaries on the Laws of England*; quoted in Carole Pateman, "Women and Consent," *Political Theory* 8 (1980): 152.

44. This securing and resolution was beautifully exhibited in the pressure exerted by his advisors on the wife of Bill Clinton, after he lost his 1980 Arkansas gubernatorial reelection bid, to take his name. In 1981, after five years of marriage, she bid adieu to Hillary Rodham and became Mrs. Clinton.

45. Even today, one hears the language of tolerance applied to women only when men are characterizing a disruption to an avowed pleasure produced by the reigning masculinism in a particular venue, such as their social clubs. In such characterizations, the *equality* of men and women is rarely at issue; rather, what is at stake is an alleged gender-based *affinity*.

46. See Nancy Fraser, "Recognition and Redistribution," in *Justice Interruptus: Critical Reflections on the "Postsocialist" Condition* (New York: Routledge, 1997).

CHAPTER FOUR. TOLERANCE AS GOVERNMENTALITY: FALTERING UNIVERSALISM, STATE LEGITIMACY, AND STATE VIOLENCE

1. Michel Foucault, "Governmentality," in *The Foucault Effect: Studies in Governmentality*, ed. Graham Burchell, Colin Gordon, and Peter Miller (Chicago: University of Chicago Press, 1991), 95.

2. As Foucault formulates the contrast, sovereignty is "the power to take life or let live," while biopower is "the power to make live and to let die" (Michel Foucault, *Society Must Be Defended: Lectures at the Collège de France, 1975–76*, ed. Mauro Bertani and Alessandro Fontana, trans. David Macey [New York: Picador, 2003], 241).

3. Foucault, "Governmentality," 87.

4. Michel Foucault, "Politics and Reason," in *Politics, Philosophy, Culture: Interviews and Other Writings, 1977–1984*, trans. Alan Sheridan and others, ed. Lawrence D. Kritzman (New York: Routledge, 1988).

5. Nikolas Rose, *Powers of Freedom: Reframing Political Thought* (Cambridge: Cambridge University Press, 1999), 18.

6. Foucault, "Governmentality," 103.

7. Ibid., 102.

8. Ibid., 103.

9. Foucault's eschewal of the problem of political legitimacy is partly the result of his critique of ideology, of the notion that regimes of power are ideological and as such persistently risk withdrawal of belief and hence legitimacy. He argues instead that regimes carry (and disseminate throughout the space they occupy and the subjects they organize) their own truth—indeed, that a regime of truth is the precondition of power, a formulation that largely eliminates the problem of legitimacy. Consider:

> There can be no possible exercise of power without a certain economy of discourses of truth which operates through and on the basis of this association. We are subjected to the production of truth through power and we cannot exercise power except through the production of truth. . . . In the last analysis, we must produce truth as we must produce wealth, indeed we must produce truth in order to produce wealth in the first place. In another way, we are also subjected to truth in the sense in which it is truth that makes the laws, that produces the true discourse which, at least partially, decides, transmits, and itself extends upon the effects of power. ("Two Lectures," in *Power/Knowledge: Selected Interviews and Other Writings, 1972–1977*, ed. Colin Gordon [New York: Pantheon, 1980], 93–94).

10. See Foucault's lectures at the Collège de France, given on 17 and 24 January 1979, transcriptions of which are published in Michel Foucault, *Naissance de la Biopolitique: Cours au Collège de France, 1978–1979* (Paris: Gallimard, 2004).

11. In addition to the problem discussed in note 9, above, this ellipsis would also seem to be the result of Foucault's stubborn refusal to foreground matters of consciousness and subjectivity in theorizing power, or indeed even to allow them much place. Consequently, Foucault's radical theories of how subjects are produced through regulatory and disciplinary power converge in certain ways with the very behaviorism they were designed to defeat.

12. David Cole, *Enemy Aliens: Double Standards and Constitutional Freedoms in the War on Terrorism* (New York: New Press, 2003).

13. Michael Ignatieff argues that "cosmopolitanism is the privilege of those who can take a secure nation-state for granted" (*Blood and Belonging: Journeys in the New Nationalism* [New York: Farrar, Straus and Giroux, 1994], 13). See also Bruce Robbins, "Comparative Cosmopolitianisms"; Pheng Cheah, "Given Culture: Rethinking Cosmopolitical Freedom in Transnationalism"; and Amanda Anderson, "Cosmopolitanism, Universalism, and the Divided Legacies of Modernity"; all in *Cosmopolitics: Thinking and Feeling beyond the Nation*, ed. Cheah and Robbins (Minneapolis: University of Minnesota Press, 1998).

14. Michel Foucault, *History of Sexuality*, vol. 1, *An Introduction*, trans. Robert Hurley (New York: Random House, 1978), 8–9, and "Two Lectures." Here is how Foucault frames the problem in the latter text:

> [An analysis of power should] refrain from posing the labyrinthine and unanswerable question: "Who then has power and what has he in mind? What is the aim of someone who possesses power?" Instead, it is a case of studying power at the point where its intention, if it has one, is completely invested in its real and effective practices. . . . Let us not, therefore, ask why certain people want to dominate, what they seek, what is their overall strategy. Let us ask, instead, how things work at the level of on-going subjugation, at the level of those continuous and uninterrupted processes which subject our bodies, govern our gestures, dictate our behaviors, etc. (97)

15. This recasting of the core question would imitate Foucault's well-known reformulation of the "repressive hypothesis" concerning sexuality: "The question I would like to pose is not: Why are we repressed? but rather, Why do we say, with so much passion and so much resentment against our most recent past, against our present, and against ourselves, that we are repressed? By what spiral did we come to affirm that sex is negated? What led us to show, ostentatiously, that sex is something we hide, to say it is something we silence?" (*History of Sexuality*, 8–9).

16. The emergence of tolerance as a badge of Western superiority in the civilizational discourse framing aspects of contemporary international relations came a bit later, and is discussed in chapters 6 and 7.

17.

. . . I still have a dream. It is a dream that one day this nation will rise up and live out the true meaning of its creed: "We hold these truths to be self-evident: that all men are created equal." I have a dream that one day on the red hills of Georgia the sons of former slaves and the sons of former slave-owners will be able to sit down together at the table of brotherhood. I have a dream that one day even the state of Mississippi, a desert state, sweltering with the heat of injustice and oppression, will be transformed into an oasis of freedom and justice. I have a dream that my four children will one day live in a nation where they will not be judged by the color of their skin but by the content of their character. . . . With this faith we will be able to transform the jangling discords of our nation into a beautiful symphony of brotherhood. With this faith we will be able to work together, to pray together, to struggle together, to go to jail together, to stand up for freedom together, knowing that we will be free one day. (from King's speech delivered on the steps at the Lincoln Memorial in Washington, DC, on 28 August 1963; in Martin Luther King, Jr., *I Have a Dream: Writings and Speeches That Changed the World*, ed. James M. Washington [New York: HarperCollins, 1992], 104–5).

18. Anne Phillips, "The Politicisation of Difference: Does This Make for a More Intolerant Society?" in *Toleration, Identity, and Difference*, ed. John Horton and Susan Mendus (New York: St. Martin's Press, 1999).

19. This is not to say that tolerance inevitably entails radical moral or cultural relativism; some avenues of retreat from universalism do not lead to indifference among various religions, cultures, or value systems but rather submit these variations to a table of values in which some are much finer than others. This is exactly the kind of retreat that tolerance stages with its double action of inclusion, on the one hand, and of fierce normativity on the other. As chapter 2 argued, while religious tolerance promotes a certain epistemological relativism, it is at the same time an intensively normative discourse that designates morally superior and inferior identities and beliefs. Moreover, the particular universalism at issue in the present discussion is ontological rather than moral.

20. For two accounts of this phenomenon from different ends of the Enlightenment/post-Enlightenment spectrum, see Arjun Appadurai, *Modernity at Large: Cultural Dimensions of Globalization* (Minneapolis: University of Minnesota Press, 1996), and Jürgen Habermas, "The European Nation-State: On the Past and Future of Sovereignty and Citizenship," *Public Culture* 10.2 (Winter 1998): 397–416.

21. Jeremy Stolow, "Transnational Religious Social Movements and the Limits of Liberal Tolerance," unpublished MS, Departments of Sociology and Communication Studies, McMaster University, Ontario, 1998, 13.

22. Ibid., 18–20.

23. Volunteerist associations of various kinds may represent the trace of such communities and certainly constitute a significant interval between state and individual; but as elements of civil society they lack corporate communities' political and economic autonomy or significance vis-à-vis the state.

24. Joseph Raz, *Ethics in the Public Domain* (Oxford: Clarendon Press, 1984), 172.

25. In a similar vein, Bernard Williams figures global capitalism as the long-term solution to "intolerant" cultures and, more generally, to extreme nationalism or other fundamentalism. Because it introduces liberalism and skepticism wherever it settles, according to Williams, global capitalism will reduce the fanaticism that arouses the need for tolerance in the first place, that creates a problem for the tolerant in its nonreciprocity, and that insulates "fanatic" or "fundamentalist" cultures or subcultures from liberalization (see "Toleration: An Impossible Virtue?" in *Toleration: An Elusive Virtue*, ed. David Heyd [Princeton: Princeton University Press, 1966], 26).

26. "Remarks by the President at Photo Opportunity with House and Senate Leadership," The Oval Office, Office of the Press Secretary, 19 September 2001 (⟨http://www.whitehouse.gov/news/releases/2001/09/20010919=8.html⟩, accessed 4 October 2005). This is only one of many such occasions on which Bush defined Islamic American citizenship through the discourse of patriotism.

27. See Mahmood Mamdani, *Good Muslim, Bad Muslim: America, the Cold War, and the Roots of Terror* (New York: Pantheon, 2004), esp. chap. 1.

28. "The Second Gore-Bush Presidential Debates," 11 October 2000, Commission on Presidential Debates (⟨http://www.debates.org/pages/trans2000b.html⟩, accessed 4 October 2005).

29. As has often been noted, most Supreme Court decisions concerned with abortion locate the state in a similar position. *Roe v. Wade* (1973) established the state's interest in protecting potential life, thus allying the state with pro-life language and interests, while at the same time circumscribing a space of privacy, and hence of nonstate intervention, in which individual women might choose to abort. The logic of *Harris v. McRae*, the 1980 decision that proscribed Medicaid funding for abortions, followed accordingly.

30. While legalizing same-sex marriage is clearly consonant with basic precepts of equality and anti-discrimination and therefore appropriate in liberal democracies founded on these precepts, I feel compelled to note that I am no fan of the gay marriage campaign as a social justice project. The campaign's inevitable fetishism, sanctification, and valorization of marriage as a legal status and of the couple and the nuclear family as a kinship form raise many concerns about sexual, gender, and kinship regulation, none of which is relevant to the discussion here. Michael Warner's polemic, "Beyond Gay Marriage," republished in *Left Legalism/Left Critique*, ed. Wendy Brown and Janet Halley (Durham, NC: Duke University Press, 2002), is a good introduction to these concerns. My favorite comment on the campaign was a *New Yorker* cartoon by Michael Shaw featuring a middle-aged heterosexual couple watching television news together. One comments to the other: "Gays and lesbians getting married—haven't they suffered enough?" (*New Yorker*, 1 March 2004, p. 8; also available at Cartoonbank.com (⟨http://www.cartoon bank.com/product_details.asp?sitetype=1&sid=69362⟩, accessed 4 October 2005).

31. "President Holds Prime Time News Conference," The East Room, Office of the Press Secretary, 11 October 2001 (⟨http://www.whitehouse .gov/news/releases/2001/10/20011011=7.html⟩, accessed 24 October 2005); "President Pledges Assistance for New York in Phone Call with Pataki, Giuliani," Office of the Press Secretary, 13 September 2001 (⟨http://www .whitehouse.gov/news/releases/2001/09/20010913=4.html⟩, accessed 4 October 2005).

32. "'Islam Is Peace,' says President," Washington, DC, Office of the Press Secretary, 17 September 2001 (⟨http://www.whitehouse.gov/news/releases/ 2001/09/20010917=11.html⟩, accessed 4 October 2005).

33. The most conservative estimates of Afghan civilian casualties have placed them at more than 1,000; others have put the figure above 4,000. In January 2002, Michael Massing suggested that civilian deaths were probably in the neighborhood of 2,000 ("Grief without Portraits," *The Nation*, 4 February 2002, pp. 6–8). In *Blown Away: The Myth and Reality of Precision Bombing in Afghanistan* (Monroe, ME: Common Courage Press, 2004), Marc Herold argues that three years into the war, the count is at least 3,000. What is most striking is that the numbers are neither tracked by the State Department or a concern of the mainstream press.

34. See Cole, *Enemy Aliens*.

35. Dan Eggen, "Delays Cited in Charging Detainees," *Washington Post*, 15 January 2002, A1.

36. Jodi Wilgoren, "Prosecutors Begin Effort to Interview 5,000, but Basic Questions Remain," *New York Times*, 15 November 2001, B7.

37. "On the Public's Right to Know: The Day Ashcroft Censored Freedom of Information," editorial, *San Francisco Chronicle*, 6 January 2002, D4.

38. "FBI and Justice Department investigators are increasingly frustrated by the silence of jailed suspected associates of Osama bin Laden's al Qaeda network, and some are beginning to say that traditional civil liberties may have to be cast aside if they are to extract information about the Sept. 11 attacks and terrorist plans" (Walter Pincus, "Silence of 4 Terror Probe Suspects Poses Dilemma for FBI," *Washington Post*, 21 October 2001, A6).

39. See "Torture Policy," editorial, *Washington Post*, 16 June 2004, A26; "Rumsfeld Sued over Prisoner Abuse," CBSnews.com, 1 March 2005 (⟨http://www.cbsnews.com/stories/2005/03/01/terror/main677278.shtml⟩, accessed 24 October 2005); and "ACLU and Human Rights First Sue Defense Secretary Rumsfeld over U.S. Torture Policies," American Civil Liberties Union, 1 March 2005 (⟨http://www.aclu.org/SafeandFree.cfm?ID=17584& c=206⟩, accessed 24 October 2005).

40. "President Discusses War on Terrorism," World Congress Center, Atlanta, GA, Office of the Press Secretary, 8 November 2001 (⟨http://www.whitehouse.gov/news/releases/2001/11/20011108=13.html⟩, accessed 5 October 2005).

41. "We are outraged at reports of attacks on Arab Americans, Muslim Americans, and their mosques and businesses. . . . Such attacks, such scapegoating, are deeply un-American" (press release, 13 September 2001, Union of American Hebrew Congregations, Religious Action Center ⟨http://rac.org/Articles/index.cfm?id=781&pge_prg_id=4368⟩, accessed 5 October 2005).

42. Dissenters and even critical intellectuals inevitably become the "weak link" in this war. Precisely this term was used in presenting a list of traitorous academic utterances in the now infamous report by the American Council of Trustees and Alumni, "Defending Civilization: How Our Universities Are Failing America and What Can Be Done About It" (Patrick Healy, "McCarthyism: Rightwingers Target Voices of Dissent," *Boston Globe*, 13 November 2001, A7). The report was authored by Jerry L. Martin, ACTA president, and Anne D. Neal, ACTA executive director, and launched publicly by Lynne

Cheney (her cover blurb appears as the epigraph to this chapter). ACTA describes the report on its website:

It was not only America that was attacked on September 11, but civilization. We were attacked not for our vices, but for our virtues—for what we stand for. In response, ACTA has established the Defense of Civilization Fund to support the study of American history and civics and of Western civilization. The first project of the Fund is *Defending Civilization: How Our Universities Are Failing America and What Can Be Done About It* [November 2001, rev. and expanded February 2002]. The report calls on college and university trustees to make sure that their institutions offer strong core curricula that pass on to the next generation the legacy of freedom and democracy. (⟨http://www.goacta.org/publications/reports.html⟩, accessed 5 October 2005)

In fact, the report is largely devoted to printing (and damning) extracts from student and faculty criticisms of U.S. foreign policy in the first two months after the attacks. The report, incidentally, does affirm "tolerance" as one of "the great ideas and central values of our civilization" (8).

43. Boyd and Bush are quoted in Shelvia Dancy, "Bush Visits Mosque, Warns against Anti-Islam Violence," Religion News Service, 14 September 2001; available at ⟨http://www.beliefnet.com/story/88/story_8801_1.html⟩, accessed 5 October 2005.

44. Advertisement, *New York Times*, 30 September 2001, B12.

45. A quick tour of the Anti-Defamation League website makes this stance clear enough. See especially the 2002 "Resolution on Iraq" (⟨http://www.adl.org/presrele/Mise_00/2002_resolution_a.asp⟩, accessed 5 October 2005).

46. In November 2001, there appeared on the Anti-Defamation League website a press release titled "ADL Poll: No Increase in Anti-Semitism in Wake of Sept. 11 Attacks" (⟨http://www.adl.org/presrele/asus_12/3948_12.asp⟩, accessed 5 October 2005). In the analysis of the poll results, anti-Semitism was indexed by "American" attitudes toward Jews and toward Israel. Thus, proof that Americans have not become more anti-Semitic as a result of the September 11 attacks was derived as follows:

1. "The basic sympathies of the American people remain solidly behind Israel. When asked whether their sympathies were closer to the Israeli position

or the Palestinian position in the current conflict, Americans supported the Israeli position by 48 percent, compared with 11 percent for the Palestinian position."

2. "The American people overwhelmingly blame the violence in the Israeli-Palestinian conflict on the Palestinians."

3. "The public supports Israel's right to use force to defend itself against terrorism. By margins of 46 to 34 percent, Americans reject the notion that Israel should limit the use of force."

47. The call for tolerance in the context of state violence bound to essentialized difference is inherently idealistic, insofar as the conflict at issue is not actually occasioned by intolerance and cannot be solved by tolerance.

48. I have made this argument in more detail in "Political Idealization and Its Discontents," in *Dissent in Dangerous Times*, ed. Austin Sarat (Ann Arbor: University of Michigan Press, 2004), and republished in Wendy Brown, *Edgework: Essays on Knowledge and Politics* (Princeton: Princeton University Press, 2005).

CHAPTER FIVE. TOLERANCE AS MUSEUM OBJECT: THE SIMON WIESENTHAL CENTER MUSEUM OF TOLERANCE

1. "About the Museum of Tolerance," Museum of Tolerance, 2004 (⟨http://www.museumoftolerance.com/mot/about/index.cfm⟩, accessed 7 October 2005). Literature soliciting membership gives a slightly different account of the museum's mission: "to ensure that the horrors and lessons of the Holocaust and other twentieth century genocides and mass persecutions will never be forgotten" (Museum of Tolerance brochure, n.d., collected in the fall of 2004).

2. Here is the Wiesenthal Center's self-description at www.wiesenthal.com (under "About Us," accessed on 28 November 2005):

The Simon Wiesenthal Center is an international Jewish human rights organization dedicated to preserving the memory of the Holocaust by fostering tolerance and understanding through community involvement, educational outreach and social action. The Center confronts important contemporary issues including racism, antisemitism, terrorism and genocide and is accredited as an NGO both at the United Nations and UNESCO. . . .

Established in 1977, the Center closely interacts on an ongoing basis with a variety of public and private agencies, meeting with elected officials, the U.S. and foreign governments, diplomats and heads of state. Other issues that the Center deals with include: the prosecution of Nazi war criminals; Holocaust and tolerance education; Middle East Affairs; and extremist groups, neo-Nazism, and hate on the Internet.

3. "The Power of Words," an exhibit in the Tolerancenter, a section of the MOT discussed later in this chapter. Also noteworthy is the complete absence of Palestinians and the Middle East conflict from the MOT website. In the search box at ⟨http://www.museumoftolerance.com⟩, I typed "Palestinian," "Arab," "occupied territories," "West Bank," "Gaza Strip," "Middle East," and "Middle East conflict." Each time, the same eerie message came up on the screen: "Museum of Tolerance Results: 0 of 0. There are no records." Nor were there records for inter-Jewish racism and intolerance within Israel, or even for "Sephardim," although "Sephardic" had one hit: the story of a victim of the Holocaust. "Palestine" brought up four records, each associated with the story of a Jewish victim of the Holocaust whose family may have gone to Palestine in the 1930s. The MOT website offers records when searches are done for Rwanda, Bosnia, Ethiopia, massacre, genocide, former Yugoslavia, civil rights, racism, prejudice, human rights violations, Jackie Robinson, hate groups, survivor, African Americans, Poles, Hungarians, Sudan, exiled, Jerusalem, refugee, Albania, trauma, terrorism, and more. But there is literally no trace of a Palestinian or of any conflict in the Middle East.

4. A professor of education at the University of Georgia, Athens, wrote of her visit to the MOT: "The power of this experience became apparent to me on my return flight from Los Angeles. . . . I heard putdowns, saw subtle sexual harassments, and witnessed insensitivity to other's feelings as I had never seen them before. I was no longer in a cocoon, protected from what was happening around me. I only have myself to blame if I should forget the lessons learned that day" (Mary D. Phillips, "The *Beit Hashoah* Museum of Tolerance: A Reflection," *National Forum: Phi Kappa Phi Journal* 74.1 [Winter 1994]: 31).

5. Jon Wiener notes that the comments in the guest books of the MOT "contained nothing about the Tolerancenter," suggesting that the Holocaust

section of the museum, generally visited after the Tolerancenter, overwhelms and overwrites the rest of the experience (see "The Other Holocaust Museum," *Tikkun* 10.3 [May/June 1995]: 83).

6. Arnold Schwarzenegger and George H. W. Bush were among those honored at Wiesenthal Center fund-raising banquets in the 1980s.

7. Wiener, "The Other Holocaust Museum," 83; "The Line Is Thin—Too Thin," editorial, *Los Angeles Times*, 21 May 1985, Sec. 2, p. 4.

8. "The Line Is Thin—Too Thin" and Mathis Chazanov and Mark Gladstone, "'Museum of Tolerance' Proposed $5-Million State Grant for Wiesenthal Facility Provokes Some Concern over Church, State Separation," *Los Angeles Times*, 19 May 1985, sec. 2, p. 1. The museum's name itself, ambiguous and inconstant, tells a certain tale about the enterprise. The official and original name of the museum, and the one still engraved on the outside of the building, is Beit Hashoah—Museum of Tolerance. In Hebrew, *Beit Hashoah* means "House of the Holocaust." But given the dash, which appears in some of the early documents as a colon or a single bullet, those without Hebrew might take "museum of tolerance" to be the English translation of *Beit Hashoah*. So why the dash, given that the two terms are not mutually defining or in sequence? In some early literature the full name is given without punctuation at all, suggesting that Beit Hashoah is the name or sponsor of this particular museum of tolerance, its proper name. Another possible reading: these are two different enterprises bound together for a purpose, a hyphenated last name given to the offspring of religious or ethnic intermarriage.

Although many of the docents who lead groups into the Tolerancenter and Beit Hashoah still refer to the museum itself as Beit Hashoah, the museum's literature and the website now identify it as the "Museum of Tolerance, A Simon Wiesenthal Center Museum." The MOT has come to constitute the whole; Beit Hashoah is but one part of the enterprise that includes the Tolerancenter, the Multimedia Center, and Finding Our Families, Finding Ourselves. Undoubtedly there are some who see this change as another status reduction for the Holocaust, its "radical relativization," as Alvin H. Rosenfeld put it ("The Americanization of the Holocaust," *Commentary* 99.6 [June 1995]: 35). Or perhaps it indicates the inevitable outcome of the kind of intermarriage that the MOT represented from the beginning. Yet the reframing surely makes possible more effective outreach to non-Jewish populations and widens of the political base of support for Israel.

9. Wiener, "The Other Holocaust Museum," 83; Chazanov and Gladstone, "'Museum of Tolerance,'" sec. 2, p. 1.

10. Edward Norden, "Yes and No to the Holocaust Museums," *Commentary* 96.2 (August 1993): 23–24.

11. Fred Diament, president of the 1939 Club, blasted Hier as a publicity seeker who was exploiting the Holocaust: "As a survivor, what aggravates me is that they collect lots of money in the name of the Holocaust. And they're using lots of it for publicizing their center and also for certain sensationalist things. . . . The style of the Wiesenthal Center [also] aggravates me. They're too commercial. You cannot package the Holocaust. It's an insult to the memory of our parents and brothers and sisters" (quoted in Chazanov and Gladstone, "'Museum of Tolerance,'" sec. 2, p. 5).

12. Norden, "Yes and No to the Holocaust Museums," 23.

13. Wiener, "The Other Holocaust Museum," 83; Mark Gladstone, "Deukmejian Gets Bill Allocating $5 Million for Tolerance Museum," *Los Angeles Times*, 19 July 1985, sec. 2, pp. 1, 2.

14. House Subcommittee on Postsecondary Education of the Committee on Education and Labor, *Oversight Hearing on H.R. 3210, To Provide Financial Assistance to the Museum of Tolerance at the Simon Wiesenthal Center*, 101st Cong., 2nd sess., 1990, 33–35.

15. MOT docent, heard on museum visit, 25 September 2004.

16. See Lessons and Activities: "Essential Vocabulary and Concepts," a worksheet from the MOT Teacher's Guide ⟨http://teachers.museumoftolerance.com/content/downloads/lesson1_2.pdf⟩, accessed 8 October 2005).

17. This formulation hardly satisfies the hard core. In a scathing denunciation of the MOT in *Commentary*, Rosenfeld writes that "the Museum of Tolerance radically relativizes the catastrophe brought on by Nazism. America's social problems, for all of their gravity, are not genocidal in character and simply do not resemble the persecution and systematic slaughter of Europe's Jews during World War II. To mingle the victims of these very different historical experiences, therefore, is to metamorphose the Nazi Holocaust into that empty and all but meaningless abstraction, 'man's inhumanity to man'" ("The Americanization of the Holocaust," 35–36).

A desire to remain technologically and politically current also appears to drive the major and minor modifications and updates the museum has undertaken since it opened in 1993. Some original exhibits were removed: a "whisper gallery," whose visitors were subjected to a variety of whispered or hissed ethnic, racial, and sexual slurs as they walked through a dark tunnel; a large cutout of a Native American declaring that "in 1492, my people welcomed Columbus—a big mistake," followed by details of the Pilgrims' massacre of the Pequots; and a film on genocides other than the Shoah, including the twentieth-century massacres of Armenians and Cambodians. Other exhibits have been radically cut back. The museum opened in the immediate aftermath of the infamous Rodney King beating and the violent response to the "not guilty" verdict for the police officers involved, and it featured these events, and the controversies surrounding them, quite prominently for its first several years; they have since been given a more minor positioning. There are also rotating exhibits on the second floor, which might feature weavings by Bosnian women in one season, Japanese American troops fighting the Nazis during World War II in another. In 2004, a new section was added to the museum: the actor-comedian Billy Crystal instigated and provided major funding for "Finding Our Families, Finding Ourselves," a walk-through diorama and video installation designed to affirm America's status as an immigrant nation and a nation in which individuals overcome hardship to do great things. Only the Beit Hashoah has remained largely the same since its inception.

18. Several critical accounts of the MOT focus on its high-tech approach; see, for example, Rosenfeld, "The Americanization of the Holocaust"; Wiener, "The Other Holocaust Museum"; Nicola Lisus and Richard Ericson, "Misplacing Memory: The Effect of Television Format on Holocaust Remembrance," *British Journal of Sociology* 46.1 (March 1995), 1–19; and Susan Derwin, "Sense and/or Sensation: The Role of the Body in Holocaust Pedagogy," in *Impossible Images: Contemporary Art after the Holocaust*, ed. Shelley Hornstein, Laura Levitt, and Laurence J. Silberstein (New York: New York University Press, 2003).

19. Rabbi May, in his testimony before the congressional committee as the Wiesenthal Center sought federal funds, made this new bearing explicit, explaining that "we will have to go outside the community" for help in building exhibits that represent other issues and reach other constituencies (House Subcommittee on Postsecondary Education, *Oversight Hearing on H.R. 3210*, 32).

20. "New York Tolerance Center," Simon Wiesenthal Center ⟨http://www .wiesenthal.com/site/pp.asp?c=fwLYKnN8LzH&b=242506⟩, accessed 8 October 2005.

21. On 2 May 2004 in Jerusalem, Arnold Schwarzenegger laid the foundation stone at the groundbreaking ceremony for the new Museum of Tolerance and Center for Human Dignity built and financed by the Wiesenthal Center. Schwarzenegger (anointed governor of California by plebiscite democracy the previous fall; his gubernatorial transition team included Rabbi Cooper, associate dean of the Wiesenthal Center), the son of a Nazi, has in recent years contributed more than a million dollars of his personal funds to the Wiesenthal Center. He has, however, also been known to express his open admiration for Hitler's capacity to move a crowd; and at his wedding, he toasted Kurt Waldheim at the very time the former UN general secretary was facing accusations about hiding his Nazi past and wartime service with a German army unit that had committed atrocities. Many have speculated that Schwarzenegger's close ties to the Wiesenthal Center helped prevent these issues from becoming significant in his gubernatorial campaign.

Schwarzenegger's most recent visit to Israel had been in 1995, when he, along with Sylvester Stallone, opened a Planet Hollywood restaurant in Tel Aviv. Fifteen years earlier, he had gone to the Holy Land to judge a Miss Teenage Israel contest. But this time, Schwarzenegger strolled about Jerusalem and other parts of Israel declaring that he would "terminate all the intolerance and prejudice in the world . . . because I'm the Terminator" (quoted in Paul Miller, "On the Road to Jerusalem with a Superstar Governor," *Carmel Pine Cone*, 7 May 2004). And with what weapon would he accomplish this mission? In addition to breaking ground for the museum, Schwarzenegger spent the four-day trip developing prospects for joint ventures and other economic deals between Israel and California, including the sale of household energy monitors and cell phone jamming devices—produced in Santa Cruz, California—that could be effective in neutralizing roadside bombs. (The latter, Schwarzenegger noted, would be useful both to Israel and to American troops in Iraq.) Along with pumping up the sagging economies of what Schwarzenegger called these "two sunny lands," promotion of such close economic ties presumably secured him support from a substantial pro-Israel electorate in California.

While the governor greeted onlookers, uttered platitudes about peace and tolerance, and chatted with Israeli Special Olympics competitors about their workout schedules, Israeli soldiers guarded the entrance of the Tel Aviv Hilton where he was staying. Dozens more armed Israeli Defense Force personnel

surrounded the hotel and crouched on the roof. A phalanx of California High-
way Patrol officers served as Schwarzenegger's personal bodyguards. Israeli
borders with the occupied territories were completely closed during Schwarzenegger's visit, preventing Palestinians in Gaza and the West Bank access to
workplaces, health care, education, daily provisions, and family members on
the Israeli side. During the groundbreaking ceremony itself, Israeli protestors
interrupted the governor's remarks with shouts of "occupation is not tolerance," but the Israeli foreign minister declared the governor "a true friend and
a staunch ally of our nation," one who deserves Israelis' "gratitude for his
fight against prejudice and anti-Semitism" (quoted in Miller, "On the Road
to Jerusalem").

The site for the Jerusalem museum is an ancient Muslim cemetery, much of
which has already been desecrated by a parking lot. The design, brainchild of
the premier architect Frank O. Gehry (known for the Guggenheim in Bilbao
and the Disney concert hall in Los Angeles), was described by one left Israeli
pundit as looking like the pile-up from a good day's bombing in the West
Bank, and by another as the "extravagant arrogance expressed in . . . geo-
metric forms that can't be any more dissonant to the environment in which it
is planned to put this alien object" (Meron Benvenisti, "A Museum of Tolerance in a City of Fanatics," *Haaretz*, 12 May 2002; read online at Haaretz
.com ⟨http://tinyurl.com/cx86b⟩, accessed 28 November 2005). The costs associated with construction of the museum are now well in excess of $200 mil-
lion, an astonishing sum—especially against the backdrop of the Israeli and,
even more, the Palestinian economy, or in contrast with the $50 million com-
mitted by George W. Bush in the spring of 2005 to the project of building
democracy in Palestine (see "President Welcomes Palestinian President Abbas
to the White House," The Rose Garden, Office of the Press Secretary, 26 May
2005 ⟨http://www.whitehouse.gov/news/releases/2005/05/ 20050526.html⟩,
accessed 6 October 2005). The museum's planners, however, have shown
some sensitivity to context: in deference to the Yad Vashem Holocaust memorial that monopolizes the role of documenting the Holocaust in Israel, the new
museum will make no reference to the Holocaust.

On the groundbreaking ceremony and plans for the Jerusalem MOT, see also
Samuel G. Freedman, "Gehry's Mideast Peace Plan," 1 August 2004, *New York
Times*, sec. 2, p. 1; and "Schwarzenegger to Visit Israel," CNN.com, 29 April

2004 (⟨www.cnn.com/2004/ALLPOLITICS/04/28/schwarzenegger.israel/⟩, accessed July 2005).

22. Mary Louise Pratt writes: "Security is one of those words, like 'celibacy' or 'short,' that invokes its opposite. As soon as you mention security, you suggest there's a danger . . . otherwise the subject wouldn't be coming up" ("Security," in *Shock and Awe: War on Words*, ed. Bregje van Eekelen et al. [Santa Cruz, CA: New Pacific Press, 2004], 140).

23. The question of how much "freedom" democracies may need to forfeit for the sake of security is posed in several of the exhibits in the Tolerancenter.

24. School visitors are often also gently deterred from writing in the museum guestbooks at the conclusion of the Holocaust section. As one docent said to a trainee while I was there, "These really aren't for them—they're likely to write inappropriate things in them. Just steer them past the books."

25. While individuals are largely left on their own after the first few exhibits in the Tolerancenter, student groups have guides throughout. The guides not only shepherd the students through the exhibits in the Tolerancenter in an efficient and orderly way, they offer additional directives about the meaning of the exhibits and conduct brief discussions with the groups that closely imitate those prompted in the interactive media exhibits. That is, the discussions are neither open-ended nor conducted with a sense of curiosity about the students' ideas; they are straightforwardly pedantic, and the students are invited to respond to factual or conceptual questions for which the guide holds the correct answer. These guides appear to be trained but not necessarily educated in the subject matter of the museum: I heard more than one offer a strikingly loose version of key episodes in American political history. I also witnessed the guides quickly set aside questions from students that fell outside of the script—for example, a question about racial profiling by the police, and a question about the victimization narrative in the Tolerancenter and why certain oppressed peoples didn't "fight back."

26. MOT docent, heard on museum visit, 25 September 2004.

27. Rosenfeld, "The Americanization of the Holocaust," 35.

28. Susan Derwin notes that this procedure is also our first induction into how the MOT "propounds it message physically. The museum does not only label its visitors 'prejudiced'; it reinforces its determination by requiring the visitors to walk through the door of the museum's choice." She also observes,

"The museum tells the visitors what they are, and if they are to go on with the tour, they must accept that judgment, or at least act as if they do; literally and figuratively, that is the only door that remains open to them" ("Sense and/or Sensation," 250).

29. Hate.com is not an actual website, though HBO used the name for a documentary in 2000. This is a small but portentous episode in the MOT's ubiquitous blurring of the real and unreal, its production of the surreal, and, above all, its substitution of a simpler and more rhetorically compelling version of reality for one that is awkward and messy. See Lisus and Ericson, "Misplacing Memory," 9–17.

30. On the last of my visits, the docent explained to a group of school students that the diner was meant to evoke a scene of struggle in the civil rights movement. Until that moment, I assumed it was simply meant to conjure public space where different kinds of people eat and talk. Others clearly made the same assumption. Susan Derwin bases part of her reading of the Tolerancenter on the fact that a diner is a place to satisfy appetites (see "Sense and/or Sensation," 251).

31. The Millennium Machine video on refugees and political prisoners runs a similar course, fanning out across a wide spectrum of issues—the dangers of land mines to refugees, different kinds of political prisoners, China's persecution of Tibetans, and forced labor practices in Brazil, China, Pakistan, Vietnam, and Myanmar—but resolving them all into the question of what Americans, as inhabitants of the world's sole superpower, can do about these problems. The choices include boycotting goods produced in bad regimes, paying higher taxes for foreign aid, and risking the lives of Americans in military excursions. Again, the narrative divides the world into good and bad and depoliticizes issues by rendering them moral, on the one hand, and as matters of personal sacrifice on the other. Indeed, it is this depoliticization that makes it possible to treat such a large and diverse range of issues under the rubric of "refugees and political prisoners." But what makes it possible to keep Palestinian refugees off the screen, especially when refugees are defined as "ordinary people caught up in political and territorial disputes . . . the true innocents in wars and ethnic cleansing"?

32. "The trick, if you want to teach people, is you have to first grab their attention, then teach them, then make sure it lasts. And this museum does all three of those things," declared Arnold Schwarzenegger at the opening cere-

monies of the MOT in 1993 (quoted in Norden, "Yes and No to the Holocaust Museums," 25).

33. See Donna Haraway, *Primate Visions: Gender, Race, and Nature in the World of Modern Science* (New York: Routledge, 1990), esp. chap. 3, "Teddy Bear Patriarchy: Taxidermy in the Garden of Eden, New York City, 1908–36."

34. Jon Wiener argues that the very existence of the Tolerancenter was driven by the quest for public funding: "Thus the decision to include the Tolerancenter in the museum grew not out of a commitment to a philosophy of inclusion but from the calculation that it would ensure state financing" ("The Other Holocaust Museum," 83). I think this view elides the other strategic purposes of the Tolerancenter.

However, what stands out in Rabbi May's 1990 testimony before the Subcommittee on Postsecondary Education of the House Committee on Education and Labor as he argued for federal funding of broad-based educational materials on tolerance, is the zigzagging between identification of the MOT as a Holocaust museum and its concern with other issues. And when he does talk about these other issues, they are often treated as the hook for interesting young people in the Holocaust. At one point, Representative Major Owens (D-NY) asked whether the Wiesenthal Center had the needed expertise to mount a successful project on subjects other the Holocaust. Here is Rabbi May's almost comic response:

> Well, clearly, we recognize, as you said, that our strength is in the area of anti-Semitism and . . . the subject of the Holocaust. In order to create the first section, the History of Racism and Prejudice in America, we've gone outside . . . to film makers such as Al Franken from Saturday Night Live, producers like Al Franken, writers like Al Franken, and those producers from McNeil-Lehrer—Mr. Sauls, Michael Sauls from McNeil-Lehrer Report—because we recognize that in order to present the subject matter we have to have a view as broad as possible and as steeped as possible. . . . We have gone outside into the broad community. (House Subcommittee, *Overnight Hearings on H.R. 3210*, 32)

35. Ibid., 31.

36. In addition to the conflict in the Middle East, two other sites of protracted conflict are notable by their absence from the MOT: Northern Ireland

and South Africa. Still more surprising in a museum that features heroes battling for racial justice around the world, neither Nelson Mandela nor Desmond Tutu are anywhere featured or cited. Would representations of the conflict in Northern Ireland or apartheid South Africa raise questions about Israel? And have Mandela's and Tutu's criticisms of Israel disqualified them from the pantheon of tolerance heroes in the MOT?

37. I am grateful to Neve Gordon for conversations about the Hebrew.

38. On relativism and tolerance, see chapter 2. Oren Baruch Stier alerted me to the metonyms but draws a different conclusion about the significance of the name, suggesting instead that Beit Hashoah is "invoked as a largely meaningless term, which is perhaps why most refer to the place simply as the Museum of Tolerance." He adds, "The museum has a certain split (and somewhat ambiguous) personality illustrated by its peculiar hyphenated title, which is no mere whim of appellation. I would argue, in fact that that split and ambiguous personality is at the heart of the museum's noncommittal program, and that the hyphen in its name is the same as that of another ambiguous concept: the 'Judeo-Christian'" ("Virtual Memories: Mediating the Holocaust at the Simon Wiesenthal Center's Beit Hashoah–Museum of Tolerance," *Journal of the American Academy of Religion* 64:4 [Winter 1996]: 839).

39. Joan W. Scott, "Experience," in *Feminists Theorize the Political*, ed. Judith Butler and Scott (London: Routledge, 1992).

40. In the museum's account, grounding the narrative's authority is also the purpose of the live survivor testimonies offered several times daily at the MOT; as one docent put it, "They establish that the Holocaust really did happen" (heard on museum visit, 1999).

41. MOT docent, heard on museum visit, 25 September 2004. The Researcher is described as reviewing "pictorial evidence to choose visual material that best represents what happened," while the Designer "selects items and interprets them into a visual experience." In addition, the Designer serves a narrative function similar to a Socratic interlocutor in the ensuing tableaux: he is the naïf who asks basic questions that permit the Historian to clarify and underscore certain points.

42. Occasionally this primer is a bit haphazard in its approach to minor facts: it describes the Depression as making "money worth nothing," thereby confusing it with inflation, and the sloppiness of its rendering of the famous

Wannsee Conference (in a simulated boardroom where the figures speak in accented English), at which the "final solution" was approved, has been criticized by several historians.

43. Beit Hashoah installation, viewed on September 25, 1994.

44. In the portion of its website devoted to teacher preparation and follow-up to visiting the museum, the MOT does define anti-semitism as "hostility towards Jews as an ethnic or religious group, often accompanied by social, economic and political discrimination." See "Definitions," under "Define: Vocabulary and Concepts" (⟨http://teachers.museumoftolerance.com/mainjs .htm?s=4&p=1⟩, accessed 4 October 2005).

45. Dialogue with Pope John Paul II on the occasion of the fortieth anniversary of the Warsaw Ghetto uprising; quoted in *Response: The Wiesenthal Center World Report* 19.3 (Fall 1998): 6.

CHAPTER SIX. SUBJECTS OF TOLERANCE: WHY WE ARE CIVILIZED AND THEY ARE THE BARBARIANS

1. Mahmood Mamdani, *Good Muslim/Bad Muslim: America, the Cold War, and the Roots of Terror* (New York: Pantheon, 2004), 18.

2. Bernard Lewis, "The Roots of Muslim Rage," *Atlantic*, September 1990, pp. 47–60, and Samuel Huntington, "The Clash of Civilizations?" *Foreign Affairs* 72.3 (Summer 1993): 31; both cited in Mamdani, *Good Muslim/Bad Muslim*, 20–21.

3. National "civic religion" was featured by the classic social contract theorists—Hobbes, Locke, and Rousseau—as a necessary *supplement* to the social contract; where did the contents of what was deposited in that supplement go, and what is the relationship of this loss to the rise of subnational identities requiring civic tolerance?

4. Immanuel Kant, "What Is Enlightenment?" in *Kant's Political Writings*, ed. Hans Reiss, trans. H. B. Nisbet (Cambridge: Cambridge University Press, 1970), 54. Kant also problematizes this very formulation.

5. On Bush's regular consultations with "rapture Christians," and the effects of these consultations on foreign policy, see Rick Perlstein, "The Jesus Landing Pad," *Village Voice*, 18 May 2004 (online at ⟨http://www.villagevoice.com/ news/0420,perlstein,53582,1.html⟩, accessed 6 October 2005). See also Bob

Woodward's *Plan of Attack* (New York: Simon and Schuster, 2004), which quotes Bush's response to the question of whether he consulted his father before deciding to launch a war on Iraq: "You know he is the wrong father to appeal to in terms of strength. There is a higher father that I appeal to" (94). Bush also told Woodward, "I believe the United States is *the* beacon for freedom in the world. . . . I say that freedom is not America's gift to the world. Freedom is God's gift to everybody in the world. . . . And I believe we have a duty to free people" (88–89).

6. A significant exception to this generalization is Chandran Kukathas, who claims that liberty of conscience and autonomy are not only not equivalent but may well conflict at times. He argues that liberty of conscience, not autonomy, is the basis of toleration and that liberty of conscience must trump autonomy when they do conflict (see *The Liberal Archipelago: A Theory of Diversity and Freedom* [Oxford: Oxford University Press, 2003], esp. 36–37).

7. Susan Mendus, *Toleration and the Limits of Liberalism* (Atlantic Highlands, NJ: Humanities Press, 1989), 56; Will Kymlicka, "Two Models of Pluralism and Tolerance," in *Toleration: An Elusive Virtue*, ed. David Heyd (Princeton: Princeton University Press, 1996), 97; Bernard Williams, "Toleration: An Impossible Virtue?" in Heyd, ed., *Toleration*, 24.

8. Michael Ignatieff, "Nationalism and Toleration," in *The Politics of Toleration in Modern Life*, ed. Susan Mendus (Durham, NC: Duke University Press, 1999), 102.

9. In his comments on my work at a symposium (at the Launch of the Center on Citizenship, Identity, and Governance, Open University, Milton Keynes, England, March 2005) Barry Hindess reminded me that the temporalization of difference is an insidious and pervasive trope in Western political and social thought, one that is not limited to liberalism or even to colonial discourse. For an elaboration of this position, see the essay he coauthored with Christine Helliwell, "The Temporalizing of Difference," *Ethnicities* 5.3 (2005): 414–18.

10. See, for example, Michael Ignatieff, *Blood and Belonging: Journeys in the New Nationalism* (New York: Farrar, Straus and Giroux, 1995).

11. Sigmund Freud, *Civilization and Its Discontents*, trans. James Strachey (New York: Norton, 1961); *Totem and Taboo*, trans. James Strachey (New York: Norton, 1952).

12. Sigmund Freud, *Group Psychology and the Analysis of the Ego*, trans. James Strachey (New York: Norton, 1959). This work is hereafter cited parenthetically in the text.

13. Freud, *Civilization and Its Discontents*, 69; *Totem and Taboo*, 144.

14. Continued revelations about the deliberate development and approval of the techniques of torture and abuse practiced at Abu Ghraib, and their continuity with those practiced both at Guantánamo and in United States detention sites for "suspected terrorists," gives little credence to initial defenses of the Abu Ghraib scenes as "animal house" behavior. For news on these links, see, for instance, Josh White, "Abu Ghraib Tactics Were First Used at Guantanamo," *Washington Post*, 14 July 2005, A1; Oliver Burkeman, "Bush Team 'Knew of Abuse' at Guantánamo," *Guardian*, 13 September 2004 (⟨http://www.guardian.co.uk/guantanamo/story/0,13743,1303105,00.html⟩, accessed 28 November 2005); Richard Serrano and John Daniszewski, "Dozens Have Alleged Koran's Mishandling," *Los Angeles Times*, 22 May 2005, A1.

15. On the "nature of the enemy," see "President Thanks Military Personnel and Families for Serving Our Country," Camp Pendleton, CA, Office of the Press Secretary, 7 December 2004 (⟨http://www.whitehouse.gov/news/releases/2004/12/20041207-2.html⟩, accessed 24 October 2005), and "President's Radio Address," Office of the Press Secretary, 15 May 2004 (⟨http://www.whitehouse.gov/news/releases/2004/05/20040515.html⟩, accessed 24 October 2005); on Abu Ghraib, see "Global Message," from interviews with Al Arabiya and Alhurra, 5/5/04, Office of the Press Secretary, 6 May 2004 (⟨http://www.whitehouse.gov/news/releases/2004/05/20040506-1.html⟩, accessed 26 October 2005).

16. The distress of isolation is one Freud makes quite concrete in his brief discussion of panic, a sensation he describes as "feeling alone in the face of danger" and which is experienced psychically whenever the emotional ties that sustain us are felt to disintegrate (*Group Psychology*, 36).

17. The idealization of the beloved gratifies the demands of the ego ideal on the ego, demands that are always punishing and that this roundabout order of love seeks to partially relieve from such punishment and failure through the idealization of the beloved. The headiness of being in love, Freud suggests, issues in part from such relief.

18. In fact, Rousseau's version of the social contract follows this model pre-

cisely. His effort to "transform each individual, who by himself is entirely complete and solitary, into a part of a much greater whole, from which the same individual will then receive, in a sense, his life and his being" parallels Freud's understanding of a group as individuals in love with something common that is also external to the group (see Jean-Jacques Rousseau, *The Social Contract*, trans. Maurice Cranston [New York: Penguin, 1968], 84). Note, too, that *commune moi* ("common me," or "common ego") is Rousseau's norm for the formation (exceeding a mere tie that binds) produced by and at the heart of the social contract (*Social Contract*, 61).

19. Presumably this relationship to the love object explains why the sexual organization of modern cults often involves injunctions to abstinence, injunctions to promiscuity, or the unlimited sexual access of the (male) leader to all women in the group.

20. "Civilization . . . obtains mastery over the individual's dangerous desire for aggression by weakening and disarming it and by setting up an agency within him to watch over it, like a garrison in a conquered city" (Freud, *Civilization and Its Discontents*, 84). Cities represent the literal conquest of man, the containment of his instincts, but Freud is also analogizing the civilized psyche *to* a conquered city. Civilization thus entails a double subjection, first by the aim inhibition required by civilization and then by the introjection of civilization's demands into the psyche. Both of these moves are challenged by the psychic undoing that produces the group.

21. This view converges with Hegel's analysis of the philosophical movement from family to ethical life: "Love means in general the consciousness of my unity with another, so that I am not isolated on my own, but gain my self-consciousness only through the renunciation of my independent existence and through knowing myself as the unity of myself with another and of the other with me. But love is a feeling, that is, ethical life in its natural form. In the state, it is no longer present. There, one is conscious of unity as law; there, the content must be rational, and I must know it. The first moment in love is that I do not wish to be an independent person in my own right and that, if I were, I would feel deficient and incomplete." He notes elsewhere, "The family disintegrates, in a natural manner and essentially through the principle of personality, into a *plurality* of families whose relation to one another is in general that of self-sufficient concrete persons and consequently of an external kind" (*Elements of the Philosophy of Right*, ed. Allen W. Wood, trans. H. B.

Nisbet [Cambridge: Cambridge University Press, 1991], addition to §158, 199; §181, 219).

22. Freud, *Totem and Taboo*, 161.

23. See George W. Bush, Inaugural Address, "President Sworn-In to Second Term," (⟨http://www.whitehouse.gov/news/releases/2005/01/20050120=1 .html⟩, accessed 8 October 2005).

24. See George W. Bush's State of the Union Address, 2 February 2005:

In the long term, the peace we seek will only be achieved by eliminating the conditions that feed radicalism and ideologies of murder. If whole regimes of the world remain in despair and grow in hatred, they will be the recruiting grounds for terror, and that terror will stalk America and other free nations for decades. The only force powerful enough to stop the rise of tyranny and terror, and replace hatred with hope, is the force of human freedom. Our enemies know this, and that is why the terrorist Zarqawi recently declared war on what he called the "evil principle" of democracy. And we've declared our own intention: America will stand with the allies of freedom to support democratic movements in the Middle East and beyond, with the ultimate goal of ending tyranny in our world. (Office of the Press Secretary ⟨http://www.whitehouse.gov/news/releases/2005/02/20050202=11 .html⟩, accessed 8 October 2005).

25. For Bush's words, see his interviews with the Al Arabiya and Alhurra television networks on 5 May 2004 ("Bush Vows Abusers Will Face Justice," CNN.com, 6 May 2004 ⟨http://www.cnn.com/2004/ALLPOLITICS/05/05/ bush.abuse/⟩, accessed 28 November 2005). I heard Blair's statement on BBC news radio between 3 and 5 May 2004, but I have not been able to find it in print.

26. Talal Asad makes a similar argument in *Genealogies of Religion: Discipline and Reasons of Power in Christianity and Islam* (Baltimore: Johns Hopkins University Press, 1993), 268, 306.

27. Convergent studies that have linked liberalism's constitutive outside with its internal operations (as opposed to treating its involvement with colonial or imperial discourses as "alien intrusions," to use Barry Hindess's phrase) include Uday Mehta, *Liberalism and Empire: A Study in Nineteenth-Century British Liberal Thought* (Chicago: University of Chicago Press, 1999); Dipesh Chakrabarty, *Provincializing Europe: Postcolonial Thought*

and Historical Difference (Princeton: Princeton University Press, 2000); Paul Gilroy, *The Black Atlantic: Modernity and Double Consciousness* (Cambridge, MA: Harvard University Press, 1993); and Barry Hindess and Christine Helliwell, "The 'Empire of Uniformity' and the Government of Subject Peoples," *Cultural Values* 6.1 (2002): 137–50.

28. Raymond Williams, *Keywords: A Vocabulary of Culture and Society*, rev. ed. (Oxford: Oxford University Press, 1983), 87, 88.

29. A decisive change, Williams argues, comes in the late eighteenth century, when Herder insisted on the pluralization of culture across nations and periods as well as among social and economic groups within any given nation (ibid., 89).

30. Ibid., 90.

31. Seyla Benhabib, *The Claims of Culture: Equality and Diversity in the Global Era* (Princeton: Princeton University Press, 2002), 106. Benhabib elaborates: "These norms expand on the principles of universal respect and egalitarian reciprocity, which are crucial to a discourse ethic. . . . [V]oluntary self-ascription and freedom of exit and association expand on the concept of persons as self-interpreting and self-defining beings whose actions and deeds are constituted through culturally informed narratives" (132).

32. Ibid., 124–25.

33. While contemporary liberal political rationality articulates such a noncultural subject, it also stumbles over and even rejects several of the implications of this articulation. First, the idea that only nonliberal peoples are organized by a "common way of life" features so blatant a conceit about the civilizational maturity of Europe and the primitivism of others that even liberals are embarrassed by it and will quickly correct themselves when these implications of their positioning of culture as always elsewhere from liberalism are pointed out to them. Second, if liberals fully endorse the privatization of culture defined as a "way of life," their position concedes a stark thinness to public life in liberal societies. Indeed it concedes that liberal public life is no way of life at all but only a set of juridical principles combined with a set of market principles that work independently of any actor. This condemns public life to a culturally impoverished, morally relativistic state whose orientation is controlled largely by legislators, lawyers, manipulated public opinion, and market forces. It confesses as well the absence of a public bond among citizens, other than that rooted in fealty to the nation-state, on the one hand,

and that which is driven by diverse *privatized* cultural-religious attachments or economic interests on the other. That is, it positions public life as buffeted between private desires and *raison d'état* and lacking any organized aim, ethos, or purpose of its own. Third, if culture is only ever something that nonliberal peoples have as a group, if it belongs only to "less mature" peoples, this stance cedes something of value—culture in the intellectual and artistic sense, and in the civilizational sense—to these peoples. Through a linguistic inadvertency that provides a window on the unconscious of liberalism, it admits what we already fear: rights and the market, and nothing more elevated or substantive, determines what we collectively share and commonly value.

In short, if, in contemporary liberal democratic parlance, culture signifies moral and intellectual advancement and knowledge, it also signifies the absence of moral and intellectual autonomy, as well as rule by something other than reason. This means that liberalism simultaneously claims and disclaims culture; culture is part of the greatness of the West and also that which liberal individuals have thrown off in their movement toward maturity and freedom, producing "cosmopolitanism" in its stead. In these two crucial and opposed implications of having culture—moral elevation and the absence of moral autonomy—the word's meanings collide in a way not accidental but symptomatic. They represent a deep and fundamental bind of liberalism in modernity, a bind at the very heart of a project of freedom rooted in reason and individualism.

34. Benhabib, *The Claims of Culture*, 105, 111.

35. Avishai Margalit and Moshe Halbertal, "Liberalism and the Right to Culture," *Social Research* 61.3 (Fall 1994): 491–510. Benhabib tries to have it both ways: culture is both something to which one has a right *and* constitutive, in the same way that persons are "self-interpreting and self-defining" while their "actions and deeds are constituted through culturally informed narratives" (*The Claims of Culture*, 132).

36. Even Will Kymlicka, who works assiduously at establishing "cultures or nations [as] basic units of liberal political theory" because "cultural membership provides us with an intelligible context of choice, and a secure sense of identity and belonging," formulates the project of "liberalizing culture" as a legitimate one even for those outside the culture at issue. Liberals, he writes, should "seek to liberalize [nonliberal nations]" and "should promote the lib-

eralization of [illiberal] cultures" (*Multicultural Citizenship: A Liberal Theory of Minority Rights* [Oxford: Oxford University Press, 1996], 93, 94–95, 105). The justification for this endeavor lies precisely in the distinction between liberal legalism and culture that we have been considering. Drawing on Yael Tamir's *Liberal Nationalism* (Princeton: Princeton University Press, 1993), Kymlicka depicts liberal nations as having "societal cultures," which provide their "members with meaningful ways of life across the full range of human activities, including social, educational, religious, recreational, and economic life, encompassing both public and private spheres" (76). Striking in their absence from this list of what "societal culture" comprises, however, are politics and law, the very domains that liberalism treats as primary domains of power. Liberalized cultures (including the "societal cultures" of liberal society) are considered to generate and circulate meaning but not power, because liberalization is by definition the devolution of power to the morally autonomous subject theorized by Kant and Freud, and to the secular state theorized by social contract theorists. Thus while Kymlicka, more than many other liberals, acknowledges that liberal societies are cultural too, he legitimates the imposition of liberal political values on nonliberals—that is, he legitimates liberal imperialism.

37. "President Delivers State of the Union Address," United States Capitol, Office of the Press Secretary, 29 January 2002 (⟨http://www.whitehouse.gov/2002/01/20010129=11.html⟩, accessed 8 October 2005).

38. The language of nonnegotiable demands, borrowed from the lexicon of labor and peace talks, is itself curious. Not only does it suggest that the United States is engaged in negotiation rather than war, it also positions the United States as righteous supplicant rather than superpower.

39. Asad, *Genealogies of Religion*, 257.

40. There is plenty of intellectual help available for such as effort. Philosophers as diverse as Jean-Luc Nancy, Emmanuel Lévinas, Michel Foucault, Luce Irigaray, and Jacques Derrida have offered critiques that figure being in terms other than autonomy vs. organicism; and post-Nietzscheans such as Foucault, Deleuze, Agamben, and Butler undo the grip of the autonomy/organicism binary in pressing a formulation of the subject in terms of "becoming" rather than "being." Edward Said, Talal Asad, David Scott, Lila Abu-Lughod, Saba Mahmood, William Connolly, Ashis Nandy, Partha Chatterjee, Rajiv Bhargava, and Dipesh Chakrabarty, among others, have contributed to

deconstructing the secularism/fundamentalism opposition. And postcolonial and cultural studies scholars too numerous to name have placed paving stones for conceptualizing the extraordinary miscegenations among cultural and political forms wrought by late modernity.

41. Justification is not to be confused with motivation. The current imperial policies of the United States are wrought from power-political motivations that have little to do with the human rights and antifundamentalist discourses I have been discussing here.

CHAPTER SEVEN. TOLERANCE AS/IN CIVILIZATIONAL DISCOURSE

1. The same associations are not conjured by the utterance "She is a tolerant woman" or even "He is a tolerant person." This differential speaks volumes about tolerance as both an effect of power and a vehicle of power, an expression of domination and a means of extending and consecrating it.

2. "President Says Terrorists Tried to Disrupt World Economy," Shanghai, Office of the Press Secretary, 20 October 2001 (⟨http://www.whitehouse.gov/news/releases/2001/10/20011021=5.html⟩, accessed 9 October 2005).

3. "President's Remarks at 'Congress of Tomorrow' Lunch," White Sulphur Springs, WV, Office of the Press Secretary, 1 February 2002 (⟨http://www.whitehouse.gov/news/releases/2002/02/20020201=9.html⟩, accessed 9 October 2005).

4. *Oxford English Dictionary*, compact ed. (1971), s.v. "civilization." Gail Hershatter and Anna Tsing remind us that the *OED* is itself no minor civilizational project in its creation of literary legacies that both set linguistic standards and define a cultural practice ("Civilization," in *New Keywords: A Revised Vocabulary of Culture and Society*, ed. Tony Bennett, Lawrence Grossberg, and Meaghan Morris [Malden, MA: Blackwell, 2005], 35).

5. Raymond Williams, *Keywords: A Vocabulary of Culture and Society*, rev. ed. (Oxford: Oxford University Press, 1983), 57.

6. Hershatter and Tsing, "Civilization," 36.

7. Samuel P. Huntington, *The Clash of Civilizations and the Remaking of World Order* (New York: Simon and Schuster, 1996), 311.

8. Ibid., 318.

9. Ibid., 321.

10. The conflation of civilization with culture in this definition is paralleled by Huntington's definition of civilization as "culture writ large" (ibid., 41) or "the highest cultural group of people and the broadest level of cultural identity people have short of that which distinguishes humans from other species" (43). However, in opposing the barbarian to one who has "sympathy with literary culture," the *OED* definition clearly equates civilization with high European culture, thus signaling its class connotations and explaining why we refer to the process of teaching children table manners as "civilizing" them.

11. "President Addresses the Nation in Prime Time News Conference," The East Room, Office of the Press Secretary, 13 April 2004 (⟨http://www.whitehouse.gov/news/releases/2004/04/20040413=20.html⟩, accessed 9 October 2005).

12. See the Teaching Tolerance website (⟨http://www.teachingtolerance.org/⟩) and the Southern Poverty Law Center website (⟨http://www.splcenter.org⟩). The SPLC has been plagued with controversy in recent years and was compromised from the beginning by the hucksterism and opportunism of its co-founder Morris Dees. The richest civil rights organization in the business, it raises astonishing sums that it never spends and consequently has been assigned one of the worst ratings of any group monitored by the American Institute of Philanthropy. According to Ken Silverstein, who wrote about the organization in *Harpers*, the SPLC spends twice as much on fund-raising as it does on legal services for victims of civil rights abuses. And while backing away from the kinds of cases, especially death penalty appeals, that might lower its attractiveness to wealthy white liberals, it exploits and sensationalizes steadily dwindling Klan activities in a manner designed to rake in contributions from whites. In 1986, Silverstein reports, "the center's entire legal staff quit in protest of Dee's refusal to address issues—such as homelessness, voter registration, and affirmative action—that they considered far more pertinent to poor minorities, if far less marketable to affluent benefactors, than fighting the KKK" ("The Church of Morris Dees," *Harpers*, November 2000, p. 56). Another lawyer who resigned a few years later told reporters that the center's programs were calculated to cash in on "black pain and white guilt" (ibid.), a calculation that is patently evident in the over-the-top stories and testimonials featured in the fund-raising literature. However, these kinds of exposés from within and without have been largely ignored by the main-

stream press, and both the SPLC and the Teaching Tolerance project continue to garner ringing endorsements from a range of politicians, educators, and media personalities.

13. K. Peter Fritzsche, "Human Rights and Human Rights Education," International Network: Education for Democracy, Human Rights and Tolerance, Podium no. 3 (2/2000) ⟨http://www.tolerance-net.org/news/podium/podium031.html⟩, accessed 8 October 2005.

14. Jay Newman, *Foundations of Religious Tolerance* (Toronto: University of Toronto Press, 1982), 3.

15. There is a certain tension in the nativism of the popular tolerance literature. Crosscutting the view that intolerance is primordial and tolerance is a civilizational achievement is another one that "people are not born as little haters, we learn to hate. And just as we learn to hate, we have to unlearn to hate" (Caryl Stern, senior associate national director of the Anti-Defamation League; quoted in "'We Are Family' Doesn't Unite All; *Chicago Tribune*, 11 March 2005, p. 2). While superficially opposite to the idea that bigotry is primitive while tolerance is civilized and advanced, the ADL formulation may well retain the nativism. The "learning" presumably occurs in the tribe, where it is considered to be transmitted and absorbed almost unconsciously or at least subrationally as part of what binds and reproduces the tribe; the "unlearning" presumably occurs in a more cosmopolitan setting, and is considered rational and deliberate.

16. Barry Hindess, conversation, May 2005; see also Christine Helliwell and Barry Hindess, "The Temporalizing of Difference," *Ethnicities* 5.3 (2005): 414–18. Much politically liberal talk of tolerance and multiculturalism participates in this temporalizing of difference even in describing the difference between liberals and conservatives: liberals self-characterize themselves as more enlightened, forward-looking, or advanced and refer to conservative agendas as traditional, backward-looking, or regressive.

17. See, for example, the following op-eds by Thomas L. Friedman in the *New York Times*: "The Core of Muslim Rage," 6 March 2002, A21; "War of Ideas," 2 June 4 2002, sec. 4, p. 19; "Noah and 9/11," 11 September 2002, A33; and "An Islamic Reformation," 4 December 2002, A31.

18. Michael Ignatieff, "Nationalism and Toleration," in *The Politics of Toleration in Modern Life*, ed. Susan Mendus (Durham, NC: Duke University Press, 1999), 85.

19. Ibid., 101, 102.

20. Ibid., 102.

21. In the Museum of Tolerance, this normative structure appears to be disrupted with one in which those who most need tolerance, for example, Jews, can become its strongest adherents and advocates (see chapter 4). But advocating tolerance is not equivalent to being socially positioned to offer it, and it is social positioning that is at issue here.

22. Recall from chapter 2 that capacity as such is the measure of tolerance in most domains of its usage: at its most rudimentary, tolerance is defined by how much error, contamination, or toxicity can be absorbed by the host without damaging it, whether the issue is alcohol consumption for a college freshman, margin of error for a statistical inference, or ethnic nationalism for a liberal society. But within a liberal regime, this capacity is not only a measure of ability but a virtue.

23. As a political rationality shaped by the Protestant Reformation, liberal tolerance presumes not only individual autonomy but also the viability of privatizing fundamental beliefs. Most of the belief structures of most of the world's peoples for most of human history do not fit with these presumptions. Reformation tolerance doctrine does not work well for the faith structures of the ancient Greeks, of Medieval Christians, or of modern Muslims, Jews, Hindus, or Catholics. It does not work well for a socialist, tribalist, or communitarian ethos or order. It was coined to solve a specific problem issuing from a specific social formation and political crisis: how to allow Protestant sectarians the right to worship God according to their own individual understanding of him and his words without undercutting both church and state authority, how to substitute accommodation of these sects for the practice of burning heretics alive, how to stem the tide of blood spilled over religious rebellion in early modern Europe.

24. Chandra Talpade Mohanty, "Under Western Eyes: Feminist Scholarship and Colonial Discourses," *Feminist Review*, no. 30 (Autumn 1988): 74.

25. Many feminist postcolonial scholars in recent years have made this point regarding the western use of fundamentalism; for three of the best accounts, see Lila Abu-Lughod, interview by Nermeen Shaikh, *AsiaSource*, 20 March 2002 (⟨www.asiasource.org/news/special_reports/lila.cfm⟩, accessed 8 October 2005); Saba Mahmood, *Politics of Piety: The Islamic Revival and*

the Feminist Subject (Princeton: Princeton University Press, 2005); and Charles Hirschkind and Saba Mahmood, "Feminism, the Taliban, and Politics of Counter-insurgency," *Anthropological Quarterly* 75.2 (Spring 2002): 339–54.

26. Thus Bush can declare, and his neoconservative and Christian backers can agree, that America stands for the principle of tolerance, even as the Republican Party is considered the party of "intolerance" by those on the cultural left, and as certain practices of tolerance are rebuked as evidence of moral decline or depravity.

27. "The End of Tolerance: Engaging Cultural Difference," special issue of *Daedalus* 129.4 (Fall 2000), and Susan Okin, *Is Multiculturalism Bad for Women?*, ed. Joshua Cohen, Matthew Howard, and Martha Nussbaum (Princeton: Princeton University Press, 1999). Okin's book is hereafter cited parenthetically in the text.

28. Anne Norton's review of *Is Multiculturalism Bad for Women?* offers a scathing assessment of Okin's Orientalist logic, poor scholarship, and ignorance of critiques of liberal feminism and of the debates surrounding her instances of the "intolerable," from polygamy to clitoridectomy (*Political Theory* 29.5 [October 2001]: 736–49). Most of the other reviews and receptions of this work have been relatively positive, however.

29. In analyzing Okin's argument about multiculturalism and feminism, we face a conundrum: whether to deconstruct her impoverished concept of culture and thereby refuse to enter the rest of the argument, or to provisionally accept her account so that we can take up other aspects of the argument. Okin is largely impervious to the past several decades of rethinking what culture is and could mean (a rethinking undertaken primarily in anthropology and cultural studies), and she is wholly unconcerned with specifying what culture is—there is a stray mention of "ways of life" on page 10 of *Multiculturalism*. To be sure, her analysis could not get off the ground if she attended closely to theorizations of culture that do not isolate it from the political, juridical, and economic; if she grasped the colonial inflection in the notion of culture she deploys (in which culture is always preliberal and liberalism is always without culture); if she recognized that the sense of culture she uses is the creation both of liberal strategies of depoliticization and of colonial discourse.

30. See Carole Pateman, *The Sexual Contract* (Stanford: Stanford Univer-

sity Press, 1988); M. G. Clarke and Lynda Lange, eds., *The Sexism of Social and Political Theory: Women and Reproduction from Plato to Nietzsche* (Toronto: Toronto University Press, 1979); Kathy Ferguson, *The Feminist Case against Bureaucracy* (Philadelphia: Temple University Press, 1985); Wendy Brown, "Liberalism's Family Values," in *States of Injury: Power and Freedom in Late Modernity* (Princeton: Princeton University Press, 1995); Joan W. Scott, *Only Paradoxes to Offer: French Feminists and the Rights of Man* (Cambridge, MA: Harvard University Press, 1996); Catharine MacKinnon, *Toward a Feminist Theory of the State* (Cambridge: Harvard University Press, 1991); Nancy Hirschmann and Christine di Stefano, eds., *Revisioning the Political: Feminist Reconstructions of Traditional Concepts in Western Political Theory* (Boulder, CO: Westview Press, 1996); and Nancy Hirschmann, *Rethinking Obligation: A Feminist Method for Political Theory* (Ithaca: Cornell University Press, 1992) and *The Subject of Liberty: Toward a Feminist Theory of Freedom* (Princeton: Princeton University Press, 2002).

31. See Brown, "Liberalism's Family Values," and Catharine MacKinnon's essay "Difference and Dominance: On Sex Discrimination," in *Feminism Unmodified: Discourses on Life and Law* (Cambridge, MA: Harvard University Press, 1988).

32. Susan Okin's own feminist critique of liberalism is to be found in *Justice, Gender, and the Family* (New York: Basic Books, 1989), which argues on behalf of treating the family as one of the "spheres of justice" articulated in Michael Walzer's book by that name (*Spheres of Justice: A Defense of Pluralism and Equality* [New York: Basic Books, 1983]).

33. Susan Dominus, "The Seductress of Vanity," *New York Times Magazine*, 5 May 2002, p. 50.

34. Karen Springen, "Kids under the Knife," *Newsweek*, 1 November 2004, p. 59.

35. Information about the nature and numbers of intersexed persons, along with the history of their treatment, can be found at the website of the Intersex Society of North America, ⟨http://www.isna.org⟩. Intersexed children, regardless of where they are on a complex spectrum of physiological sex, are more often "surgically corrected" to be anatomically female than male, because, according to the surgeons, it is "easier to poke a hole than to build a poke." This surgery, which is performed for neither the physical health nor

the future sexual pleasure of the subject, may include clitoral reduction (to make the clitoris is less penile), invagination (to produce or enlarge the vagina), and removal of undescended or "internal" testes. The postsurgical course of treatment, often lasting for years, includes stretching the vaginal cavity with successively larger vaginal inserts; the aim is to enlarge it sufficiently for penetration by an erect penis when the child reaches maturity. Since administration of these painful treatments often requires forcible restraint of the child undergoing them, it is hard to name them anything other than medically authorized rape.

36. Herbert Marcuse, *One Dimensional Man: Studies in the Ideology of Advanced Industrial Society* (Boston: Beacon, 1964); Michel Foucault, *History of Sexuality*, vol. 1, *An Introduction*, trans. Robert Hurley (New York: Random House, 1978). For a somewhat different perspective on this dimension of agency and capitalism's charms, see Jane Bennett, *The Enchantment of Modern Life: Attachments, Crossings, and Ethics* (Princeton: Princeton University Press, 2001).

37. The anthropologists David Scott, in *Refashioning Futures: Criticism after Postcoloniality* (Princeton: Princeton University Press, 1999), and Mahmood, in *Politics of Piety*, are among those who have traced the arc of colonial discourse in measuring postcolonial states against liberal formulations of tolerance and have made a compelling case for thinking about tolerance in postcolonial settings outside of the frame of liberalism—that is, a case for refusing liberal imperialism in its academic as well as political mode.

38. Even in hyperliberal societies, not all practices of autonomy are equally valued—consider the indigent person resistant to being managed by social services or the teenager hanging around a street corner with nothing to do. Nor are all associations and practices governed by the principle of autonomy and rights; familial and social bonds are based instead on relationality and need.

39. Ignatieff, "Nationalism and Toleration," 102.

40. Ibid., 94–95.

41. The quotation is from Bernard Williams, "Toleration: An Impossible Virtue?" in *Toleration: An Elusive Virtue*, ed. David Heyd (Princeton: Princeton University Press, 1996), 26. See also Joseph Raz, *Ethics in the Public Domain* (Oxford: Clarendon Press, 1984), 171–72.

42. Williams, "Toleration," 26.

43. Will Kymlicka, "Two Models of Pluralism and Tolerance," in Heyd, ed., *Toleration*.

44. See Wendy Brown, "Neoliberalism and the End of Democracy," *Theory and Event* 7.2 (2003), republished in *Edgework: Essays on Knowledge and Politics* (Princeton: Princeton University Press, 2005).

INDEX